Cloneliness

Cloneliness

On the Reproduction of Loneliness

Michael O'Sullivan

BLOOMSBURY ACADEMIC
NEW YORK • LONDON • OXFORD • NEW DELHI • SYDNEY

BLOOMSBURY ACADEMIC
Bloomsbury Publishing Inc
1385 Broadway, New York, NY 10018, USA
50 Bedford Square, London, WC1B 3DP, UK
29 Earlsfort Terrace, Dublin 2, Ireland

BLOOMSBURY, BLOOMSBURY ACADEMIC and the Diana logo are trademarks of
Bloomsbury Publishing Plc

First published in the United States of America 2019
This paperback edition published in 2021

Copyright © Michael O'Sullivan, 2019

For legal purposes the Acknowledgments on p. vi constitute an extension
of this copyright page.

Cover design by Eleanor Rose
Cover image © Getty Images

All rights reserved. No part of this publication may be reproduced or transmitted
in any form or by any means, electronic or mechanical, including photocopying,
recording, or any information storage or retrieval system, without prior
permission in writing from the publishers.

Bloomsbury Publishing Inc does not have any control over, or responsibility for, any
third-party websites referred to or in this book. All internet addresses given in this
book were correct at the time of going to press. The author and publisher regret any
inconvenience caused if addresses have changed or sites have ceased to exist, but can
accept no responsibility for any such changes.

A catalog record for this book is available from the Library of Congress.

ISBN: HB: 978-1-5013-4482-4
PB: 978-1-5013-7835-5
ePDF: 978-1-5013-4484-8
eBook: 978-1-5013-4483-1

Typeset by Newgen KnowledgeWorks Pvt. Ltd., Chennai, India

To find out more about our authors and books visit www.bloomsbury.com
and sign up for our newsletters.

Contents

Acknowledgments	vi
1. Introduction: Radical Embodied Cognitive Loneliness	1
2. Loneliness as Method: Henry James and the "Essential Loneliness" of Artistic Practice	35
3. The "Lonely Voice" and "Submerged Population" in O'Connor, Joyce, and Mansfield: How Can We Live "Alone Together"?	57
4. Loneliness Is Part of the Job: "Sentimental Loneliness" in Carson McCullers and Richard Yates	73
5. Beating University Loneliness and Workplace Boredom: David Foster Wallace on "How to Keep Yourself Open to A Moment of the Most Supernal Beauty"	91
6. Loneliness in a Selection of Japanese Philosophy and Fiction: Takeo Doi, Natsume Sōseki, Kitarō Nishida, Haruki Murakami, and Sayaka Murata	113
Section on Radical Loneliness and Shintoism by Raphael Wung Cheong Chim	144
7. Filial Piety and Loneliness in a Selection of Chinese Novels: Cao Xueqin, Mo Yan, Dai Sijie, Ha Jin, and Yiyun Li	151
8. "I Am Trash": How Student Stress and Student Self-Stratification Is Creating a Generation of "Interconnected Loners" [with Flora Ka Yu Mak]	173
9. An Erotics of Loneliness	189
Notes	201
Bibliography	229
Index	243

Acknowledgments

I thank the Department of English and the Faculty of Arts of the Chinese University of Hong Kong for their continued support and for granting me research leave to work on this book. I thank Raphael Wung Cheong Chim for his assistance with Chapter 6. I thank Flora Ka Yu Mak for all her help with Chapter 8. I thank Lexi Li for all her research assistance with Chapter 7. I also thank Haaris Naqvi, Amy Martin, and Shyam at Bloomsbury for their support and encouragement throughout. And for the warm discussions and insights on topics related to loneliness I thank Tomás Mulcahy, Tim Kelleher, Cian O'Sullivan, Eddie Tay, and Billy Ramsell, my parents Mary and Jeremiah, my brothers Dominic, Francis and Jeremiah, my sister Margaret, and my wife Irene.

An earlier version of Chapter 2, "Loneliness as Method: Henry James and the 'Essential Loneliness' of Artistic Practice," appeared as Michael O'Sullivan, "Loneliness as Method: Henry James, Individualism and the 'More Intimate Education,'" *Textual Practice*, August 12, 2018. An earlier version of Chapter 3 appeared as "Loneliness and the Submerged Population: Frank O'Connor's *The Lonely Voice* and Joyce's 'The Dead,'" In *The Irish Short Story*, ed. Elke D'Hoker (Oxford: Peter Lang, 2015), pp. 105–20. An earlier version of Chapter 5 appeared as "David Foster Wallace, Loneliness, and the 'Pretty Much Nothing' the University Teaches," *Literature Compass* 14, no. 7 (2017): 1–11.

This book is dedicated to Irene.

1

Introduction: Radical Embodied Cognitive Loneliness

Loneliness has never been so popular. And since loneliness breeds loneliness, it is now described as the "most widespread 'disorder' of our time."[1] We are also, however, still wary of loneliness; studies reveal that when people know they are speaking to someone who is lonely, they are less sociable, thereby exacerbating the loneliness of the other and denying themselves an opportunity to understand better how loneliness can afflict anyone at any time.[2] Loneliness can even be craved: John Cacioppo has researched how protracted loneliness causes people to "shut down socially" so that they become more suspicious of any social contact."[3] As Johann Hari puts it in *Lost Connections*, "you start to be afraid of the very thing you need most" and in a "snowball" effect "disconnection spirals into more disconnection."[4] Recent studies also reveal that social media use (SMU) is likely to increase feelings of loneliness, however, there are contributing factors;[5] studies reveal that although increased SMU has been linearly associated with increased "real-life social isolation (SI)" the extent to which one feels social isolation with "increased social media use" can depend on "personality characteristics."[6] Since it is also well known and well researched that GAFA (Google, Apple, Facebook, Amazon) employs behavioral algorithms and data-mining resources to both predict behavior and get us ever more connected, tailoring each online experience to each user, our SMU and the "real-life social isolation" that comes with it is only going to increase. Recent Facebook patents such as "Augmenting Text Messages with Emotion Information and Techniques for Emotion Detection and Content Delivery" reveal how, as Curtis Silver writes, "your face would eventually make it into the social network in order to serve you content based on anything from your emotional state to expression."[7] The potential for emotional feedback loops of an introspective kind is profound; real-life SI is being complemented by self-scrutiny and self-regard of an ever greater virtual nature. Hilarie Cash, a psychotherapist who has worked with internet addicts in Washington state, believes that people "are not getting the connections that they need in order to be healthy human beings." She believes that the kind of connection we need is "face-to-face, where we are able to see, and touch, and smell, and hear each other … We're social creatures. We're meant to be in connection with one another in a safe, caring way, and when it's mediated by a screen, that's absolutely not there."[8] The tailored nature of the online experience also has other consequences for today's "internauts"; in giving us what we want, navigating online becomes all about "more comfort and less inconvenience."[9] Zygmunt Bauman argues that "the more complex, problematic, challenging and straining the tasks we confront offline are, the more seductive the simplifications and facilitations that are found and always promised in the online alternative become."[10] The offline world can then come to appear as "incurably heterogeneous, heteronomic and multivocal; it necessitates continuous choosing—hardly any choice being unambiguous and all threatening to stay 'essentially contested' "; it lacks the "cosily straightforward and risk-free" feel of the online world.[11] Bauman believes this has major implications for how we deal with such social issues as the current "migration crisis" since it is one of the most complex and controversial topics confronting us today. It's much easier to retreat to the "comfort zone" where only "like-minded people are admitted" and where a "modicum of dexterity, determination and consistency in pressing the delete key will suffice to efface the controversy."[12] However, most important for the current book is Bauman's description of this generation of "internauts" as "interconnected loners." This isolation coupled with the fact that the internet has pushed us into a new kind of society, a society of performers (to replace the previous "society of discipline"), means that we are "loners in constant touch" and in "constant competition and rivalry with each other."[13] This is the result of a period of individualization built on the "progressive erosion of communal bonds" wherein individuals are abandoned to the "burdensome duties of self-definition, self-assertion and (total) self-care."[14] In Chapter 8, we present a study of teenagers in secondary schools in Hong Kong that explores some of the consequences of this age of competition and "interconnected loners."

Loneliness also has a subjective dimension; one can *feel* lonely at any time and this is the experience and emotion I hope to explore in this book through reading works of literature and philosophy on loneliness. However, the subjective element of loneliness also raises other questions since research reveals that "the lonely are gradually moved to the outer edges of social networks."[15] As Cacioppo and Williams discover, "once on the periphery, people have fewer friends ... but it also drives them to cut the few ties that they have left. But before they do, they tend to transmit the same feeling of loneliness to their remaining friends ... These reinforcing effects mean that our social fabric can fray at the edges."[16] The wording here is interesting; we speak of "transmit[ting]" loneliness almost like it is a disease or an infection. This can result in all human interaction being regarded as a form of "infection," as the protagonist of Sayaka Murata's novel *Convenience Store Woman* believes and that I examine in more detail in Chapter 6. This is also related to what Tijmen Schep calls "social cooling"; in living constantly online with surveillance and reputation scores, we self-monitor, conform and self-clone to meet social expectations (https://www.tijmenschep.com/socialcooling/). For many people loneliness is something that must be withstood; to admit to it, to let its subjective side show, is to be defeated and to show symptoms of the infection that results in you being "moved to the outer edges of social networks," as Sagan and Miller argue. The problem is that with GAFA now tracking our emotions, we inhabit a social network and peer group unlike any in history; it creates a loneliness different from that of Riesman's "lonely crowd," Moustakas's "existential loneliness," Richard Yates's "sentimental loneliness," and Frank O'Connor's "lonely voice." It is a loneliness that can kill; one study of 308,849 participants indicated a "50% increased likelihood of survival for participants with stronger social relationships."[17] However, it is also a loneliness that GAFA and big business push on us all the more so that we will give up more and more to the network. Only the strong will survive, only those with the right "personality characteristics" who are capable of withstanding the loneliness and the real-life SI of social media. Our faces, cloned so they make it into the social network to serve us content, are used then to persuade us to offer ourselves up in our loneliness as nodes for the network. One meaning of clone in the *OED* is a person who "slavishly imitates" another; denied any opportunity to understand the emotions loneliness incites many of us turn to avatars and online personas, copies of ourselves, in order to deal with the loneliness in the social isolation of SMU. W. J. T. Mitchell argues that the "time of cloning, then is now" (42) because the clone has become the figure *par excellence* for all forms of likeness production.[18] Cloning is the literalization of our "most ancient fear [...] about images, and that is that we might bring them to life".[19] The social network, the online life, reproduces us as images back to us, blurring the lines between the metaphorics of reproductive and therapeutic cloning and threatening all notions of "differentiation and identification" in the process, what once enabled us to discover the reasons for our own likes and dislikes. As Jean Baudrillard reminds us, it is "culture that clones us, and mental cloning anticipates any biological cloning. It is the matrix of acquired traits that, today, clones us culturally under the sign of monothought".[20] Loneliness is exploited and transformed as a condition of modern networked life so that the standard narrative of the clone as "organ donor" where the human organism is reduced to a "purely instrumental and commodified condition" comes to encompass the entire subject; no longer bodies without organs we become the organs that are voluntarily donated to the network in a new form of cloning.[21] It is for this reason that I use the neologism cloneliness. It is not going too far to claim that social media users are, in a sense, being cloned as "interconnected loners"; through the endless feedback loop of the online face as image we gain more strength to keep the signs of loneliness hidden. The result is that we wear masks to waylay any suspicion of loneliness; loneliness becomes the new trigger for a new kind of cloning.

Governments are recognizing the impact of loneliness on their populations. The UK government appointed its first Minister of Loneliness in January 2018. Prime Minister Theresa May said at the announcement of this new role that "[f]or far too many people, loneliness is the sad reality of modern life."[22] According to a report published in 2018 by the Jo Cox Commission on Loneliness, more than 9 million people in the UK alone—about 14 percent of the population—"often or always feel lonely."[23] And as with all such initiatives, there is a financial incentive; it is reported that the "loneliness epidemic" costs UK businesses up to 2.5 billion annually.[24] However, it is also a global problem: there is an "epidemic of loneliness" in the UK; US "[t]eens are now lonelier than at any time" since a key loneliness survey began in 1991,[25] and high suicide rates among young students in leading university regions such as the United States and Hong Kong are also being related to loneliness and stress.[26] I discuss this in more detail in Chapter 8. In a recent edition of the *Harvard Business Review*, Vivek Murthy calls loneliness a "growing health epidemic." Once again, the argument is primarily that reducing loneliness is good for business.[27]

Loneliness may be the bad faith of our age. It is a role we can assume unthinkingly as professional and online practices alienate us from the emotions loneliness conjures. Academics are not immune; driven to meet targets and respond to social events with "impact" they must comply with algorithms for public profiles that get updated when their work goes live. I have described in a previous book how the knowledge industry through a process of academic barbarism is complicit in the cultivation and promotion of a highly testocratic environment where students see each other only as competition for exemptions, grades, and academic attention.[28] Nevertheless, the book speaks for a belief that we can rise above our age's bad faith that long ago spilled out beyond the confines of our day jobs and our professions. In our bad faith, we not only assume the role our occupations and professions grant us in order to survive in our econocracy as "ECONS,"[29] we also assume the role of our identity in the social network, a social network consistently notifying us that we need more friends, more impact, more of a profile. And yet, in being conscientious enough to use aspects of the social network for our benefit we can still work to transform this invasive form of bad faith.

Jean-Paul Sartre's original existential enquiry into loneliness in *La Nausée* in the 1930s—what I will call "existential loneliness" for the purposes of this book—still holds important truths for the exploration of loneliness today. Antoine Roquentin is a man who has "no friends" and who lives "alone, entirely alone."[30] He never "speak[s] to anyone, never; I receive nothing, I give nothing."[31] However, the state of intentionally remaining on the edge of loneliness, or catching himself in the process of descending into too deep a loneliness, makes him more receptive to changes in his environment. He thinks that "[t]hrough the lack of attaching myself to words, my thoughts remain nebulous most of the time. They sketch vague, pleasant shapes and then are swallowed up."³² Through Roquentin, Sartre explores what this life of attentive loneliness can reveal for the person with a willingness to stay with loneliness:

> When you live alone you no longer know what it is to tell something ... You let events flow past; ... you plunge into stories without beginning or end ... But in compensation, one misses nothing, no improbability or story too tall to be believed in cafes. For example, Saturday, about four in the afternoon, on the end of the timbered sidewalk of the new station yard, a little woman in sky blue was running backwards, laughing, waving a handkerchief.³³

Roquentin describes the conditions of his loneliness: "I have never resisted these harmless emotions; far from it. You must be just a bit lonely in order to feel them, just lonely enough to get rid of plausibility at the proper time. But I remained close to people, on the surface of solitude, quite resolved to take refuge in their midst in case of emergency."³⁴ It is this kind of openness, of remaining "just lonely enough to get rid of plausibility at the proper time" while also remaining "close to people" that is the guiding light for Roquentin in his quest to discover his goal as writer and as artist. It is a state that gradually alerts him to the potential it can allow him for seeing things in a more perceptive and possibly artistic way. This is a great part of "the nausea" he experiences. He finally realizes how this feeling opens him up to a way of seeing that reveals truths to him that are essential for his self-awakening as artist:

> I understood the Nausea, I possessed it. To tell the truth, I did not formulate my discoveries to myself. But I think it would be easy for me to put them in words now. The essential thing is contingency. I mean that one cannot define existence as necessity. To exist is simply to *be there*; those who exist let themselves be encountered, but you can never deduce anything from them. I believe there are people who have understood this. Only they tried to overcome this contingency by inventing a necessary, causal being. But no necessary being can explain existence: contingency is not a delusion, a probability which can be dissipated; it is the absolute, consequently, the perfect free gift.³⁵

It is a realization that is arrived at after a profound period of self-reflection on existence in the act of truly perceiving an object.³⁶ Roquentin becomes fascinated by a root, a piece of "dead wood," and this incites his realization.

He has the sensation that "[t]ime had stopped" and at that moment he has a profound realization that he merges with the object: "I was inside; the black stump did *not move*." This grants him a new understanding of existence and of his place in the environment, somewhat like Baoyu and his family in *The Story of the Stone* when they try to represent in characters the true relationship between themselves and their surroundings. I examine this sense of loneliness as method for greater self-understanding and creative practice in the work of Henry James in Chapter 2. Roquention remarks, "[e]xistence is not something which lets itself be thought of from a distance: it must invade you suddenly, master you, weigh heavily on your heart like a great motionless beast-or else there is nothing more at all."[37] Time and again in the novels and works discussed in the following chapters, an openness to the experience of loneliness is found to grant insights and illuminations that are beneficial for art and for life in general. The difficulty lies in remaining "close to people" and being self-aware as one explores what loneliness is telling you. It is a difficult process that can feel frightening. This is presumably why, on some days, Roquentin's diary entries simply remind him not to be afraid. Online-inspired loneliness, the loneliness of "interconnected loners," is another beast entirely; it liquidates one of the most profound human experiences—loneliness—by lulling users into believing the "online community" can be a guard against the more harmful aspects of loneliness. Online loneliness does not even offer the feeling of being "close to people" or the "essential contingency" that Roquentin can still claim for his loneliness.

Of course, the social network as loneliness generator feeds the loneliness we cannot satiate; furthermore, it does not allow us the rich array of disinterested moments and real-life objects that Roquentin experiences in his pre-online world as contingency. Our social networks want us to be lonely so that we will keep coming back for more. We have to stay lonely in the social network in order to be driven to consume and put more of ourselves into the databank that keeps giving. In our migration online, targets, hits, evaluation scores all pit us against each other. As more of these migrate online our profile becomes a badge of honor and shame at the same time; a public Doppelgänger we must carry with us in order to get the job, win the grant, or be accepted into the remnants of offline group dynamics that still exist. Online, you cannot sit in the corner of the café, like Roquentin, quietly observing others, confident in the knowledge that you are not being observed, without being bombarded by streams of information. Roquentin would have had to walk to the National Library where he would have had to *choose* specific books for such information. In the online world, unsolicited information comes from everywhere and yet built from algorithms drawing on previous personal preferences it does not offer the "essential contingency" Roquentin finds in loneliness. We are the first generation to grow old on the social network. Our children, the iGen, the first generation to grow up on the social network, are being conditioned to see friendship differently. When we were children we liked something a friend did by high-fiving, embracing, smiling, or telling them so; they were within arm's reach when the event happened. Individualism has become a virtual profile regime built up, yes, on old feelings of predation and competition, but only as a form of individualism as 'profilism'. We have the badge but do not get any of the embodied highs of fellow feeling that once came with group membership. Whereas individualism for many evolved out of, and once seemed to be rooted in, liberal democratic ideals such as freedom of expression or freedom of movement, today our profiles are no longer derived primarily from such ideals but are instead more about making a name for ourselves. Online individualism's foundation has shifted from freedom of expression to freedom to succeed; anything but success is unforgiveable when everyone has gone live.

Loneliness Without Solitude

The solitude Friedrich Nietzsche, Thomas Merton, and Michel De Montaigne describe in earlier times seems less desired or less accessible today. As John Kaag reminds us, for Nietzsche, we can only find the sense of value that will give us reasons for why we do what we do in our "loneliest loneliness."[38] Kaag tells us that Nietzsche writes of a moment of supreme self-enquiry that hits us only in our "loneliest loneliness" when we must come to what we value on our own: "the answer cannot be given by consensus or on behalf of some impersonal institutions."[39] Whatever we do, we must do it because we chose it and can own up to it: "[i]n the story of our lives, these choices are ours and ours alone, and this is what gives things, all things, value."⁴⁰ Thomas Merton also saw a great opportunity in loneliness. For Merton, loneliness and solitude are very close; he writes, "[i]f a man does not know the value of his own loneliness, how can he respect another's solitude ... It is at once our loneliness and our dignity to have an incommunicable personality that is ours, ours alone and no one else's."⁴¹ Our values, our sense of our own dignity, are then all to be found in loneliness, and should then lead us to seek solitude in our lives: "[s]olitude is as necessary for society as silence is for language and air for the lungs."⁴²

Michel de Montaigne argues for the importance of solitude for learning how to "live in leisure at our ease."⁴³ We must "withdraw from such attributes of the mob as are within us" to "gain power over ourselves to live really and truly alone" and "in contentment."⁴⁴ In order to attain this knowledge of ourselves, Montaigne recommends that we "should set aside a room, just for ourselves ... keeping it entirely free and establishing there our true liberty"; "no commerce or communication with the outside world should find a place there; there we should talk and laugh as though we had no wife, no children, no possessions, no followers."⁴⁵ However, it takes preparation; you must "first prepare yourself to welcome yourself there."⁴⁶ It would be "madness to entrust yourself to yourself, if you did not know how to govern yourself" since there "are ways of failing in solitude as in society."⁴⁷ Today we are not only failing *in* solitude, we are failing to *find* solitude. Many people today would find it difficult to spend time alone in their rooms getting to know themselves better with "no possessions" and "no followers." Hooked up 24/7 to the portals of information our "possessions" afford us, with their steady stream of notifications and updates from "followers" and those we follow, it is impossible to find justification for why such solitude could be needed. The FOMO (fear of missing out) is too strong. Solitude is almost completely eroded today but loneliness is on the rise and the reasons are staring us in the face. Alone in our rooms, we are primed for solitude and the encounter with ourselves but we cannot switch off. Those moments when we are physically alone that should grant us the solitude to commune with ourselves are cut short. Those moments when, as Montaigne suggests, you must "first prepare yourself to welcome yourself" so you are not "failing in solitude" are not even acknowledged as necessary. And because we fail at solitude and dodge the encounter with ourselves and then still feel lonely when hooked up to all our "followers" and "possessions," we are less prepared to deal with these uncontrollable feelings of anxiety and fear that loneliness brings us. The feelings also do not compute since you can see in the palm of your hand how many friends and "followers" you have. You ask yourself, how can I feel lonely? how can I feel "socially isolated"? So you go back to the screen and your "followers" and the algorithms design more invasive ways of getting you to give up more of yourself. The algorithms want you to spend more time online; they want to help you get others hooked; they want to reproduce this loneliness that keeps driving you back online. This is the cloneliness this book argues is a new aspect of loneliness today. It is an aspect of loneliness Montaigne and Nietzsche may not be able to prepare us for.

Radical Embodied Cognitive Loneliness and the Move to Cloneliness

Recent posthuman philosophies, human–computer interface studies, and technology-inspired biopolitical discourses and practices are reinventing and reimagining loneliness in different communities. The philosophy described as radical embodied cognitive science is important for this book. Anthony Chemero describes radical embodied cognitive science as a philosophy where "cognition is to be described in terms of agent-environment dynamics, and not in terms of computation and representation."[48] It is a philosophy that follows on from the American naturalist philosophy of John Dewey that regards actions as "organic circuits" that "cannot be understood by breaking them into parts."[49] Central to Chemero's philosophy is the idea that the "cognitive system" of the agent, subject, or animal "includes aspects of an animal's environment to which the animal is coupled."[50] In other words, it works in opposition to "wide computationalism," which argues that the "cognitive system proper has to be understood as encapsulated by the organism's skin or central nervous system."[51] Radical embodied cognitive science is then a variety of extended cognitive science; agents and environments are modelled "as nonlinearly coupled dynamical systems. Because the agent and environment are nonlinearly coupled, they form a unified, nondecomposable system, which is to say that they form a system whose behaviour cannot be modeled, even approximately, as a set of separate parts."[52] I would argue that most artists and writers discussed in this book share such an aspiration in terms of human action and agency. The obvious change that has come to the environment since Dewey's day and that is not discussed in Chemero's book at any great length is the online, virtual environment. As human–computer interface studies and information ethics works suggest, the human–computer interface is the biggest determinant of future information ethics and also plays an important role in our understanding of what "moral machines" are.[53] The online, virtual environment is therefore the key element in determining the nature of loneliness today by way of an outlook that responds in spirit to Chemero's radical embodied cognitive science. For this reason, I call the kind of loneliness that is pushed on agents today through a system of cloneliness a radical embodied cognitive loneliness. This is to stress its development and enhancement by way of a cognitive system that is being more and more integrated into an environment *as* virtual online environment. It requires both a new understanding of environment to that presumed in such classic works on loneliness as *The Lonely Crowd* and Clark E. Moustakas's *Loneliness* and also a willingness to acknowledge the impact of the human–computer interface on people's understanding of embodiment and hence environment. I will discuss some of the issues this raises for information ethics later in this introduction.

Loneliness is an essential societal concept grounded in emotion that helps us understand identity and community. This book also takes a cross-cultural approach to loneliness by examining twentieth-century and twenty-first-century artistic expressions and examinations of loneliness from Western contexts alongside Japanese and Chinese explorations of loneliness in a selection of texts from the eighteenth century to the present day. Considering the global nature of social networks, virtual reality, the biopolitical commons, academic credentialization, and other issues important for loneliness, it is important to take a cross-cultural look at the experience. Japanese and Chinese explorations of loneliness in fiction and philosophy complement the Western explorations of loneliness that are perhaps better known. This book argues that loneliness is often instilled and necessitated by a late-stage capitalism or neoliberalist ethos that establishes what Hardt and Negri call a dynamic form of the common that involves "both the product of labor and the means of future production."⁵⁴ Loneliness is today nurtured by institutions as a necessary means of cultural reproduction. This results in what the book describes as *cloneliness*, an institutional practice of reproduction in society that nurtures, normalizes, and reproduces loneliness in order to create subjects who are more willing to accept and succumb to ideologies of competition, "extreme individualism," possessive individualism, and compulsive networking. A recent philosophy of cloning, Pang Laikwan's *The Art of Cloning* (2017), written in a Hong Kong and Mainland China context, also offers a new cross-cultural understanding of cloning that describes a Chinese practice of cloning during the Cultural Revolution that works very differently to Western "possessive individualism". Pang Laikwan (2017) has employed cloning to describe cultural practices in Asia in the twentieth century and Kelly Oliver (2013) has described deconstructive ethics as rooted in questions about technologies of reproduction and such oppositions as *grown* versus *made* that are fundamental to our understanding of cloning.⁵⁵ By using the term cloneliness, I am then seeking to bring this concern with neoliberal practices into conversation with biopolitical and phenomenological discourses so that the sense of neoliberalism as a lived, circuitous process involved in the daily practice of life and encounter is emphasized.

Earlier studies of loneliness, written before the age of social media, focus on loneliness as "essential loneliness" or as a foundational state for consciousness and being that is key to self-development.⁵⁶ Clark E. Moustakas's influential work *Loneliness* was published in 1961, the year before Frank O'Connor's *The Lonely Voice* and Richard Yates's *Eleven Kinds of Loneliness* appeared, two of the greatest works on loneliness and literature. Moustakas describes "existential loneliness" as an intrinsic condition of human existence that is key to discovering personal meaning in life. Such accounts of loneliness are transformed today not only by what Moustakas calls the "social urge" to retract from loneliness or by "loneliness anxiety," what is also, for Moustakas, integral to maturation, but also by the social network's surrogate community that offers the promise of contact and community. Another important book on loneliness, David Riesman, Nathan Glazer, and Reuel Denney's *The Lonely Crowd*, was also published in 1961. In many ways, one might argue that the societal change Riesman, Glazer, and Denney describe for America in the 1950s and 1960s, largely due to "mass media," where there is the movement towards a society of "other-directed" as opposed to "inner-directed" and "tradition-directed" individuals, is as important as the shift we are experiencing today in the Internet Age.[57] They describe the change from a society made up largely of "inner-directed" people who work predominantly from a position where they were guided by goals that were essentially "internalized" and "implanted" by "elders" to a society where more people were "other-directed" and worked predominantly from a position where they felt "sensitized to the expectations and preferences of others."[58] It was a "new America" in which people, as Todd Gitlin writes, "no longer cared much about adult authority but rather was hyperalert to peer groups and gripped by mass media."[59] Riesman, Glazer, and Denney's own description of what they intend by "other-direction" is revealing of how far we might have moved from such a society in what is often described as an age of narcissism:

> What we mean by other-direction (though the term itself connotes this only in part) involves a redefinition of the self, away from William James' emphasis on the externals of name, dress, possessions, and toward inner or interactional qualities. The other-directed person wants to be loved rather than esteemed; he wants not to gull or impress, let alone oppress, others but, in the current phrase, to relate to them; he seeks less a snobbish status in the eyes of others than assurance of being emotionally in tune with them ... There has been a general tendency, facilitated by education, by mobility, by the mass media, toward an enlargement of the circles of empathy beyond one's clan, beyond even one's class, sometimes beyond one's country as well.[60]

Riesman, Glazer, and Denney's understanding of mass media could never have imagined what the Internet Age would do for societal change. In reading *The Lonely Crowd*'s description of the new society appearing in America in the 1950s and 1960s, one wherein there is a move away from being inner-oriented towards a state that is more concerned with being loved than esteemed and where people seek to be "emotionally in tune" with "others" through an enlargement of the "circles of empathy," one can only feel a sense of nostalgia. In many ways, we appear to have retreated as a society to a more inner-oriented stage that focuses more on "esteem" and forms of oppression. The kind of loneliness young people experience today through the virtual "mass media" suggests that society offers them much less empathy and emotional understanding than Riesman, Glazer, and Denney had described for their day. And, of course, the authors of *The Lonely Crowd* did not have to try and understand how anyone can feel lonely with 1,000 friends. Writers on the internet such as Nicholas Carr have argued in *The Shallows* that the Internet Age requires a "new intellectual ethic." This book argues that it also requires a new ethics of loneliness. If friendship is what our phone screen tells us it is, then friendship can mean loneliness for many young people. If friendship does mean loneliness, then one is, of course, even less likely than one might have been in the pre-social network age, to own up to, or feel one's way out of, or through, loneliness and loneliness anxiety. As a result, one is also less likely to experience what Moustakas argues is unique to the experience of "existential loneliness": "I began to see that loneliness is neither good nor bad, but a point of intense and timeless awareness of the Self, a beginning which initiates totally new sensitivities and awarenesses, and which results in bringing a person deeply in touch with his own existence and in touch with others in a fundamental sense."[61]

Loneliness as friendship is disarming. Because friendship has been more of an online experience for many young people than for previous generations, young people today can lack the kind of experience with in-person, socially generated feelings that these earlier readings of loneliness are grounded on. For example, in their literary works, both Frank O'Connor and Richard Yates focus on loneliness as it is revealed through the lives of individuals associated with different professions, careers, or identities such as carer, manual laborer, or retired military man. These professions and identities were lived wholly in a non-virtual world. Feelings that linger then in the genetic make-up of the body, feelings attached to older forms of group membership and interaction, keep their potential intact today and are possibly left unrealized in what can be a less demanding and less enriching loneliness-as-friendship virtual environment. However, in acknowledging the changed professional and personal landscape, this book gives neither a treatise against new-fangledness nor a manifesto for Loneliness 2.0. It is rather an attempt to work through in literature and philosophy very real and observed loneliness issues and the resulting lack of coping mechanisms that are apparent in the young people I have come in contact with as a teacher over the last number of years in Asia and in Western countries.[62] As embodied beings, we are hardwired to recall the touch of "real" contact or embodied contact whether it be the pat on the back, the embrace, the handshake, or even the emotion channeled by seeing the embodied reaction in another's in-person face to our own presence.

This is as mentioned also a cross-cultural, interdisciplinary study. The book incorporates insights from researchers and academics working in Japan and Hong Kong. In order to develop this cross-cultural practice, I borrow from Pang Laikwan's notion of cloning to argue that certain structures and institutional practices in society can be responsible for reproducing styles of thought and practices of living.[63] The knowledge industry and the competitive knowledge economy that is grounded on a ranking philosophy is a key factor in what can be described as a testocratic cloning practice in youth development.[64] Rigorous and competitive examination and streaming policies and the privileging of entrepreneurialism and such practices as "incubation" in university-wide courses teach individualism over and above community-based bottom–up initiatives. Pang's understanding of cloning emerges from a very specific reading of artistic practices during the Cultural Revolution in China in the twentieth century. However, I believe that it can be usefully employed to bring out some of the key aspects of the relationship between social media, educational practices, art practice, and loneliness today. Pang offers various symbols and tropes derived from Chinese terms for her new and groundbreaking descriptions of cloning and copying. There is *mofan*, *yangbanzi*, and social mimesis as well as the more transcendental forms of copying that apply to Mao's unique philosophy during the Cultural Revolution. Pang describes how this philosophy, perceived as a doxa by the people at the time, can even be regarded as encompassing individuals such as the intellectuals of the Cultural Revolution. Pang reads the intellectuals of the Cultural Revolution as products that were themselves self-copies who were coaxed into the endless production of copy—rehashed statements and verifications of their "enemy" status in a form of sacrifice. In Chapter 7, I read some works of fiction that respond to this period in China. The contemporary academic and student of our own online era of academic barbarism and online conformism might feel, despite the very different social contexts, that they share some of these feelings of being "self copies" coaxed into the "endless production of copy". Pang's analysis raises important questions about the role and nature of intellectuals, students, and academics in periods of conformism and we recall how Tijmen Schep describes our current age of "social cooling" as one of self-censorship and conformism. Pang argues that the intellectuals of the Cultural Revolution were "not entirely passive" in regard to their own self-cloning through torture and ridicule at the hands of the State. Pang argues that the intellectuals could have been better able to "perform this mimetic power" of the Cultural Revolution that "ordinary people" were well used to playing out in their villages as they impersonated the "powerful officials." In the age of the non-expert and the attack on "expertism," Pang's sense of cloning can also be used to describe practices of education and reproduction in the West, practices and institutional arrangements that recall Pierre Bourdieu's focus on reproduction in education in the 1970s and Zygmunt Bauman's description of education today where even life itself is lived as a "task." Pang argues that these 'mimetic acts' become a means of play, so that the "regime of 'truth' is made to reveal its own fictive and self-referential nature," which also describes our own "post-truth" age of alternative facts and surveillance.[65] Pang finishes her chapter on the intellectuals with the suggestion that "we might start considering negating the intellectuals as the defenders of our polity and humanity" and it is an indirect warning for experts and academics working in the conformist educational age of impact, rankings, and the knowledge industry.[66] This may well be an appeal to the "ordinary people" to start defending the polity and humanity for themselves. It is clear that the kind of cloning Pang assigns to the creative efforts of individuals exploring identity during the conformism of the Cultural Revolution are, despite the obvious political differences, in evidence today amidst an online conformism that nurtures a new kind of loneliness. Pang's readings offer rich possibilities for cross-cultural work and for the application of concepts developed through the interrogation of Chinese critical thought and an Asian humanities perspective that can help us reappraise situations and histories that have for so long been read through the theories of predominantly Western intellectuals.

New philosophies and discourses such as speculative realism, posthumanism, information ethics, object-oriented ontology, and new discourses on the algorithm call for a move from the inside to the outside. Ed Finn writes in *What Algorithms Want* that algorithms "author us"; they anticipate our interests and "informational needs."[67] The age of the algorithm also reminds us that "that which cannot be computed cannot be fully integrated into the broader fabric of culture as we live now."[68] Finn argues that we need an "experimental humanities" to survive in this world and so as to monitor and influence what he calls our "love affair" with algorithms. This book offers its own contribution to this debate. It is essentially, for Finn, about the coming together of our twinned desires "for perfect knowledge of the world and perfect knowledge of ourselves" because "every step that computational systems take in mastering a new field of practice … [means] humanity also takes a step to close the gap."[69] It is therefore a "path of collaboration" we are on and that we must accept; in a society where "Google changes your memory practices" and where identity formation is transformed by social media, collaboration is essential. However, even in Finn's "optimistic vision" where "humans engage in productive collaboration with computational systems"[70] brought about by the "computation turn" or a "theology of computation"[71] we are only ever parts of new "culture machines," what Finn calls "complex assemblages of abstractions, processes and people."[72] Finn's vision says very little about how we might *feel* as collaborators. Finn extends the reading of the "culture machines" to a very limited reading of empathy. He traces empathy back to Adam Smith's notion of the moral imagination and the moral society. However, today, as Finn writes, "with computation performing crucial pieces of the imaginative work of empathy" we no longer do the "imaginative work" necessary for empathy ourselves but instead "outsource it to a culture machine built up of tailored Likert scale questions and comment forms."[73] Therefore—and unfortunately Finn uses Uber as his example of one such new "culture machine" of empathy—the "imaginative work" of empathy, what defines us as citizens and members of community, is taken out of our hands. Algorithmic love is therefore not only reinventing a central facet of "economic life," as Finn suggests, but also of communal life. Since he also notes that there is a resulting "growing dependence on algorithms to perform affective labor," this has huge implications for community, social bonds, and the resulting feelings of isolation and loneliness.[74]

Speculative realists also ask us to move beyond subjectivity so as to observe objects as they *really* are outside our representations of them. We have been misguided all along and a new Copernican revolution has snapped us out of our overly subjective, internalist ways of living. Since the external world has been there a lot longer than us and may survive us, we need to let the world be and approach it on its own terms; or possibly not even this, we must simply accept, as Graham Harman writes, that objects are split and some aspects of them "withdraw from all relations, reposing in an impenetrable reality."[75] However, this is a world that humanity inhabited all along as communities that it evolved within, adapting to this world in becoming embodied according to how it was enabling for development and growth. In other words, just as recent studies in neuroscience argue that our brains are "wired" to be "social," this book argues that if we are "wired" to be social, then it is a sociality that is informed as much by these adaptations over years of living in in-person communities as it is by how "sets of brain regions" "work together."

Loneliness, the *Homo Digitalis* and the Loss of Thought

Two recent books by French writers that have not been translated into English—one by Daniel Cohen a well-known economist and the other by Daniel Zagury, a psychiatrist—offer some reasons for why face to face (F2F) encounter in professional life is undervalued and also how this might be responsible for an era in which the potential barbarism of each one of us, something exacerbated by loneliness, is more likely to show itself.[76] Zagury argues that when we lose the willingness to truly enter into the situation of the other and to think and self-deliberate that we begin to share in, and manifest, similar characteristics to those that Zagury's work has alerted him to in the behavior of those who have committed "crimes of passion."

Another recent study on a similar topic is Daniel Cohen's "*Il Faut Dire Que Les Temps Ont Changé…*" *Chronique (Fiévreuse) D'une Mutation Qui Inquiéte*. Cohen argues that the Internet Age has given birth to many evolutions that have spawned what he describes as the "homo digitalis." He argues that the "progress of artificial intelligence (AI) has now passed a major step following discoveries that have allowed us to imitate the structure of the neural networks of the human brain."[77] Cohen also sees the concentration on technology and the machine–human interface bringing big changes to work and employment, which serves to denigrate the role of F2F encounters in the workplace:

> Human-oriented jobs are much impoverished. They do not sparkle in the radiant future of the world of work. The promises of a society maintained by the world of services, where each is the psychoanalyst or beautician of the other, have been overshadowed by the phenomenon that the economists call "the polarization of labour." Jobs of high-scale return, those of the geeks Silicon Valley, what Robert Reich calls "the manipulators of symbols," are considerably enriched, just like those of the major artists and financiers. The F2F jobs remain numerous but are very badly paid.[78]

Cohen however makes the rather sobering point that in an econocracy it is only professions of high economic return that are valued: "anything that does not bring high scale returns tends to be transferred to the consumer who must repair his own television, reserve his tickets online, and soon heal himself all alone."[79] This undervaluing of the F2F and of anything that does not bring high returns also undervalues work that seeks out the F2F experience in order to listen, right wrongs, or help with emotional distress. This transformation can then also undervalue social work, counselling, and other caring professions that not only enhance wellbeing but also enable us to experience firsthand how entering into the lives and emotions of others benefits us; such practices also implicitly train us in representing to ourselves the links we perceive between emotions and their effects so that we do not exhibit what clinicians describe as an "incapacity to use language to describe feelings ... an aptitude to differentiate feelings and emotions from bodily sensations [what leads to] a burial of internal conflicts that remain impossible to elaborate."[80] Such a lack is evident, for Zagury, then among many young people for whom there is no longer what he describes as an aptitude or willingness to engage in thought: "When the individual is desubjectivised he only uses his thought as an instrument of his power, his ambition, and especially of the collective action he has completely merged with; when the smallest doubt is lacking, the smallest hesitation, the most tenuous of distances, then the subject no longer thinks."[81] Zygmunt Bauman sees the same thing happening for today's "internauts"; research reveals that the "most eagerly shared viral moments are those that come directly from the unconscious. Loners in front of a phone, tablet or laptop screen, with only 'viral' others present, seem to put reason together with morality to sleep."[82] Of course, it is not a new phenomenon but the scale of the problem is new; we recall Simone Weil's words of 1934: "Never have men been so incapable, not only of subordinating their actions to their thoughts, but even of thinking."[83] This wholehearted allegiance to an online form of groupthink has also been documented by studies of online trolling.

Zagury goes further in observing that one of the main characteristics displayed by subjects who have been convicted of brutal "crimes of passion" is a "difference between the manner of representing themselves and their description of their circle or surroundings, through which they invariably disregard their own needs."[84] For Daniel Zagury, this lack of an ability to think and deliberate with ourselves and to "register representations and to welcome their affects in their own psychic space," what puts us in danger of losing the ability to deliberate intimately and also to think in the first person, is part and parcel of a new era of employment and technology where F2F communication is undervalued.[85] However, Zagury regards it as potentially more damaging and destructive as it is linked to our potential to commit barbaric acts of violence without knowing at any deep level why we would do so. Zagury's years of psychiatric work both with "ordinary" patients and with murderers and terrorists convinces him that we have entered an era where there is a "trouble with thought"; he writes of his experiences analyzing the thought processes of those that have committed barbaric "crimes of passion" and have been unable to think through issues of "separation, of pregnancy, [of] the offence grounded on narcissism"; this is because "thought [has] gone fallow, dissolved, [become] compartmentalized." He argues that one of the "common traits of all these mutative processes is the loss of the capacity to think, to debate with oneself, to deliberate, to discern, to inscribe representations and to welcome their affects in their own psychic space."[86]

The tendency is quite marked in the case of those young people in particular that he describes as "aggrieved narcissists" and the online, virtual world is very often an important contributing factor to such narcissism. When such people then commit barbaric acts, Zagury asks, "how does one analyse the disproportion between the act and the alleged motif, between its gravity and the personality of the adolescent or the young adult implicated" especially when "apart from any intellectual insufficiency, thought is not really a privileged exercise for them?"[87] Such young people "not only do not know the pleasure of thought but they flee it, they avoid it, it is short-circuited because it's a source of danger."[88] Many argue that the virtual world, in not allowing young people to experience fully the implications of their acts such as online bullying, in allowing them to spend so much time on their own in virtual communities, is also enabling of this lack of engagement with their own emotions and feelings and the representations these conjure inside them in relation to the consequences of their actions for others. It also raises the important related point: even if such young people or students are made aware of this lack, because this lack is itself the practice of thinking and of self-deliberation, then any process of "re-educating" or training them in the pleasures of thinking is liable to be difficult. As Zagury says, in a powerful appeal at the end of his book, how can we

> transmit this liberty of being and of thought? These are the stakes for a democratic pedagogy, an awakening to a culture which teaches us to learn, to think for oneself, to be aware of the taste of others, to agree to be shared, to safeguard a little critical doubt, to be open to conflict, to be able—if required—to give the contrary of what one receives, to disobey, and in every circumstance to think and to continue to debate with oneself. Then without doubt, [our young people] while not being totally immune to the barbarism of ordinary people, will most likely be able to steer clear of it.[89]

Discriminatory groupthink, or collective thought taken on board and professed without any real encounter with the effects of such talk, without any experience of hearing about the effects of such discourse on real victims, can "de-singularise" the individual. Zagury argues that the most extreme instances of this dissolution of individualism or de-singularization take place in terrorist groups or cells where the young person "aspires to being a clone." He or she does not want anything at all to do with "him or herself, her aspirations, her deeper sensibility."[90] This is the kind of cloning this books speaks for. In taking stock of both Cohen's and Zagury's observations, we can see a tendency for society to undervalue self-deliberation and self-examination of one's life in relation to one's own values, wants, and desires; it is essentially as Zagury argues, a denigration of thinking itself, a de-singularization and a cloning. However, since the technological firms that make the big returns Cohen mentions are run by what he describes as "geeks" or individuals who have devoted their lives to the online world, it is no surprise that their creations both facilitate and promote the kind of lives and experiences their founders know best. Their social media creations also rely on massive group membership where everyone is content to follow the same online rules and regulations about sharing, posting, and liking. The feeling of wanting and needing to be with the "in-crowd" has never been so strong. These corporations need you to be the connected loner that spends as much time as possible staring at the screen. As the MGMT song "TSLAMP" describes, through its quirky rendition of a love affair between the phone as persona and its viewer or owner, "all I want and all I know" can quickly become "Time spent sitting all alone/ Time spent looking at my phone."[91]

Daniel Cohen relates these phone practices to the macroscopic world of big business and its impact on society. He says we are being shoehorned into an "algorithmic life" by the GAFA big four: "in the algorithmic life proposed by GAFA, the 'inner self' is lost and the intimacy of the home shattered."[92] This process of giving ourselves up to the isolation of the phone and the screen is not then solely a consumer choice, or chance occurrence, but a powerful new master narrative of big business in our lives in the twenty-first century. Since privacy is now almost redundant, we must find privacy online in the selective groups we furnish with carefully arranged narratives or image-stories; even our privacy—what used to relate to our inner self—requires the validation of others we may never have met. The inner becomes outer and in the process—as Zagury argues—we lose the ability to represent our thoughts about our feelings meaningfully back to ourselves. It feels wrong; it feels like all decisions must be made according to the like-o-meter of the post; even the most seemingly profound sense of self, what Will Storr argues is conjured by our "storytelling brains" and their narratives of heroism, are now up for discussion and peer review in an online validation process before we even begin working out whether it is right for who we are.[93] The "connected house," Cohen continues, "brings a mass of potential suppliers into your intimacy."

Private life, Éric Sadin writes in *la Vie algorithmique: critique de la raison numérique*, or "supposing that a part of oneself could be excluded from the observation of others, must be revisited entirely."⁹⁴

Cohen extends this concern with the devaluation of the F2F, the revaluation of privacy, and the polarization of labor to a reading of the changes humanity must accept in the face of technological advances, artificial intelligence, and robots. He notes that the capacity of computers to decide between "contradictory imperatives" is weak because they lack something like "common sense."⁹⁵ However, he recognizes that even though robots may only really "be comfortable with other robots, the real risk is that it may be mankind that must adapt itself to the machine and not the inverse."⁹⁶ As Serge Tisseron writes in *Le jour ou mon robot m'aimera*, "we must beware of the ability of humans to get so used to robots, that they adjust to their pace and their requirements to the extent that they become robots themselves, not biologically but psychologically."⁹⁷ Transhumanists may well plead for the hybridization of the human and the numeric, the organic and the digital, but this hybridization "has already commenced," Cohen argues; "the iPhone has become a new organ of the human body."⁹⁸

Cohen contrasts the iPhone generation with the 1960s generation and its belief that it could change the world through strikes and protests. Social media sites such as Facebook try to take this optimism online. It presents itself as a platform where everyone "can create, in networks, its own social environment, by elective affinities, by proximity, without ever using visible hierarchies ... we can accept or refuse friends as we wish. Horizontality is the rule. The numerical world has imported (certain) mythologies of the counter-culture of the 60s, in place of those which formed the industrial world, itself inheriting a vertical, religious, conception of society."⁹⁹ But the truth is very different Cohen argues; we have given in to new forms of hierarchy and a new form of servitude: "in the big mirror of social networks each seeks to magnify the construction of a self visible to others." It is a new "society of the spectacle, but unlike in 1968 where, for Andy Warhol, everyone can be a celebrity for 30 minutes, today it is "about being a celebrity for at least 15 people!"¹⁰⁰ Experiments also reveal how the internet and its social networks mean young people are more and more content to spend long periods on their own. Jean M. Twenge argues in *iGen* that young people devote 6 hours a day to their phones; young adults are meeting up less, having less sex, and even regard online resources such as Netflix as having "replaced sex."[101] Children sleep with their phones, keeping them under their pillows or their mattresses. Adolescents spend 17 hours a day sleeping, going to school, studying but all the remainder is for the essential pass-times on the new media.[102] Young people are also described as victims of the *Tanguy* effect, the title of a film where the eponymous hero never wants to leave the family home, provoking the exasperation of the parents. Cohen also contrasts the iPhone generation, the iGen, with the millennials, the latter being more optimistic in "exhibiting a certain confidence in themselves and their society." The newer generation, mindful of the recession, have more difficulties expressing themselves in public (in class) and they are preoccupied with their studies." Cohen argues that this generation "are more interested in the extrinsic values of success and money than the intrinsic value of an activity itself."[103] A study from 2013 by Ethan Kross suggests that time spent on Facebook is often correlated with sadness, feelings of loneliness and less satisfaction.[104] However, other studies have demonstrated the opposite and have observed moderate increases in "life satisfaction" through "internet adoption and internet uses."[105] Many of the articles that document the positive aspects of internet use focus on the greater opportunities and resources the internet offers for promoting careers, work, education, social status,[106] and enhancing income opportunities.[107] However, even these studies spend quite some time noting the detrimental effects of internet use beyond what is described as "appropriate use." It is also possible that loneliness itself is a cause of the frequent use of the internet. However, John Cacioppo has argued that one of the reasons people are lonely is that they are "not sharing anything that matters with anyone else"; to end the feeling of loneliness one needs to have a sense of "mutual aid and protection."[108] And since Cacioppo's belief that loneliness "*leads* to depression"[109] was made against the realization that "every pre-agricultural society we know" survived through a "dense web of social contacts" and the "reciprocal commitments they maintain," how does this sense of "mutual aid" extend to social networks? A Danish study headed by Meik Witing of the Happiness Research Institute that separated a population into two groups, one that continued to use Facebook and one that is deprived of it, also found that at the end of a week those that had stopped using Facebook felt "less alone, less depressed and happier."[110] Cohen ultimately sees the social network and the internet as inaugurating a new era of addiction whereas Jacques-Alain Miller writes from a Lacanian perspective: "the general model of ordinary life in the twenty-first century is addiction. The 'One' plays all alone with his or her drug, and every activity can become a drug: sport, sex, work, smartphone, Facebook."[111] The ever-increasing consumption of drugs—consider the opiate epidemic in the United States—is then the testimony of this "revolt against the vulnerability of human happiness." Cohen argues that "humanity is not programmed for happiness."[112] This new addiction of the "One" is supported by GAFA where the "addictive need to be connected at all times" is "artificially created" by the feeling of being hooked up to a series and one simply waits for the next hit. Combined with FOMO, the digital world then creates the disease it knows only it can heal.[113] One paradox then of the digital age is that "man has never been so on display and yet he has never worn so many masks."[114] This gives people the sense, especially young people who have grown up in this world, that the "face they contemplate on the screen is not really theirs, but a digital self," and as we have seen Facebook is working out how to add your face to the network.[115] Whereas the digital age and GAFA presents itself as the inheritor of the individualist tradition (and hence the older sense of meaningful loneliness that went along with this) in reality it constructs a "hybrid being of networks and algorithms" that shatter the old foundations of meaningful loneliness, reliant as it was on more stable, less virtual notions of self, individual, and community. Cohen argues that GAFA and its digital age, in prioritizing "the direct" nature of the social networks, cut off all possibility of the superego and self-control expressing themselves, and therefore it offers to all human impulses the possibility of self-destruction." The *homo digitalis*, by these different routes, networks, and rhizomes "threatens to deprive us of ourselves."[116] Cohen argues that while it is impossible to refuse to live with the internet, that the "digital society must also learn to live with us, individuals of flesh and blood."[117] The rules and regulation of living within the digital society must be carried out in such a way as to ensure that we are "not enveloped completely by its networks of addiction and surveillance."[118] There must be checks and balances to restrict further encroachment and giving up of personal space to GAFA; for example, public institutions such as hospitals and schools must be afforded "the means to think for themselves about the solutions that artificial intelligence can bring."[119] Cohen sees the digital revolution as affecting all aspects of privacy and individualism including interpersonal communication. Therefore a "process of re-civilisation of our interpersonal relations has become essential."[120] Both Cohen and Zagury assert that society's steady, headlong run into complete immersion in the digital world necessitates stops that should take the form of promotion and sustenance of older forms of thought. Cohen argues that "the culture of writing, the book, is the other essential pillar that must be protected. It is less about making impeccable dictates than about sharing the taste of reading."[121] For Cohen, OECD studies reveal that young French students have a hard time understanding texts.[122] As Roberto Caselli argues, the book is a contract between author and reader and if the writer has to compete with the thousands of temptations on the iPad, he will end up preferring to "play on the affects rather than with the imagination."[123]

For Cohen, the kind of obedience that was integral to the old world of production is now replaced by an imperative to create that is just as demanding as the old obedience of the age of industry. Nowhere is this felt more keenly than in the universities, the knowledge industries of our times. To find one's place in the network requires feats of ingenuity and/or cruelty.[124] However, the new digital age is different from that of the age of industry because it destroys the implicit solidarity (hierarchical but solidarity still) of the industrial world. In the end, in order to preserve the sense of self from the complete usurpation by *homo digitalis* and its ever deeper promotion of cloneliness we can take some advice from Aldo Schiavone on how to manage our new digital spaces: "we cannot allow the technique, and the network of powers with which it is crossed, to decide without mediation the forms of life that we are allowed to live. It seems more and more necessary to find a point of equilibrium which, while integrating the link between technique and market, can be placed outside of it, and which then allows for the elaboration of what will appear as a common good."[125]

Information Ethics and Reinvention of Privacy

Information ethics (IE) asks us to think beyond any singular perspective that may have allowed for older descriptions of loneliness and loneliness anxiety to emerge. IE revises the subject of anxiety as "what may count as a centre of minimal moral concern." IE replaces "life" with existence and interprets the latter informationally. IE is an ecological ethics that replaces *biocentrism* with *ontocentrism* and then interprets Being (instead of conduct or becoming) in informational terms.[126] The ethical question asked by IE is "What is good for an informational entity and the infosphere in general?" Any informational entity is recognized to be the "centre of some basic ethical claims, which deserve recognition and should help to regulate the implementation of any information process involving it."[127] IE responds to the fact that "more and more commonly, moral actions are the result of complex interactions among distributed systems integrated on a scale vastly larger than the singly human being" (160). Even when IE does assign individualism to an entity it is only in terms of how it is a "packet of information" and how that "information" is being violated:

> Privacy is nothing less than the defence of the personal integrity of a packet of information, the individual, and the invasion of an individual's informational privacy, the unauthorized access, dispersion, and misuse of her information is an infringement of her me-hood and a disruption of the information environment that it constitutes. The violaton is not a violation of ownership, of personal rights, of instrumental values, or of consequentalist rules, but a violation of the nature of the informational self.[128]

The language of cognitive neuroscience also reimagines the nature of loneliness and community by directly transferring metaphors dealing with interactions between people—either online or otherwise—onto the "behavior" and electrical pulses of neurons firing in the brain. In *Social: How Our Brains Are Wired to Connect*, Matthew D. Lieberman argues: "Just as there are multiple social networks on the internet such as Facebook and Twitter, each with its own strengths, there are also multiple social networks in our brains, sets of brain regions that work together to promote our social well-being."[129]

Even as a rhetorical ploy, the comparison of a group of Facebook users to different regions of the brain in terms of how they promote the well-being of the individual sounds like a category mistake at so many levels. In reading various, unique online friendships as different parts of a brain, we not only epitomize how "existential loneliness" is being discarded by much cognitive neuroscience but we also suggest that the isolated examination of parts of the brain through fMRI scan analysis can be taken as a necessary and sufficient condition for examining how groups of people work in community and in social interactions.

It is perhaps no surprise that bodies and embodied feelings have been slow to catch up with the demands of living as an "information packet," a "centre of some basic ethical claims," or a post-human entity within programs of education that must institute practices that cater to students as information packets and informationally connected nodes. People who have had arms and legs amputated often speak of experiencing phantom limbs; perhaps in a similar way when community exchanges and in-person interactions are truncated or substituted by newer, less embodied forms of communication, we might also consider whether there is an experience of phantom feelings. However, perhaps there is as yet no serviceable prosthetic limb for the atrophied response and affect mechanisms experienced through in-person engagement. This book then reaffirms the place of a radical embodied cognitive loneliness informed by the radical embodied cognitive theories of philosophers such as Anthony Chemero. It argues that such an understanding of loneliness can restore some of the "essential loneliness" that writers such as Moustakas and Henry James describe as essential for meaningful art practice and also as a state that has to be conceived as "within life itself, and that all creations in some way spring from solitude, meditation, and isolation."[130] Older accounts of loneliness in art, such as Wordsworth's famous line "I wandered lonely as a cloud," suggest that loneliness provides us with spots of time that provide insights about self- illumination. Objects in the environment offer us the opportunity to re-experience after the initial encounter a moment of connection with the environment or with the objects themselves, objects that we don't only need to let "withdraw" as object-oriented ontology suggests. This is not to say that similar moments cannot be experienced and triggered by

Instagram photos of objects or places but that the experience is different. With people and with friends the difference is more stark. If you have ever "ended" a friendship in person, across a dinner table, a lunch table, or on an empty street at night there are glances, smiles, looks of sorrow and understanding to ease your comprehension of the experience and the transition; there is a real, embodied, in-person exchange, a back and forth, a give and take to both relive and work out when you recall the friendship. A friend lost on Facebook is lost at the click of a mouse and the two friends might not know for some time that the friendship has been cut. This is a very different experience and yet neuroscience simply tells us that the pain caused by social injury is similar, or is experienced by the same regions of the brain, as the pain resulting from physical injury. It tells us little about how differently we experience the loss of friendship on social media and the loss of a friend in the old way friends were lost; the readings of literature that follow remind us of some of these older forms of "existential loneliness."

Our Lack of Solitude

Another recent study of loneliness is Lars Svendsen's *A Philosophy of Loneliness*. Svendsen makes an interesting point in arguing that a number of studies, such as Lazare Mijuskovic's *Loneliness in Philosophy, Psychology and Literature*, reduce "the entirety of human existence to a state of loneliness."[131] This is something this book does not want to suggest. For Svendsen, such arguments might then claim that if people do not regard loneliness as such a defining state in their lives that they are "living in denial of their basic existential condition."[132] Mijuskovic even goes so far, Svendsen argues, as to suggest that interpersonal communication is nothing more than a "momentary, albeit comforting, illusion."[133] Mijuskovic claims, for Svendsen, that "loneliness is the basic structure of self-consciousness, and that when one attempts to see through themselves completely, they find an emptiness or desolation, in short: loneliness."[134] Svendsen reads such a description as suggesting that the self is "made utterly transparent to itself" and he argues that many philosophers including Kant have argued that such an idea is problematic. Svendsen also asks why such "introspection should yield a more basic truth than that revealed by extrospection," which is of course a very valid point.[135] This book focuses primarily on how literature and philosophy represent loneliness; it might be argued that the encounter with loneliness in such books, including Svendsen's, is likely to first incite an introspective deliberation on the topic. Svendsen does admit that "you are present in your own thoughts and experiences in a way that no other person can ever be" and that "perhaps our era's greatest problem is not excessive loneliness, but rather too little solitude." In other words, solitude is being threatened by many of the experiences and developments I have discussed above. Chronic interaction or chronic sociality online are, we are told, different to older forms of solitude and therefore loneliness.[136] However, one wonders how different some of the moments we spend online in a state of chronic interaction are to solitude, or whether they are giving us a watered-down version of solitude, different to what Svendsen and others find in solitude, namely moments where "one is forced to relate to oneself, and to succeed in finding peace within this self-relationship."[137]

Svendsen argues that one must learn to take responsibility for one's loneliness as one must take responsibility for one's death and that this requires a great deal of emotional maturity; the inability to establish solitude is then revealing of emotional immaturity. He would seem to suggest then that solitude seems enabling of this moment of introspection or relation to oneself where one can seek a kind of peace within this self-relationship. Of course, it must be noted that solitude can be accessed in large cities as well as in rural hideaways. Svendsen argues that you can find it in company by daydreaming and he even argues that in large cities you can enjoy a type of solitude that requires anonymity, which is more difficult to achieve in smaller locales, where the chances are greater that you will meet an acquaintance who breaks into your solitude.[138] However, anonymity and solitude seem to be quite distinct. Anonymity requires the awareness that others see you but do not recognize you; solitude seems to describe for most people a moment when you are on your own, a moment when you are not chiefly conscious of yourself as someone being observed by others without recognition. The feeling of having people around you and sometimes pressing up against you in densely crowded cities without the possibility of recognition seems to speak more of a sense of anonymity or even alienation than of solitude. The anonymity of the lonely crowd has been overdetermined and even fetishized. However, it is, I would argue, distinctly different from the type of solitude you might find in your own company, whether it is in a field, a mosque, synagogue, church, or empty art gallery. It is different again from the kind of online solitude that is described as social. Svendsen does come back to the essential difference between solitude and loneliness by suggesting that it "consists in the relationship one has to oneself in that condition, if one succeeds in remaining relatively self-sufficient."[139] However, to suggest that one can prevent oneself from lapsing into loneliness from solitude by making sure one is self-sufficient is to perhaps miss the essential point of loneliness. As so much of the literature and art of solitude tells us, no one can tell when feelings of loneliness will emerge. However, perhaps Svendsen, rather like Sartre and Roquentin earlier, is right to suggest that we can act to prevent oneself descending too far into loneliness. Too many theories of loneliness, such as what Svendsen calls "phenomenological loneliness," regard loneliness as visiting us from outside or as caused by external factors when, in truth, we may still have the ability to take control of our lives and take more of the blame ourselves. For example, the mantra he likes to return to in his book is that "you are not lonely because you are alone—you are alone because you are lonely." This refers to the argument that many sufferers of chronic loneliness may see their condition as endogenous, that is, not influenced so much by social surroundings.[140] However, this seems to be something of a chicken and egg question. Obviously, Svendsen is making a case for getting rational with loneliness, ensuring that you understand that being on your own is not the principal cause of your loneliness but that it can produce kinds of behavior that are antisocial and prevent you from wanting to meet others thus exacerbating feelings of loneliness. This is an approach to loneliness that may well incite us to learn to try and do something with our loneliness but it tells us very little about what loneliness is; it speaks more about the symptoms of that loneliness than about loneliness itself. It also appears to suggest that people can easily acknowledge they are lonely. Svendsen argues that because of feelings of shame people are unwilling to admit in public that they feel loneliness. He gives the example of asking students in his lectures to raise their hands if they experience loneliness and of seeing no hands raised. However, admitting loneliness in public to others and acknowledging to oneself that the feelings one has are loneliness or are the result of loneliness are very different. It is very easy to act in denial of the fact that one is suffering from loneliness to the extent that one never learns to employ the most appropriate coping mechanism for loneliness. This book argues that this is, more than ever, the case in the age of chronic interaction or chronic sociality. While the role of social media in increasing levels of loneliness will long be debated, it is likely that it may well increase our inability to seek and endure solitude.[141] It also may well serve to redefine sociality as a kind of aloneness or low grade solitude. Chronic interaction leads one to believe that one is connected all the time even when asleep and yet one may actually be feeling lonely or experiencing the symptoms of loneliness while connected and interacting. However, because the state of being connected, of chatting or liking, is a state of interaction one is less likely to regard one's emotions as related to loneliness. As, Olivia Laing writes in *The Lonely City*, our "rapturous, narcissistic fixation with screens" has resulted in the "enormous devolution of our emotional and practical lives to technological apparatuses."[142] The realization that one is suffering from loneliness may then be even more traumatic or shameful when it hits since we are constantly told that we have so many friends and so many connections. This is one aspect of Svendsen's study that might seem reductive in its treatment of loneliness. Svendsen does not go gently with the lonely reader; in writing of "the lonely person" he tells us "I cannot tell you why you are lonely … The fact that you are lonely does not necessarily mean that others have failed you or that they have fallen short … it can be that it is you who have fallen short."[143] The authorial voice is very much removed from the loneliness it is analyzing; it sets up an "us and them" arrangement with regard to loneliness. There are those who take responsibility for their loneliness who may well be capable of overcoming it completely and there are those like his "you" who persist in expecting too much from the affections of others and who fall short when it comes to taking responsibility. Svendsen is a philosopher and yet he uses numerous literary examples in his study to get his points across. However, literature more than perhaps any other discipline shows us that the reductive treatment of emotions and feelings by the positing of an "other" or a "you" can itself serve to exacerbate those feelings. This book focuses on literature to explore how it can both flesh out our understanding of loneliness and its cross-cultural dimensions.

2

Loneliness as Method: Henry James and the "Essential Loneliness" of Artistic Practice

Henry James's novels consistently offer us new metaphors for individualism. These metaphors take shape in an era when a distinctly American brand of individualism was also a central concern for many of his compatriots' philosophies of liberal education. In recent years, however, individualism has come to be associated with the ills of consumerist societies. Michael D. Higgins speaks of an "extreme individualism" that is a symptom of social forces that work against "the foundations of a society that is more inclusive, participatory and equal."[1] This chapter explores the context and make-up of a turn of the century individualism that was central to James and to early programs of education in the humanities and liberal arts. For James, such individualism worked through his long engagement with what he calls his "essential loneliness" and through his deep appreciation for art and aesthetic practice. This version of individualism also influences his overall understanding of the novel as a genre that in its most complete form must be removed from what he calls the "democratic example." This chapter will therefore also give a reading of James's essay "The New Novel" in relation to the version of self-education as aesthetic education that emerges in *Autobiography* and in such novels as *The Tragic Muse*.

The parallel between the individual and the artwork and the importance of individualism for aesthetic experience is consistently privileged in James. James relies on a rich array of artistic objects and practices as tropes for the work of the novelist, individualism, and the nature of the "relations" he grants his characters. Characters become portraits and sketches and their relations are encapsulated by what artistic towers, founts, temples, and bowls elicit as beautiful and mysterious artistic objects. These are, of course, symbols for different aspects of the beautiful life as conceived by James. The sacred fount, an image that haunts the novel of the same name, can be read as a metaphor both for the life-giving power of the ever-flowing imagination and the maddening mental fecundity of the narrator. It also alludes to the glorious fecundity of a young couple with all their potential before them. The golden bowl as art object is a symbol of yet more relations; it represents initially something of the grandeur of arranged marriages until its gold gilt and the crack in its crystal is used by Maggie as something to speak for her as a "document" of the betrayal of trust and promise between couples. Its deceptive grandeur also speaks for models of decorum between father and daughter that can only ever be broken symbolically in James. James's final ornament, his ivory tower, is an elaborate and intricate piece of Indian marble that, we are told, acts as a kind of altar to the spirit of society of America's new economic age, its Gilded Age.

In *The Portrait of a Lady* this parallel between individual and artwork becomes more pronounced as individuals and their "relations" are submerged by the weighty grandeur of the artwork and what art can give to society. Isabel Archer is a portrait, a sketch, a "frail vessel" while her step-daughter Pansy Osmond is an "open book," a "blank page," a "Dresden-china shepherdess,"[2] "an Infanta of Velasquez."[3] James even prefigures his golden bowl in this novel written over twenty years before with a cracked coffee-cup of rare porcelain on the mantelpiece of Gilbert Osmond, the artist and collector. The coffee cup comes to embody the cracks in both Madame Merle and Osmond's relations and Isabel's and Osmond's relations and by implication the cracks in Isabel's own person as secrets are revealed. James even goes so far as to have the stage director of Isabel's married life in the novel, Gilbert Osmond, advise Isabel to "make one's life a work of art."[4] The portrait is the portrait of a lady as James would have her in the late nineteenth century and his devotion to art leads us to believe that character, for him, exists as a worked over, lacquered, and varnished presentation for framing. Therefore, even though James tells us in the Preface to *Portrait* in the words of his friend and writer Turgenev that all he wants in his novels is "relations"—"I seem to have as much as I need to show my people, to exhibit their relations with each other, for that is all my measure"[5]—we quickly learn that what he calls the "inward life" is the subject of his portraits and that these come to take precedence over any "relations." James decouples the "inward life" from nineteenth-century narrative's often unproblematized momentum that is driven by dialogue and event and that rarely lets the character stall, reflect, and deliberate as James's characters so often do. James admits in the Preface to *Portrait* that "what is obviously the best thing in the book"[6] is a scene towards the middle of the novel where Isabel engages in a solitary, "extraordinary meditative vigil" in which James shows us "what an 'exciting' inward life may do for the person leading it even while it remains perfectly normal."[7]

James ultimately comes to see the beautiful mind as a beautiful work of art. The mind achieves this end by giving itself up to self-inspection in the course of questioning what it is that incites aesthetic interest; it is "essential loneliness" that allows for these moments. James's characters are created in a highly symbolic language forever pointing to another artwork as a benchmark for the work he is doing as author through these characters. There must be symbols dotted along the way to sustain the characters' relations and their introspective deliberations that often lead to impasses in the "real" world of human interactions. The symbolism of these ornaments and objects take on a narrative impulse of its own that can compensate for the sluggishness readers often associate with his characters' human "relations." One almost feels that the relation between the reader and the ornament, as symbol for the particular set of human relations on display, takes precedence over the novel's plot. The emphasis shifts from a focus on what an ornament as symbol can reveal about the destinies of two interested parties to a focus on what a richly mined series of events in two characters' lives can reveal about the reader's negotiation with symbol. James's fondness for intransitive verbs, for the italicized *that* or *it*, and for phrases made up of seemingly throwaway or colloquial American idiomatic expressions may even be taken as setting up the exclamatory non-object directed capacity of language as a symbol for the event of human "relations."

I want to examine how James's description of the "essential loneliness of my life" contributes to his rendering of what he calls the "inward life" and its "more intimate education." James gives us a version of individualism through the aesthetic that ultimately relies on a privileged solitary regard for existence.

James can therefore be read as offering us important lessons for education in an age that, as Higgins argues above, is devoted to "extreme individualism" and competition. James grants the reader private moments of "dawdling" as a ground to a philosophy of artistic practice. The solitary reflection on beauty allows us to reevaluate isolation and loneliness as entry points into the contemplation of the beautiful as a ground for education. The ideal aesthetic education James describes in his fiction and essays is relevant to programs of education today. It reminds us to allow students to come to terms with their loneliness as an emotion that grants them states of mindfulness and reflection that can then enable them to work out what are the reasons for their likes and dislikes. Even though James's descriptions of the inward life, and the "more intimate education" he draws from this, can be regarded as privileging a notion of individualism, it is "a sense of individualism that is rooted in self-reflection." And since James sees the work of the artist—the novel being for James the most complete artwork—as a kind of "sacred office," replete with a moral education, James's novels are also proposing an aesthetic education grounded on a notion of individualism that parallels contemporary visions of individualism in liberal education.

The kind of aesthetic education James put forward with his "more intimate education" is informed by the great American education tradition that runs from Emerson, through James's brother William, and on to Dewey. Michael Roth has recently taken us on a tour of this educational tradition, from Jefferson to Franklin and from Emerson to Rorty in *Beyond the University*.[8] Louis Menand's *The Metaphysical Club* gave us an earlier version of this academic history by relating the new kind of individualism the American university promotes to the work of the pragmatists.[9] The pragmatism of Louis Agassiz, with whom William James worked, also sought to redefine the relationship between the individual and the environment. Agassiz's theory of recapitulation sees the process by which the universe "becomes itself as replicated in the life history of the individual,"[10] and Peirce also saw "in every form of material manifestation ... a corresponding form of human thought, so that the human mind is as wide in its range of thought as the physical universe which it thinks."[11] James takes these developments in the presentation of individualism to new imaginative heights in his novels.

James believed that the ground of his art was human loneliness. However, it is a human loneliness that also draws from the "sacred" nature of the human voice, a symbol for the human that was integral to debates on language and identity in the twentieth century. However, the "sacred" nature of the voice in James that recalls earlier Christian readings of education also raises the question of what happens to the voice in loneliness and in isolation. As Derrida might ask, can the voice hear itself in this "inward life"? Or to put it more phenomenologically, is James here describing a version of the phenomenological voice, "this spiritual flesh that continues to speak and be present to itself—*to hear itself*—in the absence of the world."[12] In other words, what kind of "more intimate education" that relies on a "sacred" voice do we allow ourselves in moments of loneliness when we are reflecting on the reasons for our aesthetic interests? James consistently describes the "seeds" of this "inward life" as stemming from moments of solitary reflection on aesthetic interest. They first occur for him in the events described in the first part of his *Autobiography: A Small Boy and Others* when as a child he spends his days dawdling, gaping, and strolling outside New York theaters.[13] These are practices James later transfers to his work as novelist as he dawdles over certain details of a character's reflection and then, in turn, passes on this capacity and practice to the reader.

The Education of the Young Henry James

In *Autobiography* James writes that in growing up a "hotel child"[14] in New York there was "incomparably" the chance to "dawdle and gape … it was even as if I had become positively conscious that the social scene so peopled would pretty well always say more to me than anything else."[15] James returns again and again to a moment that he regards as his earliest manifestation of aesthetic feeling. In a scene that becomes a motif, the young James is standing alone before a theater placard or playbill from the 1850s on Fifth Avenue:

> [H]e stood long and drank deep at those founts of romance that gushed from the huge placards of the theatre. These announcements, at a day when advertisement was contentedly but information, had very much the form of magnified playbills; they consisted of vast oblong sheets, yellow or white,

pasted upon tall wooden screens ... These screens rested sociably against trees and lamp-posts as well as against walls and fences ...; but the sweetest note of their confidence was that, in parallel lines and the good old way, characters facing performers, they gave the whole cast.[16]

James returns to this memory some pages later as it assumes a similar power to Proust's madeleine or cobblestones:

Which reflections, in the train of such memories as those just gathered, may perhaps seem overstrained—though they really to my own eyes cause the images to multiply. Still others of these break in upon me and refuse to be slighted; reconstituting as I practically am the history of my fostered imagination, for whatever it may be worth, I won't pretend to a disrespect for *any* contributive particle. I left myself just above staring at the Fifth Avenue poster, and I can't but linger there while the vision it evokes insists on swarming.[17]

He returns to the scene a few pages later:

I turn round again where I last left myself gaping at the old rickety bill-board in Fifth Avenue; and am almost as sharply aware as ever of the main source of its spell, the fact that it most often blazed with the rich appeal of Mr. Barnum, whose "lecture-room," attached to the Great American Museum, overflowed into posters of all the theatrical bravery disavowed by its title ... It was thus quite in order that I should pore longest, there at my fondest corner, over the Barnum announcements—my present inability to be superficial about which has given in fact the measure of my contemporary care.[18]

The fourth time he mentions the scene it has changed again and he explains why he keeps returning to it:

The principle of this prolonged arrest, which I insist on prolonging a little further, is doubtless in my instinct to grope for our *earliest aesthetic seeds* [my italics]. Careless at once and generous the hands by which they were sown, but practically appointed none the less to cause that peculiarly flurried hare to run-flurried because over ground so little native to it-when so many others held back. Is it *that* air of romance that gilds for me then the Barnum background-taking it as a symbol ...—from the total impression of which things we plucked somehow the flower of the ideal.[19]

Todorov has argued that the theme that ties together many of James's narratives is a "quest for an absolute and absent cause"[20] and it seems that James has here applied this to, or derived this from, his own life story. James ultimately reveals that one's attempts to disentangle the "inward life" for presentation as what is "outward" become absurd and ultimately almost harrowing as one must disturb what lies "morally affiliated" with one's "inner" sense of oneself. The effort to

> record becomes, under memories of this order—and that is the only trouble—a tale of assimilations small and fine ... Such are the absurdities of the poor dear inward life—when translated, that is, and perhaps ineffectually translated, into terms of the outward and trying at all to flourish on the lines of the outward; a reflection that might stay me here weren't it that I somehow feel morally affiliated, tied as by knotted fibers, to the elements involved.[21]

James is able to access the connection between these aesthetic seeds and their moral affiliation through his "essential loneliness."

On the other side of any idealized individualism we therefore must accept loneliness. The first-person voice of *The Sacred Fount* and Lambert Strether of *The Ambassadors* realize the limitations of their perspectives that are colored by their artistic visions of how the world should be. Their realizations lead them to profound enquiries and deliberations on the nature of loneliness, solitude, and futility and James puts these concerns at the center of his work. Late modernism discovered an explicit interest in loneliness with 1962 seeing the publication of Richard Yates's *Eleven Kinds of Loneliness* and Frank O'Connor's *The Lonely Voice*.[22] However, it is Henry James who describes the "essential loneliness of my life" as the chief ground for his art.[23] James explained to Desmond MacCarthy how isolation and solitude were essential to art. When MacCarthy told James that his own writing made him feel "absolutely alone," James replied: "Yes, it is solitude. If it runs after you and catches you, well and good. But for heaven's sake don't run after *it*. It is absolute solitude."[24] James's expatriatism and his decision to leave America for good enabled him to realize the value of loneliness. In a letter to Morton Fullerton in 1900, he writes:

> The port from which I set out was, I think, that of the *essential loneliness of my life*—and it seems also ... to which my course again finally directs itself! That loneliness ... what is it still but the deepest thing about one? Deeper

about *me*, at any rate, than anything else: deeper than my "genius," deeper than my "discipline," deeper than my pride, deeper, above all, than the deep countermining of art (10/2/1900).[25]

The "essential loneliness of my life" is integral to, and constitutive of, his notions of deepness and it is precisely the deepness of the psychological and emotional explorations of character and identity in "relations" that consistently draw us back to James. Loneliness is the "deepest thing about one," deeper even for this artist who devoted his life to art than the "deep countermining of art" itself. Countermining is an interesting word; it suggests that the depth of his art is there to both counteract and also to parallel the depths of his loneliness. Without loneliness and the interrogation of this loneliness that is acknowledged by the essential parameters he grants it, one feels that his art would not need to countermine so deeply. One is reminded of Kafka's "The Burrow" and the almost unfathomable depths of narrative experimentation, as textual burrowing or mining, that the interrogation of alienation drives in the author. Without the acknowledgment, and the prior examination such an acknowledgment reveals, would the art itself be so deep? And at a time when there is an "epidemic of loneliness," high suicide rates among young students in leading university regions,[26] and a reaction from educational institutions where teachers are being advised not to promote too much "deep thinking" in students,[27] how can these lessons on loneliness from James point us back to the importance of a deep investigation of loneliness as "essential loneliness"?

A "Sacred Office" that Works Against "Irresponsible Pedagogy"

The use to be made of literature in many of the educational manifestos and programs of James's day was not always so interested in this "more intimate education." The privileging of English literature in the English university system was also slow in coming. Even though, as Alexandra Lawrie writes in *The Beginnings of University English*, John Churton Collins and Richard G. Moulton were early champions of English literature on the university curriculum in the United States and the United Kingdom, Oxford would not appoint its first Professor of English Literature until 1904. Cambridge had its first examinations in English literature only in 1919. This was late considering James's university, Harvard, set up its first Professor of English in 1876 and was already teaching the novel, even Dickens, by 1888. The British Board of Education's famous report, the Newboldt Report, published in 1921 entitled the "Teaching of English in England," privileges the capacity of English as a discipline that takes precedence over all other branches of learning.[28] However, it is to be used not for enabling this "inward voice," but for building national sentiment and for also unifying class divisions. English literature must build "national pride" and "the humanist and nationalist elements of this strategy were [to be] directed at unifying the class divided nature of British society."[29] James, it seems, had a very different conception of the role literature might play in education and in life, one far removed from such nationalist aspirations.

James reminds his readers that the novel is bound up with the "sacred" and that its potential and emergence is best destroyed through an "irresponsible" education. He argues in "The Science of Criticism" that "literature lives essentially, in the sacred depths of its being" and that nothing is "better calculated than irresponsible pedagogy to make it close its ears and lips."[30] In reminding us that language and specifically speech are sacred, he writes that "the human side of vocal sound" must be preserved and regarded as sacred.[31] All of James's novels can seem like thought experiments conducted through dialogue on the means through which individuality must be sustained in the face of loneliness for the service of art. Many of his leading characters seem to rehearse his own struggles for remaining so individual, so single, and so committed to exploring what "essential loneliness" reveals about the engagement with art. As Leon Edel writes, in his "ultimate work," *The Golden Bowl*, James was dealing with "the deepest part of his own inner world—his father having had in the house not only his wife Mary, but her sister Catherine, the loyal Aunt Kate."[32] Adrian Poole also suggests that this play between versions of the self, these separate alter egos, are all concerned with "questions of power." Poole reads his later works and this exploration of individualism through loneliness as focusing on "the inevitable reciprocity of power, whereby it is never simply given or taken but constantly passing between donors and beneficiaries, predators and prey. It is not always easy to know which it is."[33] However, it would appear that the boundaries of power in James are chiefly concerned with maintaining the space of an isolated self for the greater, possibly "sacred" preservation of the essential loneliness that directs his art.

James's later works often appear obsessed with how to maintain a productive sense of individualism in the face of failure and futility. Two of the leading characters of *The Ambassadors* try to preserve themselves knowing they are "failures." Miss Gostrey says to Lambert Strether early on with regard to hosting a party: "seems to rescue a little, you see, from the wreck of hopes and ambitions, the refuse-heap of disappointments and failures, my one presentable little scrap of an identity?";[34] we hear they are "beaten brothers in arms." Strether is also a more mature James, possibly a James still shaken by his failures as a playwright:

> He hadn't had the gift of making the most of what he tried, and if he had tried and tried again—no one but himself knew how often—it appeared to have been that he might demonstrate what else, in default of that, could be made. Old ghosts of experiments came back to him, old drudgeries and delusions, and disgusts, old recoveries with their relapses, old fevers with their chills, broken moments of good faith, others of still better doubt; adventures, for the most part, of the sort qualified as lessons ... They represented now the mere sallow paint on the door of the temple of taste that he had dreamed of raising up—a structure he had practically never carried further. Strether's present highest flights were perhaps those in which this particular lapse figured to him as a symbol, a symbol of his long grind and his want of odd moments, his want of money, of opportunity, of positive dignity.[35]

James's own "lapse[s]" were also then enabling of his "flights" of imagination because they are made into symbols for his "positive dignity"; the symbol as the driver of his "temple of taste" returns him to his core values and he discovers in it the motivation to pursue, as novelist, what else "could be made."

Strether points the way for James's later use of symbols for representing the struggle between relations and individualism. This is a practice that will keep James's own aesthetic flowing as he tries to rescue the "handful of seeds" at the roots of his own aesthetic education through the engagement with his past in narrative. In *Autobiography* James describes how this unique vision of the artist's intellectual life emerged and how it was educated into existence by receiving a rather unique, nomadic education and by finding its own means of education. However, James's description of the education of the individual mind through art also echoes his brother William's views on the contemporary problems with university education. William was also concerned with the direction education was taking in the new century. He was unsure about the connections between the kind of individuality novels could promote and the kind of person universities were producing. His essay "The Phd Octupus," given as a talk in 1903, explains how the tyrannous machine of the university was already destroying the fabric of American society and its "individuality" as well as personal and spiritual spontaneity. He argued that it was leading to an increase in academic snobbery, insincerity, and mandarinism.[36] In a work from the 1920s, *Individualism Old and New*, John Dewey also delves into the societal reasons for the tendency of the time to live out the "contradiction between our life as we ourselves live it and our thoughts and feelings—or what we at least say are our beliefs and sentiments."[37] Art, and the novel most particularly for James, assist in opening out this "contradiction." These writers bring the ideal education back to the aesthetic and to the kind of unique practice and style of deliberation that the artist is privy to. James saw his novels as explorations of intellectual life and it was a view that was shared by early academics of English literature in the American academy. For example, Richard G. Moulton's conception of literature in his collection, *Essays in Modern Novelists* (1910) describes the "modern novel" as a "manifestation of intellectual life."[38] He also taught an extension course in 1891 with the title "Story as a Mode of Thinking."[39] Arnold Bennet in the first chapter of *Literary Taste* also describes literature as "first and last a means of life."[40]

"A More Intimate Education" that Is Truly Participatory

It is James's essay "The New Novel," published in 1914, that perhaps provides the best description for how the novel is, as Moulton describes, "a manifestation of intellectual life." James brings criticism and novel work together in arguing that the "state of the novel in England at the present time is virtually very much the state of criticism."⁴¹ His writing on criticism relates directly to the work of the novel in early modernism. He argues:

> The effect, if not the prime office, of criticism is to make our absorption and our enjoyment of the things that feed the mind as aware of itself as possible, since that awareness quickens the mental demand, which thus in turn wanders further and further for pasture. This action on the part of the mind practically amounts to a reaching out for the reasons of its interest, as only by its so ascertaining them can the interest grow more various. This is the very education of our imaginative life; … Then we cease to be only instinctive and at the mercy of chance, feeling that we can ourselves take a hand in our satisfaction and provide for it, making ourselves safe against dearth […].⁴²

We see that the same motivation—to reach out for the reason of the mind's interest—drives him in *Autobiography* when he takes the reader back time and again to the scene of him as a child standing before playbills outside the New York theater houses of the 1860s in order to discover the "seeds" for what drives his initial artistic feelings. In the extract above, we have a description of the individual intellectual life that is both represented in, and engaged by, James's novels where "our absorption and our enjoyment of the things that feed the mind [becomes] as aware of itself as possible." This is a profound exploration of the individual mind in action. It is also a privileging of a unique vision of individualism that James seems to oppose to what he calls the "democratic example" and the "condition of the people," aspects that he believes are too eagerly privileged by writers at the time. He describes the "democratic example" as a kind of flood ready to lay waste to all before it:

> Beyond number are the ways in which the democratic example, once gathering momentum, sets its mark on societies and seasons that stand in its course. Nowhere is that example written larger, to our perception, than in the "new novel"; though this, we hasten to add, not in the least because prose fiction now occupies itself as never before with the "condition of the people," a fact quite irrelevant to the nature it has taken on, but because that nature amounts exactly to the complacent declaration of a common literary level, a repudiation the most operative even if the least reasoned of the idea of differences, the virtual law, as we may call it, of sorts and kinds, the values

of individual quality and weight in the presence of undiscriminated quantity and rough-and-tumble "output."[43]

Once again, James is here privileging the "individual quality" over and above the "democratic example" and the subservience to the "common literary level."[44] He goes on to describe in further "vague" detail that the novel's chief interest as a genre works only on "condition of its consenting to that more intimate education which is precisely what democratised movements look most askance at."[45] It is this "more intimate education" bound up with the novel and its exploration of "essential loneliness" that is perhaps most under threat by the "extreme individualism" of harsh meritocratic university policies that give individualism a bad name today and that lead to university provosts describing "deep thinking" as unproductive in today's entrepreneurial knowledge industries. James's "more intimate education" removed from the "democratic example" and "democratised movements" is indeed a fiction, but nevertheless a compelling fiction. James is here, in the midst of the publication and creation of some of the greatest works of modernism, describing a conflict between different kinds of novel that is also implicitly a description of different kinds of education. James is offering an alternative vision of education through his "more intimate education" that is grounded on a particular regard for the aesthetic. In presenting us with an educational philosophy where the beautiful mind, or mind contemplating the origins and meaning of its aesthetic interest, is itself presented as a work of art, James allows us to imagine how the aesthetic can become accessible to all; the "seeds" of the aesthetic are found within. We only have to train ourselves to engage in the solitary practice of reflection and contemplation making sure that the objects of our contemplation are what truly lead us to understanding our best interests.

The aesthetic is then no longer at a remove but can be found inside in the workings of the beautiful mind; the beautiful is accessible to all. It is a vision of education that enables readers or students to find in themselves the reasons for their interests and it is representative of a kind of thinking that was important to an emerging liberal education in universities. This style of education focuses on a notion of the individual as an entity that is essentially self-forming and self-educating even while proclaiming its greater democratizing ambitions.

Louis Menand's *Metaphysical Club* situates this movement in such theories as Agassiz's theory of recapitulation, a process by which the universe "becomes itself as replicated in the life history of the individual."[46] James offers an approach that aspires to the same kind of potential between the environment, particularly its artistic objects, and the intellectual life. A style of education that does not have democratic participation as its first philosophy may seem to conflict with the kind of "common" leveling and democratic participation the liberal arts are often assumed to uphold. However, James's belief in the aesthetic quality of the intellectual life that is raised on his "more intimate education" seems to presume that a collection of beautiful minds would inevitably lead to a beautiful society. It is an internal "intimate education" that also recalls Emerson in "The American Scholar": "The world is nothing, the man is all; in yourself is the law of all nature."[47]

James's autobiographical writings reveal how he understands the growth of the intellect through an engagement with life that seeks out its aesthetic seeds. James does this while describing himself as being "pragmatic." His brother William had written that the pragmatic spirit recognizes that "[m]any of the so-called metaphysical principles are at bottom only expressions of aesthetic feeling."[48] Fred Kaplan also finds a pragmatic reason behind James's early interest in art and reading: "[a]s a child, reading and writing were mostly private, solitary. They helped him escape into the inner freedom that substituted for the outer freedom that he did not have." Art also offered him the feeling of being "as free as possible from external control" with "few boundaries" while also allowing him to find in art the "formal boundaries" that were important for his "need for control" in art and life.[49] However, as Megan Quigley reminds us, the narrator's pragmatic method can often err in such novels as *The Sacred Fount* because he begins to "shield his theory from the 'stream of experience.'"[50] Quigley argues that this theory applied to life ends up isolating the protagonist from others and makes him seem "delusional."[51]

In *Autobiography* James explains in greater detail how aesthetic feeling is essential to his vision of education. James writes that his father advised against committing or "surrendering" to any single pursuit too early for fear that it would lead to a "narrowing." The James brothers' formative years were therefore chiefly concerned with learning to "be" rather than about learning to excel at any particular pursuit. James's search for, and deliberation on, the "earliest aesthetic seeds" relies on memory and focusing on what his character Lambert Strether calls his "handful of seeds." James strives again and again to describe for the reader the earliest moments of the aesthetic feeling in order to determine where its first "interest" lies. However, the fiction that a better education could be gained intimately from a communion with oneself in the presence of what is deemed beautiful, a fiction often gained and sustained through reading fiction, is also challenged in *The Sacred Fount* where James's protagonist, a committed artist-observer, realizes how his readings have taken him further from the "real thing."[52]

The means of seeing education in terms of a metaphor whereby the author can get readers to return to, what Proust calls, the "unknown book of signs" inside and, in doing so, make them better readers of themselves also recalls Schiller's notion of the "ideal man" that all possess inside. Schiller argues that "every individual man carries, within himself, at least in his adaptation and destination, a purely ideal man" (Letter IV).[53] He argues: "Cherish triumphant truth in the modest sanctuary of your heart; give it an incarnate form through beauty, [so] … that you may not by any chance take from external reality the model which you yourself ought to furnish, do not venture into its dangerous society before you are assured in your own heart that you have a good escort furnished by ideal nature."[54] James would seem to agree with much of this in privileging a form of "intimate education" that stands before the "democratic example."

Schiller explains that this approach is necessary, in echoing Higgins above, because "utility is the great idol of the time":

> For art has to leave reality, it has to raise itself bodily above necessity and neediness; for art is the daughter of freedom, and it requires its prescriptions and rules to be furnished by the necessity of spirits and not by that of matter. But in our day it is necessity, neediness, that prevails, and bends a degraded humanity under its iron yoke. Utility is the great idol of the time, to which all powers do homage and all subjects are subservient. In this great balance of utility, the spiritual service of art has no weight, and, deprived of all encouragement, it vanishes from the noisy Vanity Fair of our time. The very spirit of philosophical inquiry itself robs the imagination of one promise

after another, and the frontiers of art are narrowed, in proportion as the limits of science are enlarged.⁵⁵

However, Schiller too notes that "[t]he great point is therefore to reconcile these two considerations: to prevent physical society from ceasing for a moment in time, while the moral society is being formed in the idea."⁵⁶ Schiller therefore, like James, seems to suggest that a kind of "moral society" can come to fruition through a concentration on the "idea" and the "ideal man" inside, what James will later assign to "the man of imagination" in his *Autobiography*.

An Aesthetic Education that Promotes "Objectivity" in *The Tragic Muse*

Meghan Marie Hammond has recently argued that James gives us a new kind of empathy by "feeling into" consciousness as object through a philosophical worldview that sees no distinction between consciousness and physical objects or the external world:

> "Feeling into" objects makes more sense if we believe that thought and object are not categorically separate—that act becomes a credible possibility rather than a mere figure of speech. Indeed, if we are to believe that empathy exists as more than a capacity of the imagination ... we might need to accept that both our thoughts and the physical world are made of some prior "substance" with the potential to behave as either.⁵⁷

This recalls both the embodied phenomenology of such ontological monists as Michel Henry and also recent debates in speculative realism. However, if the "essential loneliness" that seeks the roots of a person's aesthetic seeds is to be a driver of empathy then its motivations may well have to lie, for James, with the "finer grain" and the beautiful mind. The beautiful mind must, in turn, be something like the mind or consciousness he describes for such characters as Isabel Archer where he aimed, as he wrote in his preface to the 1908 edition of *The Portrait of a Lady*, to "put the heaviest weight into ... the scale of her relation to herself" and the least weight "on the consciousness of [his] heroine's satellites."⁵⁸ In other words, it is a mind like James's own mind, a mind concerned with individualism and its relations and the act of exploring what might constitute self-relation. However, if individualism is not confined to the internal or the external then the "aesthetic seeds" of what constitutes the beautiful mind of such individualism are everywhere. The operation of a consciousness's relation to itself may only then become personalized through the acknowledgment of what incites empathy, namely a recognition of difference that comes to be associated not solely with an external environment but with other persons and other objects. Empathy requires the recognition of some difference in order for the projecting consciousness to "feel into" something at a distance that incites empathy. For James, it is "essential loneliness" that affords the space for such empathy, or for what Hammond describes as "the fundamental instability in empathic structures of feeling." Such empathy is unstable because it is an empathy that is unsure of what constitutes the domains of consciousness and yet James is convinced of the fact that the finer part of consciousness is that which "put[s] the heaviest weight into … the scale of her relation to herself" and the least weight "on the consciousness of … [our] satellites."[59] It is a plea for individualism over and above both "extreme individualism" and the individualism of the social network that may only find itself in the reflection of its "satellites." Therefore, even though James notes the instability of consciousness and of empathic structures of feeling, he is quite assured of both the central depth afforded by "essential loneliness" and of the type of focus on self-relation that consciousness, once captured, must practice.

In the fourth period of James's writing career, the period encapsulating his autobiographical works, James treats his own "man of imagination" as the object of interrogation for understanding how the "aesthetic seeds" take root. These works also then enable us to examine how the fruits of a life devoted to art through its awareness of "essential loneliness" allow James to hit upon "the prize to be won,"[60] namely "objectivity." Essential loneliness simply gives to him a sense of objectivity in relation to personality and individualism that could not have been nurtured otherwise:

> The personal history, as it were, of an imagination, a lively one of course, in a given and favourable case, had always struck me as a task that a teller of tales might rejoice in, his advance through it conceivably causing at every step

> some rich precipitation ... The idea of some pretext for such an attempt had again and again, naturally, haunted me; the man of imagination ... if one could but first "catch" him, after the fashion of the hare in the famous receipt ... It happened for me that he *was* belatedly to come, but that he was to turn up then in a shape almost too familiar at first for recognition ... He had been with me all the while ... I had in a word to draw him forth from within rather than meet him in the world before me, the more convenient sphere of the objective, and to make him objective, in short, had to turn nothing less than myself inside out.[61]

The benchmark for the "objectivity" James seeks as the "prize to be won" as artist is the objective he finds through deliberation on individualism. It is found in the detached state of self-examination of a core aspect of consciousness described as "the man of imagination." The hovering sense of detachment and non-coincidence between narrator and self-as-man-of-imagination is a less than deductive or purely rational accounting for consciousness. It differentiates James's method from those of contemporary philosophers of consciousness. It recalls what he envisaged as the appropriate work and method of the novelist in his essay "The New Novel": "This action on the part of the mind practically amounts to a reaching out for the reasons of its interest, as only by its so ascertaining them can the interest grow more various. This is the very education of our imaginative life." The education of our imaginative life is then the process James assesses for himself in the *Autobiography* in order to find the true sense of "objectivity" he craves. It is a sense of objectivity and a practice of education of our imaginative life that requires our "essential loneliness."

The Tragic Muse is a novel that gives an elaborate description of the mental struggles integral to the artistic life, however, it may also mark the point at which James begins to move inwards in his search for his aesthetic "seeds." James published the novel in 1890 at a time when he was trying to jump careers into theater. Nick Dormer, a committed artist, also deliberates on how his profession channels his own aesthetic roots in giving up his seat in the House of Commons for art. James contrasts Nick's artistic temperament with that of the diplomat Peter Sherringham:

> Nick's observation was of a different sort from his cousin's [Sherringham]; he noted much less the signs of the hour and kept throughout a looser register

of life; nevertheless, just as one of our young men had during these days in London found the air peopled with personal influences, the concussion of human atoms, so the other, though only asking to live without too many questions and work without too many rubs, to be glad and sorry in short on easy terms, had become aware of a certain social tightness, of the fact that life is crowded and passion restless, accident and community inevitable. Everybody with whom one had relations had other relations too, and even indifference was a mixture and detachment a compromise. The only wisdom was to consent to the loss, if necessary, of everything but one's temper and to the ruin, if necessary, of everything but one's work.[62]

The extract describes the everyday conflict between individualism—together with its states of solitude and loneliness—and community for a character committed to art. Nick, the artist, only asks to "live without too many questions and work without too many rubs" and yet he experiences life as "social tightness" and as "crowded." The weight of community seems impossible to shake off. This implicitly speaks for a need for an almost impossible state of isolation or for the emotional response to isolation that is often experienced as loneliness. This compulsion for the "more intimate education" sees passion as "restless" and community as "inevitable"; the basis for any democratic principle seems little more than a chore. Even this stark "indifference" to community, however, still involves the subject in a kind of "mixture" with others, so much so that the act of withdrawal from others is experienced as a "compromise." The narrator seems to be steeling the character for the loss of "everything" by recommending isolation because ultimately all that will be left is one's temper and "one's work"; James's later works will emphasize how this "work" can encompass self-examination and the "more intimate educaton." Once again, we detect here James's own vision of artistic practice as a practice for living where "loneliness" is the ground of all; it is almost as if an artistic sensitivity for the inevitability of loss has resulted in a need to detach from everything. The ability to transform this isolation into a way of life is most evident in James's artists or in a character such as Isabel Archer whose mind itself is a "work of art." James's presentation of their intrigues and styles of reflection also offers the reader the opportunity to see the fruits of such reflection and to share in this "more intimate education."

In the end it is art that is also a saving grace for Miriam Rooth, a Jewish actress and love interest of the diplomat, Peter Sherringham. Sherringham fails in his attempts to win her commitment. However, what is important is that James distills a human code of ethics, or manner of resolving "relations," out of the strictures of the art his characters give themselves up to. At times the narrator seems to share the reader's uncertainty at how to resolve the couple's slow, percolating distrust. Ultimately, it is the demands of art that decide the matter for Miriam. Miriam finds a way out of a kind of commitment to Peter through the narrator's presentation of Peter's somewhat alienated realization that art could never be for him what it was for Nick. The life of art is not for all and yet an encounter with art leads Peter's "inward life" to a life-changing realization:

> What was the meaning of this sudden offensive importunity of "art," this senseless mocking catch, like some irritating chorus of conspirators in a bad opera ... Art might yield to damnation: what commission after all had he ever given it to better him or bother him? If the pointless groan in which Peter exhaled a part of his humiliation had been translated into words, these words would have been as heavily charged with a genuine British mistrust of the uncanny principle as if the poor fellow speaking them had never quitted his island.[63]

Peter does not give himself up to art. It's "uncanny principle" elicits a groan of despondency when he recognizes his unwillingness to commit. Art is the calling that directs the sense of resolution of the actor Rooth. Art is the moral guide, what James aligns with his own "moral affiliations." In this middle period of James's career, it is almost as if those who turn their back on the aesthetic or misunderstand its claim are judged; this is a version of individualism grounded on aesthetic education that has almost vanished in today's universities. However, James's later works and his *Autobiography* reveal how this attention to art and the aesthetic can find its "seeds" not only in the appreciation of external artworks but also in self-examination, where the beautiful mind replaces the beautiful object.

Gabriel Nash, whom Fred Kaplan regards as a Wildean alter ego, is another type who is made to look somewhat ridiculous under the gaze of Nick Dormer, the true artist, as he sits for a portrait. James is finding out his characters through the lens of art by allowing his character-as-artist, Dormer, to subject his frivolous understudy to the artist's gaze:

> He was so accustomed to living upon irony and the interpretation of things that it was new to him to be himself interpreted and—as a gentleman who sits for his portrait is always liable to be—interpreted all ironically. From being outside of the universe he was suddenly brought into it, and from the position of a free commentator and critic, an easy amateurish editor of the whole affair, reduced to that of humble ingredient and contributor ... "Must I really remind you at this time of day that that term [old] has no application to such a condition as mine? It only belongs to you wretched people who have the incureable superstition of 'doing'; it's the ignoble collapse you prepare for yourselves when you cease to be able to do. For me there'll be no collapse, no transition, no clumsy readjustment of attitude; for I shall only *be*, more and more, with all the accumulations of experience, the longer I live."⁶⁴

The reader also sits uncomfortably at this point before the reflected gaze of James. Nash draws a distinction between "doing" and being when he is somehow "brought into" the "universe," where it is the artists who are committed to "doing" who are unable to use the "accumulations of experience" for the task of being. For Nash, artists as doers are removed from the "accumulations of experience" that shelter non-artists from the painful acknowledgments of old age. James is neither all Nick nor Nash; we may be witnessing here something of a struggle "inside" James. James may be realizing through this novel that art and aesthetic interest is not only the preserve of artists as doers but that it is also bound up with those who remain open to "living" and being as "more intimate education." Another presumption about art is unsettled when Peter Sherringham later returns again and again, like the young James, to dawdle over a vision of art that enables him to discover what aesthetic interest really means to him:

> It may be further intimated that Peter Sherringham, though he saw but a fragment of the performance, read clear, at the last, in the intense light of genius with which this fragment was charged, that even so after all he had been rewarded for his formidable journey. The great trouble of his infatuation subsided, leaving behind it something appreciably deep and

pure. This pacification was far from taking place at once, but it was helped on, unexpectedly to him—it began to work at least—the very next night he saw the play, through the whole of which he then sat.[65]

Sherringham makes his most profound realization in the moment when he acknowledges that Miriam is lost to him. The pacification, from "infatuation" to "something appreciably deep and pure," is only strengthened by his return, in isolation, to art. James will embody this "return to art" most concretely in his later novels and *Autobiography* but through artistic objects also found inside that act as symbols for the space of reflection and mindfulness.

The "essential loneliness" James cherishes for his art is instrumental for his understanding of individualism, an idea that also plays an important role, as we have seen, in early models of liberal arts education. As Larry Siedentop reminds us in *Inventing the Individual*, Western liberalism is very much about the invention of the individual and about how individual moral agency was publicly acknowledged and protected through art, political institutions, and culture.[66] One feels that modernism, as opposed to challenging individualism, has, in retrospect, played an important role in its preservation and promotion. Henry James is an important figure for determining what individualism and individual agency mean both for the novel and for programs of education. James grants readers the opportunity for reevaluating how "essential loneliness" offers the potential for "dawdling" and reconnecting with where our greatest interests lie. As James writes in his letters, it is his "loneliness" that sustains him and his art and yet it is a loneliness that must be withstood but never chased.

3

The "Lonely Voice" and "Submerged Population" in O'Connor, Joyce, and Mansfield: How Can We Live "Alone Together"?

Frank O'Connor's *The Lonely Voice* was published by the World Publishing Company in 1962 with two of its chapters appearing previously in the *Kenyon Review*. In *The Lonely Voice* Frank O'Connor argues that one of the characteristics that distinguishes the short story from the novel is its "intense awareness of human loneliness."[1] He also argues that in most short stories there is "no character with whom the reader can identify himself" thereby extending this unique thematic concern with loneliness, or with a sense of disconnect, to formal concerns over how to understand the reader's role in the short story. However, even though O'Connor privileges the short story as a "private art"[2] in its mediation of loneliness, he also finds it speaking, for the first time in fiction, for the "Little Man"[3] and, hence, for a "submerged population group."[4] Recent criticism would presumably rephrase this feature in terms of such notions as alterity and the subaltern. However, this chapter argues that we should not be too quick to translate O'Connor's concerns into contemporary critical language that all too often aligns elements of whatever the "Little Man" in fiction is taken to represent with politicized notions of marginalization. O'Connor's depiction of personal struggles grants his stories their resilience and yet the abstraction from this aspect to a critical approach that sees the short story as being at its finest when it speaks for a "submerged population group" is what is examined here. How does one move from the conviction that short stories typically describe a moment of "loneliness" to the critical assumption that the genre is at its best in speaking for a submerged population group? O'Connor's reading of the short story in terms of "loneliness" and the "submerged population group" is examined here through a close reading of a selection of his own criticism in *The Lonely Voice* and by seeing how his theory might apply to stories like Joyce's "The Dead" and Mansfield's "The Stranger." This comparison serves to show up the different aesthetic approaches taken by Joyce, O'Connor, and Mansfield. This reading also references the broader philosophical and sociological issues that O'Connor's concentration on submerged groups raises today. What constitutes community must be central to any understanding of how "loneliness" is to be subsumed by the group. Recent readings of the community and the "common" by writers such as Michael Hardt and Antonio Negri have alerted us to the fact that notions of community and "the common" have changed a great deal since O'Connor's day; group dynamics are as susceptible to change and adaptation as the artistic forms that represent these communities.

O'Connor's contemporaries, Joyce and Mansfield, give us a different kind of loneliness, one that reveals the "submerged population," to be the vast community referenced in the intertext of reading, one that can offer readers an antidote to this unsettling encounter with "loneliness." We must recall too that O'Connor does not see fit to extend the ability to write of this kind of loneliness to all groups of writers. O'Connor indirectly relates the experiences of the Irish "ascendancy" class about him in Ireland to the sense of isolation that an "ascendancy" class can feel among the majority population. In writing of Kipling and the British "ascendancy" class in India, O'Connor argues that Kipling's writing displays a learned "utter inability to face crises alone."[5] One must recall, of course, that O'Connor is possibly the least guarded of Irish critics whose conservatism is often most clearly on display in his criticism of women writers, as we will see later in this chapter. However, O'Connor describes Kipling's "ascendancy" class of "British colonials" in India as incapable of feeling that "essential loneliness" required for good writing.[6] This is presumably then a different kind of "essential loneliness" to that described by Henry James. O'Connor argues that this ascendancy class are unable to write of "essential loneliness" because their "circumstances do not permit them to be alone, for they live in the middle of hostile alien groups that will destroy them if ever they are left alone. Their schools, regiments, classes, races, always rise up to protect them from their essential loneliness."[7] Their sense of "the group"—O'Connor continues—makes it "almost impossible for Kipling or his readers to believe in individual loneliness, and when it does appear it is always in some monstrous disguise."[8] This group dynamic, or groupthink, would presumably apply in ways that O'Connor could not have imagined to today's online generation. However, O'Connor is writing of colonial times and political groupings of a different kind. He argues that Kipling "cannot write about the one subject a storyteller must write about –human loneliness."[9] This is an important extension of the domain of loneliness. In a sense, O'Connor politicizes loneliness but he is perhaps forgetful of the "ascendancy class" on his own doorstep, the Anglo-Irish ascendancy class in Ireland. The obvious question O'Connor is asking here is whether the "ascendancy" writing of his peer group, that of Bowen, Yeats, and others, is capable of describing this "essential loneliness." I have argued elsewhere that Bowen's writing manifests a concern for "imperturbable things," a "terrorism of innocence," and a world of domestic space and objects that raises the important question of how "people managed to understand each other" in any way whatsoever.[10] I have argued that she takes us to a ground zero of loneliness that O'Connor either cannot stomach or finds contrived. However, in this chapter, I wish to push further the exploration of how O'Connor's somewhat blinkered reduction of "essential loneliness" through such political manoeuvring ultimately limits his reading of loneliness especially when it comes to his reading of writers such as Katherine Mansfield.

We recall that O'Connor's contemporaries Katherine Mansfield and James Joyce were no strangers to the depiction of loneliness. In Mansfield's "The Stranger" and James Joyce's "The Dead" John Hammond and Gabriel Conroy come to experience a unique kind of loneliness through similar circumstances. Both are married men who have idealized their marriages in some way. The idealization becomes so strong that it feeds their desire for their partners thereby distancing them from any chance of appreciating, before it is too late, the great distance that must remain even between partners. Both stories revolve around an experience with death that cannot be shared; the inability to partake in what one party has experienced through being there in solitude with, or feeling one was the cause of, the death of another is set up as the ultimate metaphor for loneliness as inability to share one's most profound experiences.

John Cacioppo argues that one of the reasons people are lonely is that they are "not sharing anything that matters with anyone else"; to end the feeling of loneliness one needs to have a sense of "mutual aid and protection."[11] Sharing in solitude the death of another may well be the most poignant act of sharing and yet the inability to be able to share this experience with another is a powerful metaphor for the experience of loneliness. Neither character in these stories can ever give to their partners what their partners have received from someone else. Janey is alone with the unnamed passenger when he dies in her arms and Gretta tells Gabriel of how Michael Furey "died for me."[12] When the Conroys or Hammonds finally find themselves alone, it is the figure of death itself, perhaps representative of the most resilient "submerged group" of all, that alerts them to the experience of this kind of feeling of loneliness: "[t]hey would never be alone together again."[13] For Paul de Man, the figure of prosopopoeia is found in passages "in which the dead speak." It "prefigures our own mortality" since "by making the death speak, the symmetrical structure of the trope implies ... that the living are struck dumb, frozen in their own death."[14] These stories then elicit how the loneliness depicted is an aspect of a larger sense of loneliness that is bound up with the acceptance that people, no matter how close, cannot be "alone together." The very fact that loneliness gives us the desire and the sense that we can be "alone together" with those we are close to speaks for the strength of our communal bonds. However, if we presume too much for sharing and community, and regard its absence as the cause of all loneliness, we are only likely to exacerbate the loneliness through the confrontation with our existential state as individuals; it is simply impossible to share everything and thinking of it only leads us back to John Hammond: "No; he mustn't think of it. Madness lay in thinking of it."[15]

In attempting to capture this double bind through the representation of an individual encounter with death, Joyce and Mansfield prefigure what would become a popular figure for responsibility in philosophy in the nineties. In the *Gift of Death*, Jacques Derrida sets up death as the ultimate expression of one's responsibility; no one can take your place in your encounter with your own death. Or, as Paul Ricoeur suggests in recalling another death, the passenger who dies in Janey Hammond's arms "is alone in dying, but he does not die alone".[16] We are knee-deep then in an existential encounter with loneliness that seems to take us beyond O'Connor's more cultural materialist depiction of loneliness as bound up with submerged population groups. As we will see in Chapter 4, the kind of sentimental loneliness we associate with roleplaying and with the performance of parts in professional life can only serve to stymie a more authentic encounter with what loneliness can reveal to us. However, the presentation of life in terms of such existential loneliness can suggest that fulfilling, authentic relationships are impossible simply because we cannot be "alone together." We can read this as an aspect of modernism and its preference for emotional absolutes. In reading the work of David Foster Wallace in Chapter 5, we will also read about how later generations experience loneliness simply through boredom, apathy, and through being too much of an "inside-dopester" with regard to what knowledge industries and institutions of learning demand of them. However, such existential enquiries into the nature of loneliness and its representation in fiction also throw the spotlight on the reading experience itself. Perhaps it is because the reader can identify with such depictions of loneliness that the reader's time with the short story is so apprehensive. The reader knows that it will shake her and reveal to her, once more, as it did for John Hammond and Gabriel Conroy, the restorative power of the apprehension of loneliness, a loneliness that only grabs us momentarily before making us feel that soon we will be off deluding ourselves again that our deceptions will absorb us completely.

Even though O'Connor describes the role of the short story as speaking for a submerged population he writes that he does not know exactly what the term refers to. He frequently employs the term "submerged population group" to describe groups in society that are discriminated against or overlooked. It refers to prostitutes in Turgenev and Maupassant and to cooks, bell boys, and skivvies in Chekhov even though O'Connor admits that Chekhov, unlike his compatriot Leskov, was a "saintly doctor" trying "to help from without" who has "no clue to the workings of their minds."[17] How might this then lead the reader to see the representation of these groups, and of the loneliness that alerts us to the fact that they are being spoken for, as necessitating a certain amount of stylization on the part of the writer? Are we to imply that the loneliness of the individuals depicted in the stories is always representative of the group these individuals are seen to belong to even if the loneliness described is very clearly chafing against the institutions that confine individuals to an externally demarcated group membership? The principle characters of Joyce's stories, even if representative of a state of paralysis among Dublin, and hence Irish, people, do not stand out as members of any disenfranchised group in society. The boy in "Araby," Gabriel Conroy, and Corley in "Two Gallants" do not embody loneliness above all other human traits. On the contrary, Gabriel is a respected member of society who is at the head of the table of their small gathering. While Gretta's confession about Michael Furey is unsettling for Gabriel, reading Gabriel's reflection in the hotel as representative of the loneliness of a distinct submerged population group detracts from the universal existential features Joyce's characters always embody.

The difficulty involved in tracing psychologically the connection between loneliness and group membership in O'Connor's reading is matched by the formal difficulty involved in assessing how he assigns his use of these psychological motifs to distinct genre characteristics. For example, in the same paragraph he writes that "we see in the short story an attitude of mind that is attracted by submerged population groups" but that "the short story remains by its very nature remote from the community—romantic, individualistic, and intransigent."[18] In other words, O'Connor's critical reading of the genre might grant the reader a degree of security that stories themselves are most effective at challenging. It is precisely in that interstitial space between the assumption of a role required by the character who finds him or herself at the center of events and the sudden onset of alienation that stories often discover their power. The short story is most memorable when the individual's actions show up the trappings of group membership and of any sense of belonging to a "submerged population group" for what they are, that is, externally imposed constrictions on individual human flourishing. O'Connor's reading suggests that the reader can safely dispatch characters to various submerged groups that are categorized according to their work or their professional rank. I will explore in Chapter 4 how American writers of the 1940s and 1950s, such as Carson McCullers and Richard Yates, demonstrate how loneliness associated with professional roles can lead to an embrace of "sentimental loneliness." However, O'Connor is unwilling to give up his neat classification of types and the value of "submerged population groups." A certain *a priori* civic order drives his study. With writers like Joyce and Mansfield things are never so certain. They are writers who strip back the veil of social character and the public persona to present us with submerged emotions or submerged fears. There are no bands of disenfranchised populations but simply one shared human population. Insights are to be gained from shared human moments that have nothing really to do with a civic order or a professional rank, or even with a type of work, but instead with profound human emotions shared by all.

Of course, if groups that we might read as clear submerged populations do emerge in their fictions they are rarely the center of attention but are employed in an intentionally stylized way to bring a central character and perhaps the reader as well—who typically occupies a higher social and intellectual domain—to a somewhat humbling realization precisely because he or she has dispatched significant others in the story by reducing them to the clichéd characteristics of members of their work or rank. In other words, preconceptions of what submerged populations are, or should reveal, are consistently turned on their heads in Joyce and Mansfield. We might think of Mansfield's male workers in "The Garden Party" who put up the marquis and with whom Laura discovers a rare, almost epiphanic, degree of empathy or fellow feeling, or of the Scott family who also, in occupying a somewhat predictable social register and function, reveal uncomfortable emotional truths to Laura and the reader about how submerged populations must be treated. If Laura or Gabriel belong to any submerged populations it is surely that of the reader who comes to the text intent on learning something about his or her capacity for recognizing vulnerabilities in canonical fiction. Joyce and Mansfield are far less willing to allow the reader to find their stories morally edifying or to see them as validating preconceptions about disenfranchised groups in society.

This aspect of their stories may have emerged in reaction to an elite moral vanguard of critics who were beginning to acclaim the moral function of literature and its role in forming a social character that was itself supportive of social planning. I'm thinking here of the later emergence of the notion of English as a vocation in the work of F. R. Leavis. This questioning of traditional group characteristics also owed much to the move from the era of the industrial worker to that of the knowledge worker. Peter S. Drucker argues that the "knowledge worker" was already a known quantity for many decades before 1959, when Drucker coined the phrase. However, knowledge workers who were writers—together with the new common readers who read their complex works—could now begin to see themselves as a new working group and not as isolated artists. These writers needed the new kind of "knowledge worker" their works inspired *as* readers. This new group relationship was all that could "provide the basic continuity that knowledge workers need in order to be effective."[19] In other words, these new writers formed part of a knowledge industry that needed a submerged population that saw its disenfranchisement and loneliness not as an attribute of lower-class working rank, but as a universally shared, existential condition of modern life; they did not want to feel their submerged population status, if any, so keenly. Such readers wanted writers whom they did not feel were talking down to them but were instead describing shared intellectual concerns and who were taking their readers as equals. One means of achieving this was for writers in the knowledge industry to pally up to readers and to present no clear distinction between the narrative voice and the various representatives of social groups mentioned. The voice of the author then merges with that of the main character and we get the subjectivist, meta-referential works of modernist fiction that are less prescriptive about the relative attributes of professional groups in society.

It is important to remind ourselves of the kind of stories O'Connor likes. He likes stories most of all by Chekhov (who is his favorite), Turgenev, Maupassant, and Leskov that have a "submerged population group."[20] This is a group that "changes its character from writer to writer, from generation to generation. It may be Gogol's officials, Turgenev's serfs, Maupassant's prostitutes, Chekhov's doctors and teachers, Sherwood Andersons's provincials, always dreaming of escape."[21] In other words, it is an extension of the New Testament authors' employment of a system of nomenclature that sets up prostitutes, tax collectors and fishermen for the work of redemption and salvation. We know well in advance who must be spoken for and the salvation afforded the reader in having these submerged groups spoken for is almost equivalent to the lessons Jesus teaches the Pharisees when he writes in the dirt and asks the question about he who is without sin. O'Connor's submerged population is not necessarily the proletariat, submerged because of material conditions, for submerged means for O'Connor "defeat inflicted by a society that has no sign posts, a society that offers no goals and no answers."[22] However, this is not to say that O'Connor does not offer very clear goals, signposts, and answers for the writers he critiques. He argues that Joyce "took rhetoric to the fair" and that he forgoes the submerged population for style. Mansfield is an immature writer who follows a "magical approach to literature" like Joyce and Proust who try to make the printed page "not a description of something that had happened but a substitute for what had happened."[23] Kipling is a "damned liar" who does not know about "individual loneliness" and cannot know because his own very real "submerged population," the British colonials in India,[24] was never really a submerged population anyway but an "ascendancy" who had to live as expats as a group that was "never alone" because to admit loneliness would be to admit to the "nightmare" that was the reality of millions of subjugated natives outside their flimsy colonial social network. O'Connor's submerged population model therefore dangerously mixes fact and fiction. It is at once a discernible disenfranchised group in a story or group of stories, but its authenticity must be realized from, and depend upon, real contact with a real-life submerged population that have enough emotional savvy to accept loneliness for what it is.

O'Connor saves his most pointed polemic for the work of Mansfield and his reading here is perhaps most problematic of all. He writes that she writes stories that he "reads and forgets." Her work is the work of a "clever, spoiled, malicious women"[25] and she possesses "emotional immaturity." He writes: "that clever, assertive, masculine woman was a mistake from beginning to end, and toward the close of her life she recognized it herself."[26] It is the type of criticism that makes one appreciate the advances of new criticism and post-structuralism. He argues that even though he "knows nothing that would suggest she had any homosexual experiences, [that] the assertiveness, malice, and even destructiveness in her life and work make me wonder whether she hadn't?" He reads Mansfield's understanding of what he calls "experience"—and this is taken from her work and her life—as something through which she justifies what he calls her "occasionally sordid love affairs."[27] This "idea of experience" he argues "is a typical expedient of the woman with a homosexual streak who envies men and attributes their imaginary superiority to the greater freedom with which they are supposed to be able to satisfy their sexual appetite."[28] He continues:

> The trouble with "experience" in the sense in which Katherine Mansfield sought it is that by being self-conscious it becomes self-defeating. The eye is always looking beyond the "experience" to the use that is to be made of it, and in the process the experience itself has changed its nature, and worldliness no longer means maturity but a sort of permanent adolescence.[29]

With such psychological sensitivity it is no wonder that we have to take a second look at O'Connor's understanding of loneliness. If O'Connor reads the experience of having the psychological sensitivity and courage to be sufficiently self-conscious to examine all aspects of one's sexuality as "self-defeating," is it any wonder that he is seeing loneliness through clearly demarcated submerged populations almost everywhere? Mansfield is one with Joyce and Proust, for O'Connor, because she attempted a "magical approach to literature by trying to make the printed page not a description of something that had happened but a substitute for what had happened."[30] However, to conceive of the motivation for writing as simply getting down the "description of something that had happened" is to reduce the short story to naturalistic storytelling, what he admits in the beginning of his collection is never the case.

O'Connor does tell us that he does not "profess to understand" fully the idea he is putting forward about this submerged population, about these figures "wandering about the fringes of society, superimposed sometimes on symbolic figures whom they caricature and echo—Christ, Socrates, Moses," but that they must embody, as must the good short story, "an intense awareness of human loneliness."[31] The novel can still adhere to the classical concept of civilized society, of man as an animal, as he puts it, who lives in a community, as in Jane Austen and Trollope it obviously does (and one must admit that descriptions of animals living in community is a novel description of Austen) but the short story can never do this. It remains remote from such notions of community that the novel promotes and is yet "romantic, intransigent, and individualistic" as we have seen.[32] In this context it is also interesting to note that Sean O'Faolain has also argued in his book *The Irish* that the Irish psyche itself is opposed to the notion of civility and social order that O'Faolain traces back to Roman culture. O'Faolain argues that the "Irish mind can be described following its golden period that ended about the eleventh century as somewhat primitive."[33] What lay in the Irish mind and what may still lie there, O'Faolain continues, is "atavistically indestructible"; it is a mind that "clung to the family unit." He argues that "Roman law which was to come in with the Normans had another idea."[34] One wonders what this implies about the Irish writer's ability to conceptualize and represent social groups in terms of civility and civic order. There are of course many broader questions then to be asked of O'Connor's model not least of which is the question of what an intense awareness of human loneliness means both for the submerged community in a story and for the author writing about this population.

The Lonely Crowd, published a decade before O'Connor, would change irrevocably our understanding of loneliness, and works by Albert Camus and Richard Wright that describe a new kind of "outsider" in fiction would also align solitary existential angst with both a new kind of philosophy and with new forms of segregation and discrimination in society. It is worthwhile reminding ourselves too of how social environment can influence the political understanding of group dynamics. O'Connor came from a small city in a relatively small and impoverished country that had been torn apart in sectarian struggles in which he himself had fought. As an adult, he moved to London to work during World War II. His own society in Ireland would have been slow to experience the kind of societal changes that Riesman et al., for example, outline in *The Lonely Crowd*; I will examine how American writers dealt with some of these shifts in Chapter 4. However, one aspect of this societal change occurring in the 1940s and 1950s, for Riesman et al., is the shift from a world dominated by the "inner-directed character" who expresses himself in politics in the style of a "moralizer" to a world populated more and more by the "other-directed character" who tends to express himself politically in the style of an "inside-dopester."[35] Perhaps it is because of the make-up of the society O'Connor lived in when he read these stories that one can still hear some of the tone of the "moralizer" in his readings. *The Lonely Crowd* argues that this shift in character in society is also marked by a "shift in political mood" one that Riesman et al, describe as a shift from "indignation" to "tolerance." If there is any overriding tone to some of the comments we have read here from O'Connor in reaction to loneliness, it is more likely to be read today as "indignation" rather than "tolerance." Since *The Lonely Crowd* is concerned with the "process by which people become related to politics,"[36] it is also at times revealing of the history and politics of its own era. Descriptions of loneliness, even by writers as gifted as O'Connor, when they become political can tell us quite a bit about the "process by which [writers themselves] become related to politics." These are simply some of the sociological and philosophical currents swirling around the notion of loneliness when O'Connor was writing his collection of essays. However, I now want to examine how his reading of loneliness and the submerged population might fit one of the greatest stories of one of his strongest precursors.

James Joyce's "The Dead" is a story that attempts to get the dead speaking with the living and, in so doing, it raises important questions about the role of the dead in fictional representation. It explores another important issue that arises when we attempt to ground a fictional genre on a perceived ability it has to speak for submerged population groups. Katherine Mansfield's "The Stranger" and James Joyce's "The Dead" share certain thematic concerns that challenge O'Connor's reading of the short story. John Hammond and Gabriel Conroy come upon life-changing experiences through similar circumstances. As we learn in both stories, when the desire to shake off the crowd and be "alone together" has been physically realized, both realize that proximity with a loved other only heightens the complexity of loneliness; they realize they never will be "alone together again." Maintaining a comfortable feeling of being "alone together" as partners is a difficult task and the "The Dead" is speaking for this realization. However, there is also another sense here; the appearance of the dead in the story in the guise of Michael Furey has introduced a new element, a new persona and trope, into the relationship between Gabriel and Gretta. Just as Eliot begins "Prufrock" with a voice from Dante's world of the dead that had only spoken because it had assumed its voice would never be heard among the living, so does Joyce now realize that the presence of Michael Furey and how he had "died for" Gretta also introduces a haunting voice that will prevent Gretta and Gabriel from ever being "alone together" again. Both stories revolve around an experience with death, perhaps the ultimate expression of loneliness. Neither character can ever give to their partners what their partners have received from someone else through death. Janey is alone with the unnamed passenger when he dies in her arms and Gretta tells Gabriel of how Michael Furey "died for me."[37] When the Conroys or Hammonds finally find themselves alone, it is the figure of death itself, perhaps representative of the most resilient "submerged group" of all, that alerts them to the necessity of loneliness in even the most intimate of couples.[38] The psychological necessity of navigating a way through it reveals that it speaks for a submerged population that is not categorized only according to class or station.

For Paul de Man, the figure of prosopopoeia is found in passages "in which the dead speak." It "prefigures our own mortality" since "by making the death speak, the symmetrical structure of the trope implies ... that the living are struck dumb, frozen in their own death."[39] In "Shelley Disfigured" he argues that in our "endless prosopopoeia [giving a voice to the absent or dead] ... which is not *our* strategy as subjects, since we are its product rather than its agent," it "*would* be naive" to believe that its meaning "can be a source of value."[40] De Man argues that this form usually occurs in what he refers to as autobiography, what only presumes to reveal a "reliable self-knowledge but what instead demonstrates the impossibility of closure and totalisation."[41] Prosopopoeia is then a unique trope, often used in autobiography, and it typically de-faces or confers a mask. It is duplicitous and it returns us to the concentration on language, a language post-structuralism reveals as a perpetual process of dissimulation and deferral. O'Connor does not like to think of stories at this level; he never questions the ability of language to represent human analogues representative of character traits that can then be subsumed within submerged population groups. In a sense, one might say, in recalling De Man's reading of the trope of prosopopoeia, that O'Connor's reading of the short story remains perpetually susceptible to "the closure and totalisation" that the critic must presume when he grounds a reading of literature on the prior assumption that the text only confers meaning on groups already deciphered and labelled outside the text. One is reminded here of Walter Benjamin's warning about the aestheticization of politics; he writes: "the increasing proletarianisation of modern man and the increasing formation of masses are two sides of the same process ... The logical outcome of fascism is an aestheticizing of political life."[42] If we reduce art to the political message implicit in a reading that regards its *sine qua non* as its ability to speak for preformed submerged population groups, how far are we from what Benjamin advises against? Is O'Connor mindful of what the hovering submerged population present in the Intertext of all stories—the dead—prefigures, namely this aversion to totalization? O'Connor appears to suggest that some implicit model of human value is what is gained from writing of the submerged population. However, when the submerged population is the dead, is there any system of values that we can safely assume they speak for? Stories that speak of the encounter with the dead and with death show up how the short story is best at calling into question presuppositions in regard to categorizations in community. If we open up to them are we left "frozen in [our] own death," as de Man suggests?[43] In the end, this would most likely be representative of a degree of lack of control that O'Connor would be unwilling to admit is workable for the critic.

Death, like the snow, is "general all over Ireland" and falls "through the universe" in "The Dead."[44] It is a story about the possibility of truth and communicative authenticity. It questions whether truth can exist even between those who love each other. Joyce will go on to discover his own unique sense of truth in the later devotion to the singular voice as he gives up dialogue for the stream of consciousness, word association, and interior monologue. If there are any truths in Joyce's later work it is that found in the singular conversation with the Intertext over and above any belief in reported dialogue as revealing of truth. Joyce then asks whether loneliness is in truth the point at which the short story's authentic modus operandi must come to the fore. Loneliness presumes a certain unhappiness with others with whom one attempts to communicate. It presumes a person-oriented approach to meaning. We are never wholly understood and can never hope to be and therefore loneliness results. However, Joyce goes further than this and I believe Mansfield does too. Compassion, generosity, and love are discovered by Gabriel when he has resigned himself to the power of miscommunication and inviolable incomprehension between people. Snow covers our tracks and makes all lose definition and yet the vista that remains is a thing of beauty. Personal fulfilment or authenticity works similarly. Joyce recognizes in this the last of his short stories that the urge to compulsively idealize is always there when we regard loneliness and a failure to understand each other as the ultimate incentive or stopgap on the way to artistic representation. Joyce and Mansfield take up the loneliness and run with it and transform it into the kind of gait Kierkegaard suggests the Christian believer must have in bearing a sense of absurdity in the face of the teleological suspension of the ethical. O'Connor argues that Joyce's characters are "not characters but personalities" and that Joyce would never again after "The Dead" be able "to deal with characters, people whose identity is determined by their circumstances."[45] But we must ask how do writers since Joyce understand literary character in the wake of his psychological rendition of consciousness and can the representation of the "circumstances" of a character's identity, whatever that might mean, ever be the same again in light of the psychological and phenomenological experiments of Modernist writers such as Joyce, Proust, Woolf, James, and Kafka? And it must be noted that these are writers of short stories whose formal experimentation O'Connor barely mentions in *The Lonely Voice*? This might also remind us of Bowen's description of Joyce. Bowen argues that Joyce's "Dublin days," the days his readers came to imaginatively construct from his early works, now live "for very few people."[46] This is so, for Bowen, because "[i]t is surroundings that tie us closely to people, that are the earth of friendship. And that physical, associative tie with his countrymen Joyce broke when he went to live abroad."[47] Joyce does not persist with neat dialogic stories—the ones O'Connor likes—grounded on only the presentation of loneliness. Surprisingly most of O'Connor's critiques end when he has discerned the loneliness he privileges—he does not examine the nature of the loneliness or how it can still offer potential or somehow lead the writer to further experimentation. Joyce does not have dialogue as his chief tool; he complements it with an interest in the polyphonic conversation between text, style, and community, between the Intertext and the reader. This forms a new background against which new encounters or collisions with loneliness play out. Analogically it can be compared to the polyphony of voices in real-time today in conversation between tweets, android communication, voice–voice communication, and visual stimulation. Joyce found this living polyphony in the Intertext, a grand dialogue broader than any one individual and therefore difficult to assign only to the purely emotional construct of loneliness.

We recall Joyce's lines: "Other forms were near. His soul had approached that region where dwell the vast hosts of the dead … the solid world itself which these dead had one timed reared and lived in, was dissolving and dwindling."[48] What happens in fiction at these moments "when the dead speak" as Paul De Man argues? How does this openness to this most submerged of populations, to use O'Connor's criteria for the good short story, upset our sense of security before categories of representation since it is a region from which "no traveller returns." How does it upset any civilizing or levelling function that we had hoped this representation of the submerged population might offer, since the giving of a voice to the dead cannot be equivalent to the giving of a voice to the impoverished of nineteenth-century Russia or to the soldiers of 1920s Ireland?

4

Loneliness Is Part of the Job: "Sentimental Loneliness" in Carson McCullers and Richard Yates

So much of the fiction of modernism is concerned with the streetwalker, flâneur, or existential city-dweller. It is a well-known figure of the modernist narratives we are told writers use for the "observer-effect." When we read Carson McCullers and Richard Yates, the individual's loneliness is often recorded by way of descriptions of feelings of being "lonesome," "alone," or a "stranger" in a strange town. And yet these feelings emerge through interactions with others in bustling city streets, market towns, busy public beaches. Many of the moments of enlightenment, clarity, and self-deliberation or self-awareness characters experience about their states of being "lonesome" or estranged emerge after conversations or interactions with workers and other tenants in these towns and villages. They are always face to face encounters and one can hear, reading between the lines of the shared dialogues, the often shared understanding of what is expected in these societies to earn a living or get by. The individual's wandering through the thoroughfares, main streets, and markets of these towns and cities in the first half of the twentieth century is then well documented; we have a good archive of how feelings of being "lonesome," "alone," or lonely in these streets emerge and how they affect the fictional individuals concerned. The reader understands that the authors may also have experienced such states and feelings and that they are assigning them to the characters they create—we think of Mick Kelly in *The Heart Is a Lonely Hunter* (1940) and of Lenehan in Joyce's "Two Gallants." However, for millennials and for the iPhone generation, the thoroughfares and streets of loneliness are very different. We know from various academic studies already mentioned—what did not exist for the lonely crowds of Joyce, Yates, and even McCullers—that young people are just as lonesome—possibly more so—than they were during modernism. However, where are the narratives and shared fictional accounts of the means through which encounters in these digital highways shape and mold their experiences of loneliness through self-deliberation and self-questioning? Recent novels such as Gail Honeyman's *Eleanor Oliphant Is Completely Fine* and John Boyne's *A History of Loneliness* do offer us contemporary pictures of loneliness but once again these authors most often retreat to everyday work encounters, chance encounters on streets in public life, and also to encounters with older people and the elderly, people who do not live in the digital world. Where then is the fictional archive that affords young people an opportunity for finding relatable accounts of struggle and personal trial due to loneliness and feelings of being "alone" in the streets of the digital landscape? We can look to online forums and blogs[1] and Netflix series such as *13 Reasons Why* and the fan fiction that has sprung up around such series and around the superhero genre;[2] however, these are often written by fans and young people who are as confused about their feelings of loneliness as the characters in the series. Daniel Cohen has argued for the urgent preservation of the culture of reading and of the book as an essential pillar of society as it is enabling of self-examination and of an ability to live with a sustained account of life from the perspective of a fictional character or persona, what many believe is then enabling of empathy as the ability to step into the thoughts and feelings of another. However, are we expecting too much? Is the new kind of loneliness experienced by those who have grown up walking digital streets and highways so different from what has been charted by modernist writers that it does not need to be recounted and captured in novels and stories? It is a consideration that we must be willing to accept.

In this chapter, I look therefore at a selection of works that deal with the representation of loneliness in America during modernism and at how these stories grant insights into the experience of loneliness. Novels were hugely important for Riesman, Glazer, and Denney's sociological study *The Lonely Crowd* that was published in 1950. They regard books, novels, and biographies primarily as hugely important in shaping young people. They go so far as to describe how the

> inner-directed youth was made to leave home and go far both by directly didactic literature and by novels and biographies that gave him a sense of possible roles on the frontiers of production. In contrast to this, the other-directed person has recourse to a large literature that is intended to orient him in the noneconomic side of life.[3]

The authors describe a change that came to people's reading habits in the 1930s and 1940s. Whereas "earlier books are directly concerned with social and economic advance, dealt with as achievable by the virtues of thrift, hard work, and so on," in later publications such as Dale Carnegie's 1937 *How to Win Friends and Influence People* "wealth was to be achieved no longer by activity in the real world but by self-manipulation."[4] In Carson McCuller's *The Heart Is a Lonely Hunter* we witness the shift from one worldview to the next as the protagonists battle within themselves and without in struggling to fit together profound metaphysical questions about self and society and the desperate economic conditions of work and labor. However, perhaps surprisingly for a book entitled *The Lonely Crowd*, there is not a great deal in it on loneliness; the authors do warn against being what they call "lonely successes," types best captured for them in comics and "modern popular culture that stresses the dangers of aloneness and, by contrast, the virtues of group-mindedness."[5] They note how in such works the gangster's success ultimately spells his undoing as it "cuts him off from the group."[6] In fact, there is a passing comment towards the end of the book, *The Lonely Crowd*, that appears to suggest that loneliness is simply "part of the job," a consideration I will discuss in this chapter in the work of McCullers and Richard Yates. At one point in their book, Riesman et al. are turning to the future and speculating on what the future holds for an America that is "not only big and rich, it is mysterious."[7] They argue that "other-directed people"—the kind of people they have argued are coming more to the fore in American society—"should discover how much needless work they do, discover that their own thoughts and their own lives are quite as interesting as other people's, that, indeed, they no more assuage their loneliness in a crowd of peers than one can assuage one's thirst by drinking seawater, then we might expect them to become more attentive to their own feelings."[8] This is a somewhat dramatic revelation coming towards the end of *The Lonely Crowd* that sums up the perils of too close alignment with the lonely crowd and yet it is precisely the kind of realization that Frank and Anne Wheeler are faced with in *Revolutionary Road* at a time in their lives when they feel there is no way back.

When characters in the modernist narratives of McCullers are alone or feeling lonesome in a new environment they often call on speech and they talk aloud to themselves; Jake Blount sits alone having just found a new job at a fun fair in *The Heart Is a Lonely Hunter*:

> Words came to him and dreamily he spoke them aloud to himself. "Resentment is the most precious flower of poverty, Yeah." It was good to talk. The sound of his voice gave him pleasure. The tones seemed to echo and hang on the air so that each word sounded twice. He swallowed and moistened his mouth to speak again. He wanted suddenly to return to the mute's quiet room and tell him of the thoughts that were in his mind. It was a queer thing to want to talk with a deaf-mute. But he was lonesome.[9]

This is both a physiological and a psychological experience. Hearing his own words aloud while feeling "lonesome" draws him back to the contemplation of the need for human company and communication in a shared, quiet space. One wonders whether those on the digital thoroughfares, in growing up in a society where the majority of their conversations and communication is silent and runs across fibers that speak of physical distance, are also more at a remove from the benefits offered by both the sound of a voice—even if it's your own— and the comfort brought through the contemplation of a quiet place where vocal communication takes place? In growing up with such a barrage of silent communications have younger generations lost the sense that even speaking out your words to yourself is enlivening or fulfilling in any deep sense?

McCullers tells us that Jake Blount finds that "the loneliness in him was so keen that he was filled with terror."[10] He looks to alcohol as a way out:

> [h]e drank the raw liquor and by daylight he was warm and relaxed." However, the loneliness is so "keen" that he returns "out into the narrow, empty streets." Once again he finds release in talking: "He talked. The winter

dawn was white and smoky and cold. He looked with drunken urgency into the drawn, yellow faces of the men." He also finds relief in his work in the bustling fun fair: "The noise, the rank stinks, the shouldering contact of human flesh soothed his jangled nerves."[11]

However, he also returns to Singer's room and the quiet and peace of the communications and talks they share: "They would idle in the quiet room and drink the ales. He would talk, and the words created themselves from the dark mornings spent in the streets or in his room alone. The words were formed and spoken with relief."[12] It is the loneliness then that has created these words. Once he had shared them aloud with Singer "[t]he fire had died down." The prospect of communication provides a reason for the words that form within him in the moments of loneliness. Without that release, without that sharing, where he talks and Singer listens, he would not have been able to calm the fire inside. McCullers describes here an experience shared by many migrants in big cities; how can they ever find likeminded people with whom to share their most secret thoughts? For many young people addicted to virtual and online communications, the strain can become unbearable and the impossibility of ever finding someone to talk to or listen becomes too much. However, loneliness itself feels different if one has the experience that its state of despair will later be transformed into words spoken, exchanged, and listened to in person; it is a more directed loneliness, one that can sense the warmth of sharing that is just around the corner. Without this prospect loneliness becomes suffered for its own sake; it may lead to a state of resignation. Olivia Laing writes in *The Lonely City* of the city streets and bars of Edward Hopper's paintings, streets and bars McCullers also would have known since she grew up on the same street as Hopper. Hopper's *Nighthawks* may well capture the early morning exchanges of Biff's New York Café in *The Heart Is a Lonely Hunter*. Laing writes that Hopper captures

> loneliness as a large city, revealing it as a shared, democratic place, inhabited, whether willingly or not, by many souls? What's more, the technical strategies he [Hopper] uses—the strange perspective, the sites of blockage and exposure—further combat the insularity of loneliness by forcing the viewer to enter imaginatively into an experience that is otherwise notable for its profound impenetrability."[13]

The experience of art is then enabling of the dissipation of loneliness's impenetrability. The reader might also perceive the moments of empathic communication between Jake and Singer as somewhat impenetrable for Singer and yet it is the representation of such communication in a space where the reader might not expect it to take place that brings home all the stronger the potential of talk and communication for breaking down the barriers that loneliness sustains and is sustained by. Laing also explains the "terror" that McCullers assigns to Jake Blount's loneliness in his room. In referencing the words of Frieda Fromm-Reichmann, who suggests that the "second person's empathic abilities are obstructed by the anxiety-arousing quality of the mere emanations of the first person's loneliness," Laing suggests that this is what is so "terrifying" about loneliness, that it appears as "literally repulsive, inhibiting contact at just the moment contact is most required."[14] Hopper, Laing argues, then gives us paintings and representations—rather like McCullers does with words—where loneliness is not only seen as something "worth looking at" but is represented as if looking itself could combat loneliness; we learn to come to terms with a way of looking that can unsettle loneliness's "terror." It is a looking focused on the artwork and on the kind of "dawdling" Henry James describes in Chapter 2 for those early seeds of aesthetic life; it asks us to search for what breaks the spell of loneliness in the reasons of one's own interests.

The Heart Is a Lonely Hunter is a book that presents us with scenes of communication that also challenge Laing's "insularity of loneliness" and its "profound impenetrability." As we have seen, the main character, Singer, is deaf and he cannot speak and yet he becomes the center of "talk" and the go-to person for communication. The loneliness and muteness of Singer is what allows others to find solace in speaking to him; when the other chief characters of the novel find themselves with Singer in his room, characters who "always had so much to say," they "were silent." It is almost as if their collective loneliness finds the means to break out of its own "insularity" when they are confronted with the person who, for them, cannot communicate as they do. And yet the emptiness of loneliness still spreads in Singer when he is alone walking the streets of the town:

> The emptiness spread in him. All was gone. Antonapoulos was away; he was not here to remember. The thoughts of his friend were somewhere else ... The emptiness was very deep inside him, and after a while he glanced up at the window once more and started down the dark sidewalk where they had walked together so many times."[15]

Singer too must strive to shatter this "insularity" of loneliness by finding something within it that speaks for a move beyond its apparent "impenetrability." Both friends are deaf and cannot speak, and Singer also likes to write to Antonapoulos who himself cannot read:

> The fact that Antonapoulos could not read did not prevent Singer from writing to him. He had always known that his friend was unable to make out the meaning of words on paper, but as the months went by he began to imagine that perhaps he had been mistaken, that perhaps Antonapoulos only kept his knowledge of letters a secret from everyone.[16]

The mystery surrounding the question of how much these lonely characters can understand by way of the different forms of communication employed about them, also leaves room for questioning how "locked-in" their loneliness is. The "emptiness," darkness, and terror they inhabit through their loneliness occasionally appears as less consuming than it should be because of this uncertainty with regard to how much they really understand of the communications that take place around them. However, it is the face-to-face encounter, the memory of it, or the self-deliberation incited through the memory of it, that manifests this uncertainty. The lonely digital streetwalker who spends up to six hours or more a day wandering online streets may not place the same emphasis on the memory of such face-to-face encounter. This outlet for interrogating the parameters and contours of their loneliness may be very different and may not have the same possibilities for release. Marina Keegan, a millennial and iPhone generation writer, says that it is "the opposite of loneliness" that she hopes she can take with her after her university days, a feeling that is "not quite love and it's not quite community; it's just this feeling that there are people, an abundance of people, who are in this together."[17] Despite the years between McCullers and Keegan, it is the kind of feeling that many of McCullers's characters also yearn for and yet cannot find; Jake Blount yearns to find someone else who "*knows*" and yet when he finds him in the shape of the physician Copeland they end up having a violent argument. Singer too longs to be reunited with his old friend Antonapoulos so that they feel that they are "in this together." Biff and Mick yearn for a kind of companionship, even if it is based on misunderstanding or idealization, where there is a feeling of being "in this together." *The Heart Is a Lonely Hunter* ends with Biff once again feeling "the peaceful silence of the night settled in him" in his bar—The New York Café—the only café in the town to stay open all night; but as he ponders it further "loneliness gripped him" again. However, it grants him the experience of a moment of extrasensory perception or enlightenment—rather like Gabriel Conroy's in the dark of a Dublin hotel or of Mersault in the prison cell where he experiences and opens himself up to the "benign indifference of the universe":

> For in a swift radiance of illumination he saw a glimpse of human struggle and of valor. Of the endless fluid passage of humanity through endless time. And of those who labor and of those who—one word—love. His soul expanded. But for a moment only. For in him he felt a warning, a shaft of terror. Between the two worlds he was suspended. He saw that he was looking at his own face in the counter glass before him."[18]

He asks himself how "this terror," a terror that arises from the loneliness that "gripped him," could "throttle him like this when he didn't even know what caused it?"[19] He again falls to self-deliberation based both on the enlightenment and the terror he has experienced, an experience that leaves him "expanded" and "suspended" between the "two worlds" of superhuman enlightenment and the terror that comes with it. It is the grip of loneliness that grants him this moment. It recalls Sartre's Roquentin and his desire to stay "close to people" even in the contemplation of the effects of loneliness:

> And would he just stand here like a jittery ninny or would he pull himself together and be reasonable? For after all *was* he a sensible man or was he not? Biff wet his handkerchief beneath the water tap and patted his drawn, tense face. Somehow he remembered that the awning had not yet been raised. As he went to the door his walk gained steadiness. And when at last he was inside again he composed himself soberly to await the morning sun.[20]

The loneliness that affords him such self-deliberation through the terror unleashed calls him back to himself and to his daily routine. Habit is the saving grace. It has not yet become the existential stage prop that it becomes in Beckett. Both Hopper and McCullers then leave us with a portrait of a café on an American street corner, with its inhabitants leaning into the counter glass, as a symbol of loneliness as the world enters into a prolonged period of war. When asked whether his painting *Nighthawks* was about portraying a night street as "lonely and empty?" Hopper replied: "I didn't see it as particularly lonely. I simplified the scene a great deal and made the restaurant bigger. Unconsciously, probably, I was painting the loneliness of a large city."[21]

This spirit of loneliness is very much in evidence in works published by Richard Yates and Theodore Roethke, American writers writing at the same time as McCullers and O'Connor who make loneliness a central theme of their work. The loneliness one discovers in these writers or sees represented can be encapsulated by what Moustakas has described as "existential loneliness." For Moustakas, this kind of loneliness describes a feeling where the subject begins to "see that loneliness is neither good nor bad, but a point of intense and timeless awareness of the Self, a beginning which initiates totally new sensitivities and awarenesses, and which results in bringing a person deeply in touch with his own existence and in touch with others in a fundamental sense."[22] There are two components to this kind of loneliness: first, it brings an intense awareness of the Self; second, this awareness brings a person deeply "in touch" with others in a fundamental sense. I would argue that loneliness today often fails to bring such a deep awareness and sense of connection with others. Of course, not all these writers allow for their descriptions of loneliness to bring their characters deeply "in touch" with others; loneliness is often pushed down, a cause for pretense and a spur to fleeing the self in these works. However, there is a residual sense in these mid-century works that if only loneliness had been confronted, if what it was trying to tell its characters was acted on, then the calamity might not have ensued. As we will see when we read the work of Sayaka Murata in Chapter 6, such existential loneliness is inaccessible to many young people today who feel they are most content merely channeling the information and commercial streams of industry as social network. In other words, we still read in these works of late modernism about how loneliness offers clues for how life with others can be lived to the full if only we are strong enough to heed the calls. If we resist, we will instead most likely continue to engage in what Alice Wheeler in *Revolutionary Road* (1961) calls "sentimental loneliness" whereby we give ourselves up to the role of husband, lover, wife, or worker in order to flee the uncomfortable truths our feelings of loneliness intimate to us. Murata's *Convenience Store Woman* cannot even withstand such "sentimental loneliness"; the roles and societal expectations sometime-friends and others push on her ultimately swamp her and she only feels "reborn" channeling the convenience store jungles, promotional pitches, and commercial temporality. What Laing calls the shame and seeming impenetrability of loneliness are the factors that cause Yates's characters to give themselves up to these pretenses. However, even in acknowledging this, there is still a residual sense in the works on loneliness by O'Connor, Joyce, Yates, and McCullers that loneliness teaches essential truths that need to be heeded. In the Information Age, because loneliness is often experienced in complete isolation most of the time, it can become detached from its cause; young people fail to see that engaged human contact face-to-face and in-person with a living human voice can shatter the spell of impenetrability surrounding loneliness; they fail to see the lack of this engagement in their lives as a cause for their feelings of loneliness. Loneliness then becomes a condition without a cause; it becomes a mental health issue detached more and more from societal causes. In a sense then we are left with the husk or hull of loneliness, a loneliness as grinding as ever before but without the connection with societal causes that allowed us to still devise stories and artworks around what it was telling us and around what our failure to heed those calls might bring down upon us.

Richard Yates gives us many different faces of this existential loneliness and yet in making loneliness his main theme he also begins to demonstrate clearly to us how Moustakas's description of "existential loneliness" can often fail to bring characters closer to a more integrated understanding of others. However, Yates's readers know that the loneliness he describes from so many different perspectives still informs them about the peril of not facing up to loneliness in their lives. Yates, like O'Connor and Joyce, gives us various roles and occupations—army sergeant, newlyweds, teachers, freelance writers, failed company clerks, salesmen—for whom it is already too late in terms of how they deal with loneliness. These are types and the reader knows they are types used by the writer to say something about the kind of jobs and occupations society is now asking people to take up. They do not give us any truly successful professions or caring professions; we begin the narratives of these tired schoolteachers, army sergeants, army veterans expecting the authors to demonstrate for us how certain professions can be unfulfilling or emasculating. In a sense, we the readers need to read these narratives to feel validated about our professions that we must feel and know are different. In more recent accounts of loneliness such as Sayaka Murata's *Convenience Store Woman*, Gail Honeyman's *Eleanor Oliphant Is Completely Fine*, or John Boyne's *A History of Loneliness*, loneliness is very much the result of a lengthy internalization of institutional norms and expectations that seems to run deeper than the kinds of performances Yates speaks for. This might be because these three later novels deal with the issue of abuse and mental illness and in doing so the authors employ narrative techniques that bring you inside the narratives of characters who are initially somewhat oblivious to the trauma and how it has marked them. Loneliness in these novels is very much a lived condition of life and work that has nothing to do with performance; it is either how society now educates its young people (as in David Foster Wallace), part of the daily routine one enacts in order to feel more oneself (as in Sayaka Murata), or the result of an underlying mental health condition that the novel reveals only much later (as in Gail Honeymoon). These twenty-first-century descriptions of loneliness do not then presume the kind of engagement with the self or with others that Moustakas assigns to "existential loneliness."

The kind of loneliness Richard Yates describes in his collection *Eleven Kinds of Loneliness* (1957) is often impossible to throw off for his characters; it is indeed impenetrable because his characters have most often been given no way out. For example, the TB patients in "No Pain Whatsoever" and "Out with the Old" are confined to hospital wards and the possibility for growth is presented as limited. When they do encounter people outside the hospital, there is a great gulf between their perceptions of relationships and their abilities to influence and understand events even in their own family settings. McIntyre tries hard to come to terms with his daughter's teenage pregnancy in "Out with the Old"; he begins writing a letter to her but can never get beyond the third page and he cannot even describe the kind of knowledge to effect change that life experience has given him: "Your old dad may not be good for much anymore but he does know a thing or two about life and especially one important thing, and that is."[23] Harry, another TB patient in "No Pain Whatsoever," is also described in such harrowing terms that we are concerned chiefly with his quality of life when we meet him; how he engages with feelings of loneliness is secondary: "When he bent forward to take the match the yellow pajamas gaped open and she saw his chest, unbelievably thin, partly caved-in on one side where the ribs were gone. She could just see the end of the ugly, newly healed scar from the last operation."[24] Harry's wife Myra is also barely developed beside the harrowing descriptions of her husband and the description of the amorous antics of her friends, the couple Irene and Marty.

Yates describes his lonely characters with such evocative language and imparts to them such deliberate intent and such singular motivations that we get no sense that there is any possibility of them ever experiencing anything but disappointment in relation to the gap between their desires and what they actually experience. John Fallon, the discharged soldier in "The B. A. R. Man" has such violent intentions during even the most casual of encounters with a woman: "And the images that tortured him now, while he stood in line at the makeshift bar, were intensified by rage: there would be struggling limbs and torn clothes in the taxi; there would be blind force in the bedroom, and stifled cries of pain that would turn to whimpering and finally to spastic moans of lust."[25] The characters are so wedded to their descriptions that we fail to see how they might be anything but lonely. We fail to see how they might possess the other-related awareness that Moustakas assigns to "existential loneliness."

Sentimental Loneliness in *Revolutionary Road*

The Wheelers of *Revolutionary Road* are very different; they are full, rounded characters, characters the novel can give us over and above the short story. Alice Wheeler recognizes that she had given in to a "sentimentally lonely time" in telling herself that she loved Frank Wheeler. As she prepares for her self-induced miscarriage she thinks back on why herself and Frank had got together:

> And all because, in a sentimentally lonely time long ago, she had found it easy and agreeable to believe whatever this one particular boy felt like saying, and to repay him for pleasure by telling easy, agreeable lies of her own, until each was saying what the other most wanted to hear—until he was saying "I love you" and she was saying "Really, I mean it; you're the most interesting person I've ever met."[26]

She realises what a "subtle, treacherous thing it was to let yourself go that way! Because once you'd started it was terribly difficult to stop."[27] Alice's interior thoughts, given to us in a second-person, free, indirect discourse, explain how the self-harm of this performance in the face of loneliness evolves:

> [T]he next thing you knew all honesty, all truth, was as far away and glimmering, as hopelessly unattainable as the world of the golden people. Then you discovered you were working at life the way the Laurel Players worked at *The Petrified Forest* ... earnest and sloppy and full of pretension and all wrong; you found you were saying yes when you meant the very opposite; then you were breathing gasoline as if it were flowers and abandoning yourself to a delirium of love under the weight of a clumsy, grunting red-faced man you didn't even like—Shep Campbell—and then you were face to face, in total darkness, with the knowledge that you didn't know who you were.[28]

Feelings of sentimental loneliness then, we are told, lead the subject to take up the performance; sentimental loneliness is a kind of loneliness that is associated with youth. The suggestion might be that each age brings with it its own version of loneliness; whether we listen to the loneliness at each stage of life and weather its waves of attack or give in to its sentimental variety and then persuade ourselves to perform against our best interests, a more authentic version of loneliness is waiting to engulf us either way. At this point, we are very close to describing self-awareness and self-reflection themselves, what bring home to us our irrevocable existence as individuals beset with individualism, *as* loneliness. However, as Lars Svendsen reminds us, it is foolhardy to reduce all forms of self-reflection to a kind of loneliness. How many of us are indeed capable of never giving in to what Alice berates herself for, namely the tendency to persuade ourselves for a time in our lives that being with certain others we may not love is beneficial? However, it is at this point in the exploration of loneliness incited by the novel that the reader is urged to examine what storytelling itself tells us about loneliness. We are inclined to read this section on Alice as her getting to the heart of her loneliness through this second-person, free, indirect discourse.

Narrative and the Performance of Loneliness

However, storytelling itself offers a unique textual performance; it asks the solitary reader to perform the impression that he or she is really engaging with another consciousness—the author's impressions mediated through a fictional character—in determining or working out what loneliness is. Reading then, in a sense, is the archetypal performance made in full awareness of our individualism or solitude; while it necessitates a kind of solitude it also asks us to play at sustaining the fiction that there is something to be learned about loneliness. It asks us to sustain the fiction there is something to be learned through it about how to move beyond individualism to authentic existence with others by engaging in a mental enquiry or "conversation" with another textual persona. If loneliness as sentimental loneliness—what Yates very often seems to reduce loneliness to in describing the necessary performances individuals engage in that ultimately dupe them—is not to be given in to, then surely the play and performance of giving oneself up to long narratives describing fictional characters being duped in this way is precisely the kind of practice that is likely to nurture a susceptibility to such sentimental loneliness? In other words, we are close to the point at which loneliness and our need for narrative and storytelling in self-understanding intersect. In running up against reading as performance in the sense of sustaining a "conversation" with an imagined textual other, we begin to realize how much of our encounter with loneliness is shaped by how we have learned to internalize narrative for self-reflection. We end up feeling we need to work out a phenomenology of loneliness. We are close to the point at which we must draw back and ask ourselves how narrative and the stories it has enabled us to tell ourselves over the years is itself a factor in enabling us to be susceptible to sentimental loneliness. And if this is the case, the question is then how loneliness evolves in an age when the need for narrative has changed. When young people's means of adopting and sustaining enquiries with fictional personas in narratives that enable them to deliberate on such important subjects such as identity is made through online channels and resources, how different is it from Yates's sentimental loneliness? And since the kind of performances we engage in to deal with the kind of loneliness Yates describes better than anyone—performing in the day job, the role of husband or wife, the role of army veteran, of budding writer—require institutions of practice to make them seem viable, how realistic is it to posit that today's institutions sell us performances that are asking far more from us in terms of accommodating loneliness? Whereas the era of military patriotism and of the national patriotism embodied through large national companies such as General Electric or General Motors, an era that has all but passed in the United States, demanded daily performances of roles we could switch off when we left the office or escaped to the woods or the bedroom, the online performances incited by today's version of sentimental loneliness in young people are more pervasive and they do not get switched off. In other words, there are less opportunities today for discovering how such performances might even be rooted in feelings of loneliness and therefore less opportunities for encountering those moments of insight that non-sentimental loneliness affords us for discovering how we are being duped. There is also the sense that online communities today often require a certain performance from young people in order to keep the social network profitable. Therefore, built into this 24/7 hooked up online performance generator are also the instructional and motivational cues and rubrics that keep us performing and keep us online, thereby isolating loneliness as a condition no longer rooted in the lack of community.

Frank and Alice Wheeler know that they are surrounded by deadening jobs and also by what he calls "hopeless emptiness." He also then accepts that part of each day must be given up to such performances:

> Intelligent, thinking people could take things like this in their stride, just as they took the larger absurdities of deadly dull jobs in the city and deadly dull homes in the suburbs … the important thing was to keep from being contaminated. The important thing, always, was to remember who you were.[29]

However, in the novel such performances are nearly always enacted in the face-to-face encounter with other people. The Wheelers and the Campbells meet to gossip about their fellow neighbors and their "extreme suburban smugness."[30] Frank then extrapolates from their smug neighbours: "It isn't only the Donaldsons … It's all the idiots I ride with on the train every day. It's a disease."[31] Then the authorial omniscient voice steps in, with only a hint of free indirect discourse, to say: "They would all agree, and the happy implication was that they alone, the four of them, were painfully alive in a drugged and dying culture. It was in the face of this defiance, and in tentative reply to this loneliness, that the idea of the Laurel Players had made its first appeal."[32] The community's desire to set up a performance group is then the result of a shared loneliness. Yates makes loneliness the ground of all their disquiet; it is a lot for loneliness to shoulder and its prominent place in the novel recalls the use of loneliness in his later short story collection *Eleven Kinds of Loneliness*. It is another example of the power of loneliness in Yates's works. However, when loneliness is this big and this all-consuming we are once again, as readers, brought face to face with the performative consolations of fiction; we are made to examine how much of our own understanding of self and identity comes to us through the fictional personas we sustain and help build and then commune with in enquiring into individualism and community. The sense we get then in reading Yates in an Internet Age is that we must come to some new understanding of loneliness; loneliness in Yates sometimes seems as dated as the creased suits and the petticoats his characters wear. Perhaps he is right to see loneliness first as a philosophy and as the ground of all performance and self-delusion, but it has today taken on new forms and young people have ever greater demands made on them in terms of how they navigate loneliness and how much they put into their performances that both consolidate loneliness and yet also detach its emotion from its ground, a connection that would enable them to understand it better. Whereas for Frank and Alice, the loneliness they feel is pushed under by the pleasure they can each give each other and through the gossip about the "suburban smugness" of an outgroup, for online communities the "smugness" of the outgroup becomes so all-consuming precisely because the individual faces of the outgroup are numberless and faceless. Frank assigns names to the outgroup; he speaks of the Cramers and the Donaldsons, people he has met and talked with. For many online groups targeting outgroups, the faces are never known and face-to-face conversation between groups is impossible. Therefore, the nature of the outgrouping that an allegiance to "sentimental loneliness" incites today is detached from any causal connection with feelings of loneliness; it instead becomes justified on the basis of how this all-encompassing outgroup is defined. The effects of the gossip or hatespeech is harder to see firsthand or even imagine. However, this "sentimental loneliness" *as* a loneliness that has been detached from its roots in a lack of fellow feeling then only serves to prevent young people from ever realizing the benefits of the "existential loneliness" Moustakas describes.

Considering the fact that Moustakas describes this ideal kind of loneliness as "existential loneliness" it is interesting to read that Frank then, in looking back at his days in college, describes himself as a "John-Paul-Sartre sort of man."[33] Yates, writing in the late 1950s and early 1960s, is then already lampooning the popularity of existential philosophy among college youth. Frank muses:

> as an intense, nicotine-stained, Jean-Paul-Sartre sort of man, wasn't it simple logic to expect that he'd be limited to intense, nicotine-stained, Jean-Paul-Sartre sorts of women? But this was the counsel of defeat, and one night, bolstered by four straight gulps of whiskey at a party in Morningside Heights, he followed the counsel of victory.[34]

The Sartrean "counsel of defeat" is already being caricatured by Yates. Perhaps Frank is a bad reader of Sartre in summing him up with the phrase "counsel of defeat": as we recall from Roquentin's deliberations in Chapter 1, he never feels defeated by loneliness but instead uses it to inspire himself to write, what Frank cannot work himself up to despite his wife's support. However, even though Frank is owning up to this admission in these reflections, he later also demonstrates an existentialist attitude towards work when he goes looking for assistance from his friend Sam, a philosophy graduate now working in the "student placement office":

> All I want is to get enough dough coming in to keep us solvent for the next year or so, till I can figure things out; meanwhile I want to retain my own identity. Therefore the thing I'm most anxious to avoid is any kind of work

that can be considered "interesting" in its own right. I want something that can't possibly touch me. I want some big, swollen old corporation that's been bumbling along making money in its sleep for a hundred years, where they have to hire eight guys for every one job because none of them can be expected to care about whatever boring thing it is they're supposed to be doing.[35]

Frank is no slouch and he cannot be accused of Sartrean bad faith on the job. He wants to keep his identity but he seems oblivious to the fact that giving up all that time in a job that is not "interesting" is precisely how the national or multinational company makes you lose your own identity. The "hopeless emptiness" that he tries to escape by not deciding on what he wants to do, that is essentially another name for the "sentimental loneliness" his wife has given herself up to, will only become ever more apparent in a job that asks you to give up the best days of your life to something that is not "interesting." Frank seems to believe that occupation and identity can be kept apart, however, even Thorstein Veblen had predicted at the turn of the century that leisure itself would soon become only an extension of the institutional life of labor. In the next chapter, I will examine how David Foster Wallace describes boredom as offering us moments of salvation in the workplace.

Ultimately, Yates's work moves us on from the existential loneliness of existential philosophy and the humdrum nihilism of Beckett in late modernism to a close exploration of the impact of loneliness on the American postwar baby boom generation. Yates's work comes at the end of this generation and thus its ideals are being challenged in the face of the postmodern turn waiting in the wings. Yates's realist and deeply psychological engagement with themes of disillusionment in suburban American life also asks us to reflect on the role narrative plays in our understanding of individualism and the move out of the self. His works look forward to the postmodern works of Pynchon, late Nabokov, and Barth, works that demonstrate that loneliness as first philosophy in the novel can very often draw the reader into a rigorous questioning of the role narrative plays in our determination of identity. Inspired by post-structuralism, postmodern novels will demonstrate that reader–response relations and the human–text interface is no solid ground on which to ground a philosophy of loneliness as existential loneliness or sentimental loneliness.

5

Beating University Loneliness and Workplace Boredom: David Foster Wallace on "How to Keep Yourself Open to A Moment of the Most Supernal Beauty"

David Foster Wallace describes a very different kind of loneliness in his post-postmodern or "new sincerity" works. He also describes a new relationship between the author and the reader. He is willing to admit that the relationship between the author and the reader is "more like a late-night conversation with really good friends, when the bullshit stops and the masks come off."[1] Of course, the kind of conversation one has with Wallace in such works as *Infinite Jest* can be a long and demanding conversation, one that very few young readers will take up. It also rails against minimalism and postmodernism in demanding a willingness to engage with the new hypermediated and hyperaware sincerity Wallace offers. As the character in his 2000 story "Good Old Neon" notes, "What goes on inside is just too fast and huge and all interconnected for words to do more than barely sketch the outlines of at most one tiny part of it at any given instant."[2] However, in a long conversation Wallace had with Jonathan Franzen in early 1992, as they drove from Syracuse to Swarthmore, Wallace argued—as D. T. Max records in his biography of Wallace—that the purpose of literature was to "alleviate loneliness and give comfort, to break through what he characterized in *Infinite Jest* as each person's 'excluded encagement in the self.'"[3] Wallace has also been described by D. T. Max as outlining a new kind of institutionalization for the kind of sentimental loneliness Richard Yates describes in *Revolutionary Road*. Whereas Frank Wheeler wants a job that "can't touch me" so that his identity remains untouched, in *The Pale King*, when Wallace describes the tedium of working for the IRS, it is, for D. T. Max, the dullness that ultimately sets the characters free.[4] In his notebooks, Wallace describes how boredom and tedium can give way to this sense of freedom:

> Bliss—a-second-by-second joy and gratitude at the gift of being alive, conscious-lies on the other side of crushing, crushing boredom. Pay close attention to the most tedious thing you can find (Tax Returns, Televised Golf) and, in waves, a boredom like you've never known will wash over you and just about kill you. Ride these out, and it's like stepping from black and white into color. Like water after days in the desert. Instant bliss in every atom.[5]

Wallace had a team of researchers working on boredom. They assembled hundreds of pages of research on the topic, "trying to understand it at an almost neurological level."[6] He also had four offices in which he wrote his novel of boredom, *The Pale King*. He had his black room in his house, a university office that was rarely used, a room "put aside for him in Francis B's mother's house, and a rented space."[7] As Wallace described to the Kenyon students he gave the graduation address to in 2005, to navigate loneliness and the solitariness of existence and consciousness was about "being aware enough to *choose* what you pay attention to and to *choose* how you construct meaning from experience"[8] Such choices confront us daily almost at every waking moment. Wallace gives the example of standing in a supermarket line. While standing in line, students can choose to "experience nothing but the anxiety and irritation their college augmented sense of superiority would entitle them to or they could, in the midst of that same experience, open themselves up to a moment of the most supernal beauty—on fire with the same force that lit the stars—compassion, love, the subsurface unity of all things."[9] Wallace tells the students that if you have really learned how to think, how to pay attention, "then you will have other options."[10] This then is a plea to engage with the ordinary and not to dodge it like so many of us do in the first years of college where we learn a kind of academic arrogance that is hard to shake. To once open yourself up to a "moment of the most supernal beauty" recalls Camus, a writer Wallace was reading in the final months of his life, a writer he describes as "very clear, as a thinker, and tough"; his writing "makes my soul feel clean to read him."[11] Camus's Mersault has a moment when he lies in his prison cell before his own death when he too opens himself up to "the benign indifference of the universe" and gives up on the anger he had seen erupt from him when the priest visits him in his cell.

The kind of moment that Wallace and Camus describe here and that they both seem to arrive at through the engagement with solitude and loneliness—and whether it is equivalent to Moustakas's existential loneliness is unclear—also resonates with what Takeo Doi describes as "Nishida philosophy" in the Japanese tradition. Wallace practiced Buddhist meditation to try and "slow down his whirring mind."[12] In an age of hyperstimulation and 24/7 infotainment feeds, Wallace recognized that "the lack of stimulation" gave his IRS characters the "chance to open themselves up to experience in the largest sense of the word."[13] It is one of the reasons the novel itself, *The Pale King*, is a novel which he described as "a series of setups for things to happen but nothing ever happens";[14] the reader as an "old friend" can share in this experience. Doi also regards Kitarō Nishida's philosophy as being built around a notion of "pure experience" similar to the experience Wallace describes, one Doi himself reads through his own philosophy of *amae*. I will return to this concept in Chapter 6. However, Doi reads this "pure experience" of the philosophy of Kitarō Nishida, a leading member of the Kyoto School, as centering around the concept of *mu*, "void," and as allowing for the merging of the subject and the object.[15] Doi believes, writing in 1971, that such a focus on the "Zen world of identity between subject and object" will not be sufficient for "the Japanese of the future"; it will be "necessary to transcend *amae* by discovering the subject and object: to discover, in other words, the other person."[16] How are we to find these moments in the online world when it is very difficult to decipher where the boundary between subject and object lies? How do we learn to choose how to allow ourselves to remain open to "a moment of the most supernal beauty"? For Wallace, digital connection did not offer the answer as it did not help him learn more about "how to feel connected in your own life."[17] As D. T. Max writes for Wallace, the "Web might offer a different hope of escape from the self, but actually escaping was no less futile."[18] Wallace writes to his friend and fellow writer Jonathan Franzen in the final years of his life that he had much written for the last novel but that the question of connection was again the problem: "What's missing is some … thing. It may be a connection between the problem of writing it and of being alive."[19] This takes us back to Johann Hari's *Lost Connections* that I discussed in Chapter 1. It seems that Wallace's own interest in what boredom offered, and his own interest in what the everyday offered in the shape of opening "up to a moment of the most supernal beauty—on fire with the same force that lit the stars—compassion, love, the subsurface unity of all things" had blossomed to the degree that he had possibly lost the ability to connect the writing on that experience with the experience itself. How difficult is it then for a writer to give up on the critical eye that might prevent this connection with the "subsurface unity of all things"? Wallace was, rather ironically, described as the writer of the cyber generation even though Wallace wrote to a graduate student in 2001 that he only allowed himself to "Webulize" once a week.[20] He is described as writing the novel of "protest against the future they were creating" with technology and yet Max writes that the "web seemed made for [his] multiple conjunctions at the opening of sentences."[21] Was Wallace then describing a future condition that the internet would normalize but that he himself had experienced through his hyperawareness in the offline world? Does he describe an offline hopelessness of finding a connection to oneself when forever bombarded by streams of knowledge and hints of perspectives that barrage our senses daily in the online world? Was his consciousness and his own "new sincerity" somehow open to, or sensitive to, this state even though he had principally experienced it offline? Wallace was able to capture a sense of information overload in the 1990s that we would all have to adapt to in the Internet Age and yet he describes the feeling of not being able to find a connection to oneself because of the normalization of the anxiety high the connection to hypermedia as an infinity of information has engendered. Wallace was surprised to learn he had written a "cybernovel"; when asked by the *Chicago Tribune* whether his book was meant to reflect life as it was experienced in the Internet Age, he replied: "This is sort of what it's like to be alive ... You don't have to be on the Internet for life to feel this way."[22]

The field of David Foster Wallace Studies has been growing rapidly in recent years. It may have emerged as a field only as recently as 2010 when Adam Kelly's article "David Foster Wallace: The Death of the Author and the Birth of a Discipline,"[23] published in the online *Irish Journal of American Studies*, gave what he described as "an initial map of the territory of what might be termed "Wallace Studies." For Kelly, this refers to the "network of interest in David Foster Wallace's *oeuvre* that ranges through but also well beyond the traditional academic channels." Kelly argues that the field had arisen in a far more "democratic vein" to that in which discourses and genres have evolved around other great writers such as Joyce and Nabokov. However, given that netizens, "amateur" critics, "skillful and committed nonprofessional readers," and internet sites devoted to Wallace such as *The Howling Fantods*[24] have done the hard work in creating this vibrant field, it is no surprise that professors and academics now appear to be taking up the slack and creating their own professional discourse around Wallace, one that academic publishers are always eager to make less "democratic" than any online sites of enquiry and public discussion. New academic books on Wallace and philosophy[25] also demonstrate the highly philosophical nature of Wallace's writing and his interest in freedom in an age that he regarded as mediated too much by the college experience. Wallace's archive is also now safely housed at the Harry Ransom Center at the University of Texas, Austin. The curator of his archive revealed that "Wallace was born 10 years later than any other writer whose archive we house." Wallace has then truly entered the Academy, an Academy he taught in for many years at Emerson College and the University of Arizona, an Academy whose selection and admissions procedures he brilliantly mocks in *Infinite Jest*. The academicization of Wallace since his death would surely have amused him and possibly saddened him at the same time especially considering that so many of his characters are both wounded and scarred by their own experiences in college. I will return to this aspect of Wallace's work later in this chapter. However, Wallace did not intend simply to "dramatize how dark and stupid everything is"; he strongly believed, as he told Larry McCaffrey in the *Review of Contemporary Fiction*, that "the definition of good art would seem to be art that locates and applies CPR to those elements of what's human and magical that still live and glow despite the times' darkness."[26] This is what Wallace speaks for; in being hyperaware and sometimes hypercritical of the most mundane of objects, institutional tics, and consumer practices he shines a light on the indomitable human spirit of curiosity and he reminds us to check whether we have really *chosen* to do what we are doing.

Wallace's work always explores the links between literature and philosophy. Since Wallace was a high-achieving philosophy undergraduate student at Amherst, where his father—a philosophy professor—also studied, and later a gifted graduate student in philosophy at Harvard, it is no surprise that critics have been looking for the philosophical in Wallace's writing. Robert K. Bolger and Scott Korb's edited collection *Gesturing Toward Reality: David Foster Wallace and Philosophy* and Steven M. Cahn and Maureen Eckert's *Freedom and the Self: Essays on the Philosophy of David Foster Wallace* include many insightful essays that demonstrate clearly both how philosophical approaches to Wallace can uncover hidden dimensions of his texts and how Wallace's work helps open out philosophical ideas such as sincerity, loneliness, bad faith, and even religious investigation. Andrew Bennett's chapter "Inside David Foster Wallace's Head: Attention, Loneliness, Suicide, and the Other Side of Boredom" relates Wallace's concern with boredom to Schopenhauer's work on boredom and suffering. Bennett describes how Wallace recognizes the paradoxical nature of boredom, a state that compels us to endure, and perceive, the "human condition" in terms of the repetition of the dullest of tasks while also recognizing that the feeling of "flow" that can sometimes manifest in the midst of such tasks also offers us the potential for a degree of transcendence in "self-overcoming," that is, a state of "quasi-spiritual self-denial."[27] Maria Bustillos's chapter "Philosophy, Self-Help, and the Death of David Wallace" is another recent important intervention. Bustillos argues that Wallace was keenly aware of the limitations that philosophers such as Alain be Botton perceive in the current university teaching of the humanities. She argues that Wallace recognized that universities should not overlook what is today left largely to the self-help domain. His work promotes the idea that literature should nurture "a strong, seeking and inventive mind operating freely in a condition of eternal doubt" but also recognizes that our "pedagogical methods, including those employed in the teaching of philosophy, seldom favor the development of such minds." Bustillos writes that the student of philosophy "who wishes to excel as Wallace did isn't taught to seek or to ask new questions, but rather to produce what is required or expected within increasingly challenging fixed parameters. A particularly gifted student like Wallace performs like an Olympic athlete in a dazzling routine. It's a competitive sport, in fact—one where the 'best' will 'win.'"[28] However, not all recent books on Wallace relate his work to what we are told is the ever-diminishing return to be got from traditional pedagogical values. Jeffrey Severs's recent *David Foster Wallace's Balancing Books: Fictions of Value* reads Wallace in terms of value, ground, and balancing books. He argues that Wallace writes "moral fiction within a postmodern United States" as "a matter of restoring readers' sense that beneath what has been sold to them as infinite choice lies an ancient moral image: the balance scale, a primitive computer with two options, clearly seen and objectively weighted."[29]

Academic Cloneliness

For the rest of this chapter I want to build on new philosophical and pedagogical readings of Wallace by examining Wallace's obsession with how education and the arts have fostered a form of blinkered competition that promotes a destructive form of loneliness and an unwillingness to examine such loneliness. Wallace's *oeuvre* can be viewed as an ever more elaborate and yet concentrated exploration of cycles of repetition. In early works such as *The Broom of the System*, routine and repetition are less evident, there is less talk of the "corrective discipline" and "drills" that loom over all aspects of life in *Infinite Jest*.[30] His final work *The Pale King* brings us up close and personal with the drills and corrective discipline of one of the most notoriously inward-looking bureaucratic institutions, the IRS. All the time this ever-recurring and ever-deepening focus on drills and corrective discipline is also referencing the work of writing, reading, and rewriting, what Mark McGurl argues has been transformed into an "institution of nothing" thanks to the prevalence of the writing program in today's universities. However, Wallace was a humanist and a proponent of what has been called "new sincerity" and thus the individual must still come first before the institution no matter how much she is defined by it. While McGurl's institution of nothing would then presumably give us a kind of individualism of nothing, a new kind of positive barbarism or loneliness that sustains itself through ever more self-reflexive institutional checks and balances, I believe that Wallace tries to preserve individuality from what he often describes as an "arts-inspired loneliness is hip movement" evident in elite universities by detailing how the most mundane of routines such as an IRS job can be material for an art that celebrates the normal and not the "nothing" or the "best." Critics have also begun to note the important epistemological and metaphysical questions that Wallace tackles thematically and stylistically through his ground-breaking narrative experimentation. Brian McHale has argued that postmodern novels privilege the ontological above the epistemological and it is an opposition that Wallace's work challenges; Wallace reveals that the kind of person we see ourselves as is directly related to how we negotiate and internalize our daily routines, our encounters with both people and consumable objects, and our personal hang-ups, embarrassments, and weaknesses in our work spaces and living spaces. Like Elizabeth Bowen, Wallace acknowledges that our world is not only our globalized city or country but a locus or habitus that is determined by how we negotiate the furniture of everyday life about us whether it be a pile of tax returns, an undergarment, a new brand of chocolate treat we have been tasked with promoting, or a new art-form made entirely from human excrement.

Wallace does not meticulously detail the impact of this world of objects and practices on consciousness in order to discredit it. On the contrary, he demonstrates through the long, rich trajectory of his work how this daily interrogation of seemingly pointless endeavor is in fact the means to the only end, perseverance. For one of his middle-aged father characters in *The Pale King*, Wallace describes how such perseverance becomes key even to our dealings with others; this father has so many secret sexual obligations with different women that all he finds in the relationships is "a sort of dutiful tedium of energy and time and the will to forge on in the face of despair."[31] Wallace is not speaking for the "hollow hypocrisy" of the postwar generation.[32] His leading male protagonists are not even trying to negotiate the tired midlife crises and normative family constraints that so many male American writers, from Updike to Bellow and from Richard Yates to Roth, feel the need to document. Relationships are so painful, idiosyncratic, and self-interrogative in Wallace as to feel fictional. For Wallace, the suburban moral vacuum is not a given since the subject is still negotiating his or her place in the world through college interviews, board meetings, drug treatment clinics, counselling sessions, or intensive tennis coaching classes. There is no spurious identity to be parodied with anti-epiphanies since identity has been replaced by endless competition, office routine, approval mechanisms, and self-help resources. Wallace hits the ground running with a consumerist pragmatism and a heightened psychological sense of what it means to be American—and it *is* nearly always American—in the age of the sports celebrity, the prescription nation, and the shopping channel. Wallace's place in the canon of American novelists is assured and yet still being configured precisely because his work is so rich and in offering the kind of "new sincerity" that postmodernism had always taught us was defunct, Wallace sends literary critics back to review their postmodernism course readers.

    Mark McGurl reads Wallace as a "Program Man," a product of the Writing Program scene, or the Program Era, in American universities, a writer "whose situation marks a further step toward the thorough *normalization* of the emergent conditions of institutionalization that that term tries to name."[33] He argues that Wallace "could not have been more deeply embedded in the culture of the school, or more conversant with the folk-ways of university intellectuals";[34] his works, for McGurl, speaks for a "commitment to the necessity of institutions in making and maintaining a 'meaning of life.'"[35] However, this institutionalization is built on nothing and is sustained by nothing since the "blank 'inhumanity' of the outside encloses the interior, infiltrating it, threatening at any point to reveal that infinity of meaning as nothing, as zero."[36] The institution then becomes a "safe space in between interiority and exteriority, a kind of turnstile," it becomes like the place Beckett's speaker longs for in "my way is in the sands flowing"[37] when he finds "my peace" is there "in the receding mist/ where I may cease from treading/ these long shifting thresholds/ and live the space of a door/ that opens and shuts." The difference is that whereas this space of nothingness once described a kind of alienated consciousness today it describes an institutionalized consciousness. However, if Wallace does write as what he once described as a "complete just total banzai weenie studier" then it is of course as a unique, competitive and privileged, prestigiously educated, middle-class American white male. McGurl argues that "nothing" is the "seductive object—or nonobject—of a death drive, a destination of pure authenticity" and that "its fatal attraction can be avoided only by getting with the program, submitting to a Higher Power, ad infinitum. The problem being that, ultimately, the 'program,' too, is revealed as nothing, a congress of empty formalities."[38] This is an appealing and tidy argument and yet in its privileging of institutions it runs them all together in seeing them as equivalent. The tennis academy, the writing program, the IRS are institutions of a kind and we can look to organizational theory for ways to code and equate their practices. However, Wallace spent most of his creative hours outside these institutional walls and inside what Andrew Bennett calls his "own head" and within the four walls of his home, writing. The private institution of writing may embody all the drills and the corrective discipline of other institutions, it may even display a fondness for OCD, but it is, no matter how enthralling we find Wallace's poeticization of an institution as mundane as the IRS, never equivalent to the IRS. The nothing one keeps at one's door while writing is very different to the stress-fueled, competition-reeking, paranoid imaginings of "blank 'inhumanity' on the outside that encloses the interior" of an institution. Wallace poeticizes the most mundane of institutions and the practices that most epitomize the Yeatsian "fumble in the greasy till" to remind us, in the old way, of the beauty to be found in the most repetitive of tasks. It is only by offering up writing as a practice captivated by the institutionalization of everything that we can see what has not yet been institutionalized. The institution by its very nature can never allow for the kind of perspectives literature grants us; there is no sky hook within institutional thinking from which to imagine an outside to institutionalization. However, this is not to say that the nothingness and the competition Wallace describes in the different institutions is any less real and Wallace's depiction of it any less scathing.

Jennifer Howard's article, "The Afterlife of David Foster Wallace"[39] from *The Chronicle of Higher Education*'s *Chronicle Review*, documents how Wallace's work was then, in being read from a range of exciting, new perspectives from within the academy, slowly being fed back into the system it challenges.[40] Whereas the early focus in Wallace criticism was on his links to postmodern writers, critics such as Marshall Boswell acknowledged that Wallace clearly had a "new ethically charged agenda." Wallace is a very different writer from the champions of postmodernism such as John Barth and Thomas Pynchon. He describes both the unremitting ease with which we grant institutions ever more privileged access to our private lives and what he describes, perhaps most beautifully in his story "The Suffering Channel," as the "single great informing conflict of the American psyche," namely "the conflict between the subjective centrality of our own lives versus our awareness of its objective insignificance."[41] The careful inspection of the "problem of other minds" and the anxiety raised by the impossibility of ever being able to fathom the space between self and other (nicely lampooned by the obese character Norman in *The Broom of the System*) are everywhere in Wallace. Wallace also does not care much for the "highbrow" ultra-referentiality of canonical European modernists like Joyce and Eliot or for the "highbrow" pastiche-driven, intertextual flippancy of canonical American postmodern writers like Nabokov. He wears his canonical erudition lightly even though it is woven through every fiber of his style. It is also important to note that Wallace's work is firmly rooted in American life. While the story "Another Pioneer" does take off from solid ground in being set on a commercial flight and does cast a wide net historically and even anthropologically, the majority of Wallace's protagonists and narrators embody the insights and hang-ups of a persona that most often comes across as white, American, and male (one obvious exception being Lenore Beadsman).

In a sense, Wallace prefigures many of the epistemological insights that have been recently claimed for speculative realism. Speculative realism is a new discourse in philosophical studies with important ties to literary theory, and it preaches a new theory of attention to objects and one might even suggest the institution becomes a kind of object for Wallace. Speculative realism argues that the "object" of phenomenology was overdetermined and that the object of postmodernism was too often underdetermined. Philosophy for too long has been correlationist; there is no world other than the world as it is mediated through consciousness. Speculative realism has been developing various theories to unshackle perception from such presumptions in redefining objects as capable of "withdrawal" and "inaccessibility"; it wants to set the object free. The same lack of attention to the object has been perceived in much twentieth-century American fiction. Adam Kelly, in a recent essay on Wallace and the "novel of ideas," reads Wallace as presenting us with a new style of novel of ideas that turns its back on the Henry James-inspired American novel of the twentieth century that was always too thin on philosophy and too thick on psychology; it neglected the object and the "idea" in favor of the "feelings" evoked in the character. Kelly argues that Wallace insists on the centrality of "abstract structures that transcend the individual's psychology" and I would add to this Wallace's concern with the object.[42] Wallace may not be describing objects such as tax returns, infant carriers, chocolate treats, or Simmons Beauty Rest mattresses so that they "withdraw" or become "inaccessible" but his careful description of these objects and their physical make-up, ingredients, wrappers, terms and conditions, promotional campaigns, salesmen and women, company profiles, all alongside dense footnotes and asides on the social context of their emergence and the nature of the paperwork assigned to them, makes the object encroach on the space of the subject to the extent that the boundaries blur.

However, the need to speak for an ethical imperative rather than a purely aesthetic experimentalism is always evident in Wallace. Stephen Burn argues that Wallace tackles "the central issues of his time," including how mass media "shapes modern culture and how difficult it is for people to connect with one another."[43] Whether it be the painful trials and tribulations of Hal Incandenza and his relationship with his father in *Infinite Jest*, the deranged and possibly overworked school teacher in "The Soul is not a Smithy," the despairing couple in "Incarnations of Burned Children," or the popular boy two years ahead of David Wallace who kills himself in "Good Old Neon," one always feels that at the center of Wallace's quietly polemical prose is an assault on an institutional discourse mediated through work practices, gestures, and the description of mass-produced trinkets that has hoodwinked ambitious, aspiring Americans into parting with "what's really inside."

In *David Foster Wallace on the Good Life* (2014), Nathan Ballantyne and Justin Tosi bring together new readings on topics such as irony, narration, hedonism, and fatalism. Ballantyne and Tosi argue that Wallace "sees serious flaws" in what they describe as popular views associated with irony, hedonism, and narration.[44] Put very simply, irony describes a popular approach to life whereby we distance ourselves from everything and put on what Wallace often calls a "mask of ennui."[45] Hedonism, on the other hand, is, for Wallace, a mode of life that revolves around one's own pleasure, while "narrative theories" relates to our tendency to still believe in grand master narratives in life such as the celebrity lifestyle or the consumerist utopia or the education narrative and to then live our lives according to such narratives. These narrative theories describe, for Ballantyne and Tosi, how society has fallen for the idea that "a good human life is characterized by fidelity to a unified narrative."[46] They argue that Wallace's fiction essentially rails against any blind or considered allegiance to such narrative theories and McGurl's institutionalization narrative is another example of such a "narrative theory" Wallace does not embody but challenge. Wallace offers us a new method for pursuing moral questions. In comparing Wallace to Wittgenstein, Ballantyne and Tosi argue that Wallace is a thinker who wishes to prevent people becoming distracted by pseudo-problems. For Wallace, they argue, a "meaningful human life need not be special; it need not be characterized by commitment to values or projects that are unique, unusual, or extreme. There is value in ordinary, everyday, and even seemingly banal experiences."[47] In an age of celebrity, university rankings, tiger mamas, and cutthroat competition it is a message that people are losing sight of.

The academic reach into his life and work continues with Columbia University Press's recent publication of the undergraduate thesis Wallace wrote as a philosophy major at Amherst College: *Fate, Time, and Language: An Essay on Free Will*. It is interesting to read this thesis now mindful of the character Rick Vigorous and his deliberations on his return to Amherst 20 years after graduation in *The Broom of the System*. The thesis is a critique of the philosopher Richard Taylor's work on fatalism. The recent collection *David Foster Wallace and the Long Thing: New Essays on the Novels* responds to Wallace's thesis on fatalism and introduces Wallace to a wide range of new academic arguments. Wallace's novels are seen as promoting greater empathy, new sincerity, a new model of community, a new paradigm of consciousness, and a form of "trickle-down citizenship." In an essay from the collection *The Broom of the System*, Clare Hayes-Brady makes the case that the less-studied novel deserves more attention because it "explores the philosophy of language that so intrigued its author" throughout his life. Hayes-Brady examines the influences of such academic behemoths as Ludwig Wittgenstein, Paul Ricoeur, and Richard Rorty on Wallace's writing and his ideas on language.

Wallace and the University Loneliness

However, Wallace's importance for education and for the university runs much deeper. Wallace's depiction of young, psychologically vulnerable Americans battling with college admissions, college life, frat parties, competition, and the resulting job market reveal Wallace as a historian, sociologist, and psychologist commenting on the effects of late stage capitalism or neoliberalism in American society. I have previously aligned Wallace with the new breed of late twentieth-century and early twenty-first-century world literature writers who are challenging the university as disseminator and custodian of knowledge. I read Wallace as a pioneer in a kind of literature that I describe as a "literature of concealment" after Roberto Bolaño, a kind of literature that presents the university and all it represents in terms of meritocracy, credentialization, competition, admissions, personal statements, reading strategies, test strategies, research protocols, adjunct teaching, and rankings rubrics as destructive of the artwork, Bolaño's "flower of winter."

Together with Bolaño, Sebald, and Houellebecq, Wallace's work again and again challenges the academicization of society and by implication the university's culture of competition. The gaps in income between the different attainment levels at universities and colleges have kept growing over the last 50-year period[48] and economists such as Thomas Piketty argue that the "huge change in the social representation of inequality"—from the rentier system to the elite university meritocratic system—is in part justified but that it rests on a number of misunderstandings. Piketty gives historical evidence to demonstrate that the advent of the meritocratic age, which would work its power through the universities, often did not even try to hide its attempts at "justifying the position of the winners" as a "matter of vital importance."[49]

Wallace responds to and details for American society, how such practices have scarred American students and professionals, through a system that Lani Guinier has recently described as the "tyranny of the meritocracy." One might argue that this glorification of the "winner" is simply an aspect of neoliberalism, a philosophy that most individuals and nations have subscribed to. Wallace describes this highly competitive "winner" mentality in US society with tragic humor in *Infinite Jest*, *The Broom of the System*, and other works. Here is his narrator in *Infinite Jest*: "Be constantly focused and on alert: feral talent is its own set of expectations and can abandon you at any one of the detours of so-called normal American life at any time, so be on guard."⁵⁰ For Wallace, this social system has led to generations of US students who have "given themselves away to an ambitious competitive pursuit" to the extent that the antihero of *Infinite Jest*, a character named Hal, ends up "[l]ike most North Americans of his generation" knowing "way less about why he feels certain ways about the objects and pursuits he's devoted to than he does about the objects and pursuits themselves" and the virtual age exacerbates the dangers of this distance between feelings and knowledge.⁵¹

The result of such practices of competition is a culture of loneliness, what Wallace tells us Hal has been conditioned to feel and to also mask. However, at the heart of Wallace's Hal is a conflict that never really gets resolved in the novel. We are told that Hal suffers from a kind of anhedonia, a low-grade depression, that leaves him acknowledging that he "hadn't had a bona fide intensity-of-interior-life-type emotion since he was tiny"; he finds terms like *joie* and *value* to be like so many "variables in rarified equations, and he can manipulate them well enough to satisfy everyone but himself that he's in there, inside his own hull, as a human being—but in fact he's far more robotic than John Wayne."⁵² This leads Hal to also acknowledge that "inside Hal there's pretty much nothing at all, he knows." However, later we get a sense of how Hal has been duped by the education system that abides by and has adults perpetuate the "queerly persistent U.S. myth that cynicism and naïveté are mutually exclusive."⁵³ Hal therefore "who's empty but not dumb, theorizes privately that what passes for hip cynical transcendence of sentiment is really some kind of fear of being really human."⁵⁴ The narrator, a Wallace alias, intones: "It's of some interest that the lively arts of the millennial U.S.A. treat anhedonia and internal emptiness as hip and cool."⁵⁵ The voice argues that it is the art written and taught by older people believing this myth that is then consumed and internalized by "younger people who not only consume art but study it for clues on how to be cool, hip."⁵⁶ In other words, the institution can end up teaching the value of loneliness. Young people "enter a spiritual puberty where we snap to the fact that the great transcendent horror is loneliness, excluded encagement in the self";⁵⁷ we are taught to run from painful feelings, from feelings that tell us we are being truly affected by something. The narrative voice argues that "once we've hit this age, we will now give or take anything, wear any mask, to fit, be part-of, not be Alone, we young."[58] We are taught to turn from sentiment and naivete, "the last true terrible sin in the theology of millennial America." The arts, then instead of cultivating the soul, become "our guide to inclusion. A how-to. We are shown how to fashion masks of ennui and jaded irony at a young age where the face is fictile enough to assume the shape of whatever it wears."[59] This is all fine until we realize that the culture of competition and goals does not offer the emotional highs and sense of assurance we were promised. We look inside but we are empty; we no longer know how to seek out meaning. This is obviously a point where Wallace is appealing to his readers and to his society. Whether we call it a "new sincerity" or an old-style morality, it describes an intricate web of collusion between education, the arts, and society at large. This is why Wallace gives us Hal as a conflicted teenager, he is empty and yet he recognizes that all this is because of some "kind of fear of being really human." He is unaware that he is disconnected from his emotional life and this is why loneliness when it hits is so destructive. The "pretty much nothing" Hal acknowledges as being "inside Hal" is not nothing and it is definitely not the "nothing" that McGurl assigns to Wallace's institutions; Hal is not the robotic voice of the machine. But Wallace also cannot continue to peddle the myth of the "great transcendent horror [that] is loneliness"; he looks deeper in order to explain that even within our daily practices and our daily routines, routines as mundane as going through tax returns or writing again and again about this culture of myth in the United States, the suspicion that there is beneath all this "some kind of fear of being really human" will show through. This is a great deal more than nothing and it is the arts that Wallace believes can transform this "pretty much nothing" into a transcendent acceptance of loneliness as part of being really human.

Wallace's targeting of the University for its role in cloneliness or the reproduction of loneliness is also savage in *Infinite Jest*. Wallace describes the experiences of an anxious student faced with the admissions committee at the University of Arizona, a process I will look at in more detail in Chapter 8 in relation to university admissions in Asia. The student, Hal Incandenza, finally erupts into a stream of verbiage, deeply insightful and intelligent, that his interviewers take for the words of a beast. Hal's words speak for a generation of students faced with such interview boards:

> But it transcends the mechanics. I'm not a machine. I feel and believe. I have opinions. Some of them are interesting. I could, if you'd let me, talk and talk. Let's talk about anything. I believe the influence of Kierkegaard on Camus is underestimated. I believe Dennis Gabor may very well have been the Antichrist. I believe Hobbes is just Rousseau in a dark mirror. I believe, with Hegel, that transcendence is absorption. I could interface you guys right under the table, I say. I'm not just a creātus, manufactured, conditioned, bred for a function.[60]

Hal Incandenza is sitting before the selection committee at the University of Arizona. He greets their "expectant silence" with his "silent response."[61] His Uncle Charles does all the talking. At the end of the interview, one of the Deans finally comes clean: "Look here, Mr. Incandenza, Hal, please just explain to me why we couldn't be accused of using you, son. Why nobody could come and say to us, why, look here, University of Arizona, here you are using a boy for just his body, a boy so shy and withdrawn he won't speak up for himself."[62] Hal, conditioned to compete and socially awkward, explodes into a stream of verbiage that ends with the above monologue. In a scene of incredibly cruelty, Hal is then dragged through the Administration offices to an "old-fashioned men's room" and "rolled over supine on the geometric tile."[63] The Deans, dismissive of the student in their care who they believe has had a "seizure," are equally socially awkward and are cut off from any real understanding of the tortures their system puts students through. They can only describe his response and breakdown as "[s]ubanimalistic noises and sounds"; he was "like some sort of animal with something in its mouth"; he was a "writhing animal with a knife in its eye."[64]

This episode is a more elaborate, tragicomic detailing of the theme of educated and institutionalized national anxiety that is depicted in a nostalgic and perhaps traditional manner in the earlier novel *The Broom of the System*. The leading male character Rick Vigorous has just returned to Amherst College after 20 years to seek out the initials he had carved on various objects around the campus. He is hit by an overwhelming sense of "fear" that "accompanied and was in a way caused by the intensity of the wash of feelings and desires and so on that accompanied even the thought of a silly men's room in a silly building at a silly college where a sad silly boy had spent four years twenty years ago."[65] He comes to the sobering realization that "Amherst College in the 1960s was for me a devourer of the emotional middle, a maker of psychic canyons, a whacker of the pendulum of Mood with the paddle of Immoderation."[66] Vigorous further explains how college devoured his "emotional middle": "it occurs to me now in force that in college things were never, not ever, at no single point, simply all right. Things were never just OK. I was never just getting by. Never. I can remember I was always horribly afraid. Or, if not horribly afraid, horribly angry. I was always desperately tense. Or, if not tense then in an odd hot euphoria that made me walk with the water-jointed jaunt of the person who truly does not give a shit one way or the other."[67] Wallace therefore describes university and college for a whole generation, a generation of Americans and international students who contributed to the internationalization and commodification of the American dream as, in Richard Rorty's words, the "right kind of education." Wallace Studies has much to say in so many fields, however, it is in the fields of education, pedagogy, and educational philosophy that Wallace's work may yet have most potential. The university has become ever more competitive and ever more profit driven since Wallace's own college days and his fiction can help remind us of how education marks young people for life and that it can take a whole writing career to write those marks out of your system.

The Pale King, Loneliness, and Mental Health

Wallace's final, incomplete work *The Pale King* is also the work of a man who had undergone extensive treatment in mental health institutions, numerous sessions of electroconvulsive therapy,[68] years of Nardil medication for depression, and long periods in institutions for those with severe mental health issues. In many ways, it is a work that reveals the struggles and fears of an artist aware that his powers are diminishing. The work is perhaps overall less interesting than the earlier work not only because its theme is boredom. Sometimes it reads like the work of a writer who is trying hard to throw off the self-referential, hyperaware narrative pyrotechnics of a younger self so that a different kind of writing can emerge. Wallace's early high-octane, hypercritical work can only be sustained for so long; it always has the tinge of the radically brilliant, youthful intellect that kicks against the pricks of institutional life. In *The Pale King*, Wallace is almost desperate in his efforts to make captivating narrative out of the imagined tedious lives of middle-aged office workers. It is a kind of employment he could never hold down for very long himself and therefore the detailed description of the saving graces of boredom, or of being "unborable," by way of the description of such a world rings hollow at times. A mockumentary like Ricky Gervais's and Simon Merchant's *The Office* gives perhaps a better account of how office work in the context of office politics, relationships, midlife crises, and narcissism is not chiefly about shaping oneself according to the demands of boredom. Readers of Wallace's biography quickly realize how broken he was by the end in terms of mental stability, motivation, and capacity for work. He described the efforts of the numerous psychiatrists who were medicating for his condition as "like they're throwing darts at a dartboard."[69] It was not then a sudden change but a gradual decline. In this context, it is both revealing and painful to read that one of the final sections of *The Pale King*, the last long section of the novel, is a lengthy discussion and dialogue on boredom and loneliness. Two IRS workers after having finished work at their tingles, discuss loneliness, boredom, and psychiatric institutions over drinks at Happy Hour in Meibeyer's. Meredith Rand and Shane Drinion discuss Rand's history of cutting herself and her time at the Zeller Center where she stayed briefly as a teenager and where she met her future husband. Their discussion revolves around what Rand calls the "self-nourishing institution of the mental health system"[70] and its "big lie" about harmful practices and how "if you knew why you did it you'd magically be able to stop."[71] Rand says she cut herself as a young person because of loneliness brought on by the feeling that no one could "love you for who you are." But then she realized that the "loneliness is stupid and banal even while you're feeding it, the loneliness, so you don't even have sympathy for yourself."[72] However, she describes how it was this realization that enabled her to view the cutting as "letting the unbeautiful inside truth come out."[73] However, she also realizes in the Zeller Center how the talking cure can become its own drug; she thinks about getting "kept in the nut ward a little longer" to still get the informal sessions with her future husband, only to realize it would be "completely nuts."[74] Rand ultimately sums up the problem of immaturity as "wanting to be distracted from what you've lost and fixed and saved by somebody. Which is pretty banal."[75] During the conversation Meredith Rand keeps asking Shane Drinion "[i]s this boring?" David Wallace reminds us in an earlier section of the novel that he learned at "just twenty-one or twenty-two, at the IRS's Regional Examination Center in Peoria" that the "underlying bureaucratic key is the ability to deal with boredom":

> To function effectively in an environment that precludes everything vital and human ... The key is the ability, whether innate or conditioned, to find the other side of the rote, the picayune, the meaningless, the repetitive, the pointlessly complex. To be, in a word, unborable ... It is the key to modern life. If you are immune to boredom, there is literally nothing you cannot accomplish.[76]

However, despite this awareness, characters such as Meredith Rand—who have given themselves up to this institution, the IRS, that epitomizes said boredom for Wallace—are consistently nervous, telling life stories in case they are being "boring." They do not want to be boring even if they should know that they themselves and their coworkers, people like Shane Drinion, have become "unborable." The questions about being boring should then be redundant. However, it is precisely when Wallace lets us in on the institutional treatment and advice he may also have received for his own depression, and when he discusses the link between the banal, the boring, and loneliness, that we become interested and learn to see that he was unable, rather like his bureaucratic characters, to remain on the "other side of the rote" or "the meaningless." In describing the novel as being about boredom because it sets up a series of big events that never happen, he perhaps downplays the capacity of his descriptions of emotions and of mental health conditions to be interesting and illuminating. Wallace's attempt then, in this final work, to write for boredom and to translate the saving unborability of life into narrative ultimately cannot keep the reader on the "other side of the rote" precisely because his narrative is too perceptive and not sufficiently banal. In undermining what appear to be the narrative's objectives by giving us seemingly unborable types who are yet self-conscious about whether they are boring, Wallace reveals that his work still harbours a concern, possibly confessional, about how opening up about loneliness and mental health issues can still be regarded as boring. As a teacher, Wallace knew that students need to feel that any kind of loneliness they admit to is not boring; they might be told it is common and nothing to be ashamed of, but it is never boring. If there is then anything of the younger "David Wallace" in the younger Meredith Rand, the 17-year-old "drama queen," then perhaps he needed to be reassured that loneliness was never boring. Unfortunately, Shane Drinion is not the character to do this. Ultimately, the conversation between Drinion and Rand reveals how two somewhat stereotypical American co-workers, Rand the female "drama queen" and Drinion the male "total nerd and dweeb" never fail to misunderstand each other. They are never on the same wavelength when it comes to discussing emotional life. Drinion displays through his questions a deep-seated incapacity to convey emotion—"So there is a very intense emotional conflict going on?"—and Rand enjoys toying with his interest in her emotional life so long as she is interested in his attention. In the end, their conversation may reveal how straitjacketed American young people are by the discourse of medicalization and mental health; in spending a whole evening discussing experiences of being institutionalised over mental health issues, they remain as far apart as ever emotionally. The story demonstrates how Wallace continued to dramatise what he felt was a "tragic and universal conflict" at the heart of life right up until the end, an idea he expresses most clearly in the story "The Suffering Channel": "The conflict between the subjective centrality of our lives versus our awareness of its objective insignificance".[77] It is a conflict that the iGen's avid social media use takes to a new level. Wallace, in being unwilling to perpetuate the university's myth of the "great transcendent horror [that] is loneliness," has his characters time and again seek professional help for the pain of a loneliness they need to share. The problem is that this complementary form of institutionalization, mental health institutionalization, leaves them, like the protagonist of "Good Old Neon," "pretend[ing] to myself that I was taking steps to becoming more authentic".[78] In the end, it would seem that, as with Montaigne, and as the recent movie *The End of the Tour* reveals in taking the viewer momentarily into the darkened room in which Wallace wrote, it was the time spent communicating with himself and his legions of eager readers through his writing that granted Wallace those "moment[s] of the most supernal beauty."

6

Loneliness in a Selection of Japanese Philosophy and Fiction: Takeo Doi, Natsume Sōseki, Kitarō Nishida, Haruki Murakami, and Sayaka Murata

As we might expect, the basic societal presumptions for loneliness are different for different cultures. Takeo Doi, for example, writes in his 1971 work *The Anatomy of Dependence* that Japan has failed both "to establish the freedom of the individual as distinct from the group" and "the type of public spirit that transcends both individual and group."[1] This is of course different from what Larry Siedentop says of early European forms of individualism in *Inventing the Individual: The Origins of Western Liberalism*. Siedentop describes the origins of Western individualism in Greece and in early Christian culture. He argues that monasticism's vision of the "soul," the "Lives of the saints," and the biblical narrative of the passion of the Christ helped people to conceive of how the "immortal soul, rather than the immortal family"[2] was the "primary constituent of reality." Monasticism's egalitarian conception of society saw the "proper unit of subjection—the true subject of claims in justice" as the individual or "soul" rather than "lordships or the patriarchal family"[3] thus leading to a weakening of the "claims of family, clan and caste."[4] Siedentop then sees this as influencing how government would later emerge as "no longer primarily a rule over families, clans, or castes" but as "rule over individuals."[5] However, this easy ride to individualism in Europe is being challenged today not only by a return to nationalism and groupthink but also by theorists such as Bruno Latour who asks have we ever been modern? In *An Inquiry into Modes of Existence*, Latour assesses the plight of "the Moderns" in terms of how they are perceived to have "discovered—most often as borrowings from other civilizations, moreover—a number of values that they hold dear and that constitute, as it were, their very self-definition, even though they have never had an entirely firm grasp of these values."[6] Because "the Moderns" have always possessed this "lack of assurance" about these values they have not managed to "find a way to *respect* their own values—and still less, then, to respect those of others."[7] This might be one reason why those who believe in the authenticity of "the Moderns" keep establishing university centers and research institutes for things like "values" and "human values."

Siedentop's persuasive reading of the move from early Christian culture to the various European governments of individuals also perhaps overlooks how many modern democracies such as Ireland chose to make the "family," not the individual, the basis of society in their constitutions. The family also became the cornerstone of European psychology and particularly of psychoanalytic counselling. However, treated as it was as a religiously sanctioned *sine qua non* of society, it served to stunt the growth of individualism through the very real emergence of the return of the repressed. When all neuroses and psychoses are traced back to familial structures and their individual object cathexes to the extent that individualism can only ever take shape against family as first philosophy then one needs to ask how strong and how modern individualism is in the European context. Latour also reminds us of the feelings of disquiet that the lonely modern subject of today, a subject nurtured on the gristle of the hollow individualism of "the Moderns," experiences in counselling:

> They're telling me that the emotion I feel, this rage that makes my heart rate go way up, lies within me and that I have to go through a lengthy analysis and plunge deep into myself, myself alone, to master it. And yet I can't keep from thinking (everyone is trying to keep me from thinking!) that I am threatened by forces that have the objectivity, the externality, the self-evidence, the power of a storm like the one that tore the tops off the trees in my garden, just a few days ago.[8]

Society both needs and must produce lonely individuals in order to function today and so notions of collectivism and the social contract are downplayed. However, because modern liberalism as one discourse of "the Moderns" is now also challenged from a number of fronts, a discourse built on individualism, modern Western liberalism leaves people flailing inside loneliness without them knowing how to form the communities that they believe should be at the centre of their societies. As the notebooks of Latour's anthropologist doing fieldwork suggest: "I guess it's not surprising that I so often feel mistaken: what seems to me to come from the outside—my emotion just now—actually comes from the inside, they say, but what I was attributing unhesitatingly to the great outdoors is now supposed to be the result of the collective will of the narrow human world."[9] The coffers and financial algorithms of the crisis of Western liberalism also seems to cash out on the legions of lonely incels, isolates, and celibates that its philosophies have left stranded. As Sayaka Murata suggests in *Convenience Store Woman*, we are now happier as "animals" and not humans in the sense that human here refers to all the various narratives we tell ourselves we must conform to in order to feel normal—hollow and empty—but normal nevertheless. Both "normal" humanity and the animal state of being rooted in being part of an industry or institution leave us lonely, as we have seen in Wallace, but the pain of battling all those who have given themselves up to the dream of these human narratives is far harder to take than the comfortable, reliable machinations of the industry life where we recognize ourselves as "cogs."

The stories Siedentop and Latour tell of modern Western individualism also differs from what Natsume Soseki, Takeo Doi, and Kitarō Nishida describe for Japanese society. Recent Japanese works of fiction such as *Convenience Store Woman* and Haruki Murakami's *Men Without Women* describe how certain jobs and certain practices actually produce the kind of lonely individuals that society now needs to function, even at the level of the much-needed service industries. The protagonist of Murata's novel describes how she was "reborn" as a lonely shop worker with no friends as a service worker and of how she loves this role.

In engaging with different cultures on individualism we are still likely to come across works that make somewhat sweeping statements about East–West differences and very often read different Asian cultures with perhaps too much emphasis on the writings of Confucius. For example, Will Storr writes in *Selfie: How the West Became self-obsessed* that "In the East, it's those who neglect their duty to bring harmony to the group who are more likely to be considered failures";[10] "East Asians tend to be more aware of what's happening in their environment";[11] "[t]he Asian self melts, at the edges, into the selves that surround it, whereas the Western self tends to feel more independent and in control of its own behavior and destiny."[12] Perhaps it is a confirmation bias; such authors clearly demonstrate that they have internalized the "independent" Western self "in control of its own behavior" that brings them to make such claims. However, in denying "East Asians" or "Chinese" the same kind of individualism and "self," one on a parallel with that of "Westerners," they perpetuate a long line of commentary designating Asian identity as other or simply different.

Loneliness is a prominent feature of Japanese fiction. Recent work by Haruki Murakami discusses new metaphors for loneliness. Recent trends and practices in society such as *hikikomori* (shutting oneself off from others), *kodokushi* (the lonely death), and even the "salary men" may have their origin, or at least a very strong tributary root, in Japanese society. Psychiatrists such as Takeo Doi have long highlighted differences between cultures in relation to the conflict between Self and Society. However, these distinctions often become most clear and their context most apparent in representations of these differences in fiction. Descriptions of loneliness, individualism, and nothingness in such writers as Soseki and Kitarō Nishida are also representative of differences between these writers and their European existentialist contemporaries on such themes as identity.

Doi's *The Anatomy of Dependence* is a milestone work on Japanese philosophy and identity. Published in 1971, a few years before Edward Said's *Orientalism* (1978), and written in a clear, accessible style, perhaps unlike earlier works on Japanese identity by Nishida, Kuki Shuzo, and Hajime Tanabe and other members of the Kyoto School, it was described by Ezra Vogel as "the first book by a Japanese trained in psychiatry to have an impact on western psychiatric thinking." However, in also being an early cross-cultural work in these fields, it makes general statements that would be more difficult to make today and would require greater research support. In discussing the importance of *amae*, a word used to "indicate the seeking after the mother that comes when the infant's mind has developed to a certain degree and it has realized that its mother exists independently of itself,"[13] what Doi also describes as "emotional dependency" that can be exhibited at any age, Doi makes the claim that "in the West with its emphasis on the freedom of the individual, people have always looked down on the type of emotional dependency that corresponds to *amae*."[14] While this is a broad claim, *amae* has clearly had a huge influence in Japanese society in relation to individualism and thus loneliness. In this chapter, I will first explore individualism and loneliness in Japanese sociological and philosophical texts. I then read a selection of Japanese novels and stories dealing with these themes. Finally, loneliness is located in early Shinto texts in the context of exploring a radical loneliness.

Doi makes a connection between loneliness and what he calls "homosexual feelings" in his treatment of individualism and *amae*. Doi writes:

> "[H]omosexual feelings" referred to here are not homosexuality in the narrow sense. The word homosexuality usually refers to the experience of sexual attraction and the inclination to sexual union between members of the same sex, but I use "homosexual feelings" here in a broader sense, to refer to cases where the emotional links between members of the same sex take preference over those with the opposite sex.[15]

Doi further clarifies that "these homosexual feelings may exist in conjunction with homosexuality in the narrow sense" but that "they do not always necessarily develop into this restricted type of homosexuality" and that "[t]hese homosexual feelings, in themselves, fall within the province of the normal, and are experienced by everybody in the course of growing up."[16] However, Doi's assertion that "it is possible" for an individual "who is sexually normal and already leading a normal married life to be emotionally under the dominance of homosexual emotions"[17] clearly demonstrates that he is writing as a psychiatrist at a time when same-sex marriage was unavailable and when it was still acceptable to make such claims about what is "sexually normal." He also looks to fiction and in particular one novel by Natsume Soseki, *Kokoro*, to explore how such "homosexual feelings" have been integral to the exploration of loneliness and isolation. He writes that he knows "no literary work that portrays so accurately the nature of homosexual emotions in Japanese society."[18] However, these "homosexual feelings" that are integral to the exploration of loneliness and isolation in the novel, for Doi, are noted by the older man in the novel, Sensei, who comes to be a kind of mentor for the younger man, the hero of the novel. Sensei says to the protagonist at one point: "You came to my place, a man of the same sex ... as a stage on the way to making love with the other sex."[19] Doi argues in his treatment of emotional attachment and dependence through *amae* that such "homosexual feelings" have been at the heart of explorations of loneliness in Japanese society. He writes of the "accurate account" *Kokoro* gives of the "precedence given to homosexual feelings in Japanese society." However, for Doi, the novel also criticizes this state of affairs in being an "eloquent testimony to the fact that exclusive concentration on male friendship can frequently drive those concerned to destruction."[20] At one point, Sensei tells the hero a story from his past about how he became jealous of a young man he had once been close to when this young man began to show affections for someone else. He then advises the hero: "You shouldn't place too much reliance on me. You'll regret it later, and then you'll take some cruel revenge for the way you've been deceived." Sensei adds:

> The memory of having kneeled before someone makes one want to trample him underfoot at a later date. I prefer to forego the reverence of today and avoid the insults to come. I'd rather put up with being lonely now than have to put up with being still more lonely in the future. We live in an age of freedom, independence, and the self, and I imagine this loneliness is the price we have to pay for it.[21]

It's a stark note of warning to the young acolyte or student intent on giving himself up to a world of ideas in which he looks to an older figure for both guidance and validation in terms of the ideas being explored. Doi sees *amae* at the root of such "homosexual feelings" that lead to shame and distrust for Sensei in Soseki's *Kokoro*. Even though Doi argues that such close bonds between students and teachers and between juniors and seniors are considered "utterly natural" in Japanese society,[22] the novel warns how "easily this *amae* can turn to hatred."[23] *Amae* is unstable because we live in an age "full of freedom and independence and self." For Doi, then, Soseki's novel demonstrates that *amae* is very much associated with mentoring and would have a kind of corollary in the Western practice of *paideia* and the kind of mentoring relations it describes. Padraig Pearse believed *paideia*, as "fostering," was important for the education of the young. However, for Doi, Soseki's novel describes how such longings and yearnings are "unable to cure man's basic loneliness and only make him unhappy."[24] The satisfaction is temporary and "invariably ends in disillusionment." Doi argues that in "a modern age of 'freedom, independence, and self'" the sense of solidarity with others that comes from *amae* is ultimately no more than a mirage. If we do not wish to suffer from disillusionment, we must be resigned to putting up with the truth about ourselves and with the "loneliness of isolation."[25]

However, the novel *Kokoro* is also a commentary on the transition taking place in Japanese society as it moves from the Meiji Era to a period of modernization, described by people at the time as "the new awakening."[26] Sensei's letter to the hero reveals how he has been wracked with guilt all his married life because of how he treated another man, K, who had spoken of having feelings for Sensei's future wife Ojosan. K committed suicide shortly after he heard Sensei would marry Ojosan. In the end, Sensei asks himself if K had experienced the same "unbearable loneliness" that he had felt for most of his married life and whether it was this that made him contemplate suicide. However, because Sensei is still a man who is wedded to the Meiji Era practices, he can only see the events of his youth and the guilt he feels for those events in terms of "the nature of human sin."[27] He longs for the punishment he feels he deserves. His only comfort comes when he decides to "live as if I were dead" and to force down any "urge to break through my deathly impasse and act."[28] Sensei's letter then reveals the heart—*kokoro*—of a Meiji Era man who cannot modernize. *Kokoro*, like Mo Yan's *Red Sorghum*—a novel I will read in chapter 7—can be read as an allegory of modernization. In the end, the failure to move on and change with the times, leads to the characters being consumed by this "unbearable loneliness."

The sense is, then, as we have perhaps also seen in Wallace, that the relationship with ideas and with the text can become a replacement or displacement for the fear we possess in real relationships in the face of such potential disillusionment. As Wallace writes, writing and reading the novel can become like a "conversation with old friends." However, in turning to Soseki's own essay on individualism and to Kitarō Nishida on nothingness and on the "pure experience" as the perfect merging of subject and object, we can learn more about the representation of loneliness and emotional dependence in Japanese writing.

Soseki and the "Solitude of Individualism"

Soseki's essay "My Individualism" and the novel *Kokoro* were both published in 1914 and in many ways the essay responds to the same kind of loneliness that we see explored in *Kokoro*. Soseki's life coincided almost exactly with the reign of Emperor Meiji, a period that saw the samurai ousted from their seats of power and a promotion of Western-style education. Soseki was then living through an era of modernization and Westernization that would have left the average person dazed and confused in relation to identity and individualism. Once again, the line from *Kokoro* is apt in looking at the major themes of the essays "My Individualism" and "The Philosophical Foundations of Literature": "You see, loneliness is the price we have to pay for being born in this modern age, so full of freedom, independence, and our own egotistical selves!"[29]

Soseki's talk was given to staff and students at the Gakushuin. One of the main arguments in the essay is that to truly be content in your own skin and with your individualism you must find a profession that nurtures this individualism—"when your individuality and your professional activity are in perfect harmony, you may say for the first time that you are satisfied."[30] Soseki found his way through to his own individualism through the study and teaching of English literature. He was the first Japanese student abroad to study English literature at University College London. He admits that he had studied the subject for three years before he left for England and yet "had understood nothing about literature."[31] He says that he did not really choose to become a teacher but that "circumstances led me into that profession."[32] It was in his early days as a teacher, bored with the profession, that he felt "turned in on myself." He felt "paralyzed, like an isolated being surrounded by mist."[33] He decides after two more years studying abroad in London that "I no longer saw any reason to read the books," a sentiment that is even more common today among young people and among academics in English literature.[34] He then realized that he had "no hope of finding salvation if I did not formulate my own basic concept of what literature was."[35] He had, until then, "floated at random, like a rootless aquatic plant, relying entirely on the opinions of others" which is what our education system still asks us to perfect. He describes himself as "strutting around wearing other people's clothes" while "deep down inside me were the early stirrings of anxiety."³⁶ He realized that if he did not "go back to something more authentic, the anxiety would never disappear." In order to begin this professional and personal journey, Soseki asks himself why he found it impossible to "reconcile myself with English critics." He then decided that the best way to understand why was to engage in a period of "introspection" and to read works that had nothing to do with great literature. He decided to begin "pondering on the expression 'self-centered'"; "it was this concentration on myself [that] set me in motion ... and pointed out the way to me."³⁷ The journey into understanding and finding a contented sense of individualism came first then with the recognition that the professional pursuit and the personal must be in some way integrated and that this must be followed by a scientific and philosophical analysis of introspection, the self and self-centeredness. He discovered that concentration on oneself was integral to finding a workable sense of individualism and that the "conviction that I acquired at that time, that the Ego is the essential ingredient and that others are merely secondary, brings me today great self-confidence and a deep feeling of peace."³⁸ He also advises the students listening to his talk that "you should identify in it some relationship to your own situation."³⁹ He describes his own relationship with the English critics he eventually deposed and with the students listening as one of "power," where power is an "instrument that allows us to infiltrate ourselves to some extent into the head of someone else."⁴⁰ However, he reminds the students that this power should not be misused; "if we look at things fairly and if we have a sense of justice, as we develop our own individuality to attain happiness we must at the same time guarantee to others the same freedom as we grant to ourselves."⁴¹ Soseki believes the study of the arts and also the study of the sciences were integral to him reaching a "certain level on the speculative and conceptual plane" that enables "the act of developing our individuality" to have the "least value" to enjoy its privilege fully.⁴² At a time when current university presidents are advising teachers to not let their students think too deeply at the expense of thinking broadly, and when, as Susan Cain notes, provosts at such places as Harvard University are instructing admissions officers to reject applications from "sensitive" applicants,⁴³ we must recall Soseki's insights about introspection and examining our own condition authentically in being "directed by the humanity in our personality."⁴⁴

The other check on individualism is what Soseki calls "duty." In referring to his time in England he begins to realize that "there is no true freedom with the notion of duty."[45] In recognizing then our duty to country, nation, and community he says we must "establish a form of freedom that can be exercised without hindrance until it begins to affect others."[46] In speaking of nationalism and political sectarianism, Soseki says that "what I call individualism can in no way constitute a danger to the State."[47] When circumstances make it impossible for people to remain in harmony, he argues, this is when we "feel solitude." And it is a "solitude, of which others cannot be aware."[48] He says that we can have "divergences of opinion among [our] closest friends" and know full well that we can do nothing about it; therefore we must "genuinely recognize the existence of others" and "because of that recognition" grant them freedom. Whatever insults we may endure we should never request the assistance of anyone who is unwilling to help. These instances reveal to us that "the solitude of individualism lies in this."[49] However, perhaps Soseki also intimates here that the shift toward the "solitude of individualism" can be curtailed by the recognition that there should be no excess of individual freedom; he writes that this "freedom rises and falls like a thermometer according to the prosperity or poverty of the country ... If the country is in danger, the freedom of the individual is restricted."[50] This is a sense of individualism and freedom of expression that is very much in the spotlight in Hong Kong at the moment, a region that never had a clear sense of itself as a "country" prior to the Handover and that struggles today to conceive of itself as wholly part of the larger "country" of Mainland China. In drawing this connection between individualism and the "country" or the nation, Soseki also recognizes that "when there is little chance of being attacked, nationalist ideas must retreat and individualism must fill the vacuum."[51]

Combatting Loneliness through the "Continuity of Awareness" the Arts Offer

Individualism and the kind of identity a congruent individualism brings—one able to withstand these moments of solitude, isolation, and loneliness—is, for

Soseki, integrally connected with what he calls a "continuity of awareness" best nurtured through the philosophical analysis of literature. He writes in his essay "The Philosophical Foundations of Literature" that even "what is commonly called 'I' is not something that exists in this world on an objective level but something that results from a continuity of awareness which we call 'I' for convenience."[52] Soseki argues that it is the "man of letters or artist" who has the capacity to engender a feeling of enlightenment in the other and in doing so dispel some of the isolation of individualism: "when the ideal that has appeared in these arts and letters, reaching perfection, is combined with the ideal of our own Ego, or even the case when the ideal of our own Ego, fascinated by the ideal of arts and letters, attains perfect truth, either in novelty or in profundity, at the time it sees the Light."[53] Soseki believes that arts and letters can therefore teach and incite how to transcend this limit "between the Ego and external beings or objects"[54]; it occurs through the "continuity of awareness" the arts and letters nurture and rely on. It is while "reading or while looking at a painting" that the "awareness of our Ego and that of the artist ceaselessly separate and conjoin"— what Wallace describes in terms of the conversation with old friends. It is this sense of speculative communion with the other that the arts and letters offer the subject. Soseki goes so far as to call those who have never once managed "to cross the frontiers of impersonality to idle in a state of ecstasy" through the arts and letters "slaves of things."[55] Perhaps this is a prescient description of the cloneliness that today promotes "slavish imitation" for many "interconnected loners." However, Soseki's description of the "state of ecstasy" arts and letters affords would today have to include film, video games and virtual reality. Soseki describes clearly the kind of cognitive benefit literary works and paintings offer with regard to this state of ecstasy; he writes that for a literary work the ideal is manifested by "favouring the continuity aspect of the 'continuity of awareness'" but when the "ideal is manifested by favouring the content of awareness itself, a painting can be achieved."[56] Therefore literary works enable readers to "experience the reducing influence of movement" while the person contemplating the painting experiences the "reducing influence of serenity."[57] The "stasis" afforded the viewer of the painting gives an experience with serenity that is not always offered by the literary work, given the concentration on flow and movement that narrative privileges. Soseki is, of course, of the generation that believed that arts and letters offer an "ideal [that] is much higher" than that of the businessman. He argues that if it is "impossible for us to adopt this attitude with confidence, however much we may use a particular technique our writing will lack quality."[58] However, even the artist who manages to attain the level of speculation and contemplation required for the ideal will only be "skating over a smooth surface, connecting the words just to make sentences" if the words are not rooted in our personality."[59] He argues that if the continuity of awareness, the correspondence between our work and the other, is even achieved for a very few then "we will have made a small contribution to the enhancement of Truth."[60] Soseki believes that if our ideal is grounded in a deep appreciation for how individualism is rooted in the congruence between ourselves and our professional lives then the resulting "arts and letters can exercise a great and intangible influence on society."[61]

Kitarō Nishida and the "Pure Experience"

The Kyoto School is regarded by many as the most important philosophical school in Japan and in Asia. Kitarō Nishida is one of the school's leading philosophers and he was a contemporary of Soseki. In reading Nishida's philosophy one is reminded of the self-reflexive philosophies of the middle and late twentieth century, very often phenomenologies, that become most pronounced in writers like Maurice Merleau-Ponty and Michel Henry.[62] Nishida critiques Kant as a philosopher of the transcendental subject who in recognizing others as ends in themselves—Kingdom of ends—was yet "limited to the transcendental standpoint."[63] Nishida's concentration on the "human-historical world" and on the subject as "an expressive monad of the world"[64] where the subject as a "conscious world" "expresses itself through self-negation and creates itself through self-affirmation"[65] recalls his contemporary Husserl's privileging of expression while also moving us along to the sense of "auto-affection" evident in the work of Henry. While Nishida does not go as far as Derrida in challenging expression with a radically new reading of textuality and a metaphorics of inscription through trace, he does try and speak of "the grammatical subject" in describing "self-determination."[66] His privileging of "mutual negation" in the interaction of subject and object in giving a new description of nothingness through a reliance on what he calls "the religious form of life" may well describe contemporary feelings of dislocation, competition, and rootlessness. However, the difficulty lies in his reliance on the "religious life" and on categories such as "evil";[67] in what Charles Taylor describes as "the secular age" such religious expressions have lost much of their relevance and their former meaning. Nishida even goes so far as to suggest that the very "problems of philosophy" arise when "the sorrow of human life is reflected on at a profound level" and "the problem of religion arises."[68] Nishida grounds this experience with religion on profound self-examination where "to realize one's own death is simultaneously to realize the fundamental meaning of one's own existence. Only a being that knows its own eternal death truly knows its sheer individuality."[69] One might argue that this capacity to realize one's own death as "eternal death," as a profound awareness of mortality in the ability to represent it to oneself, is missing in today's online and 24/7 livestream existence. The consistent pressure to be live and "up for it" and hooked on to the life support machine of the information stream prevents one from internalizing this self-expression of mortality; as Nishida argues, "the self truly realizes its own temporal uniqueness as it faces its own eternal negation."[70] Do we ever represent to ourselves the experience of our "eternal negation" and thus do we ever grasp our "own temporal uniqueness" in this way? In inhabiting the virtual, the virtual becomes the paradigm from which we set off; everything must from now on be a more engaging living-out of a copy of some tedious "real." European philosophers such as Jan Patočka have related this concentration on "inauthenticity, technology, boredom individualism, masks, roles" to the reign of a "metaphysics of force"[71] where being has "allowed itself to be determined as a calculable force; and man, instead of relating to the being that is *hidden under* this figure of force, represents himself as quantifiable power."[72] Jacques Derrida, in also writing of a kind of "eternal negation" that he associates with individualism and a relation to self, associates philosophy with the individual's approach to death or "vigil over death"; "[s]uch a caring for death, an awakening that keeps vigil over death, a conscience that looks death in the face, is another name for freedom."[73] However, for Nishida, the "eternal negation" and our "own temporal uniqueness" only assume their embodied impact as self-representations when we know full well what living in the real feels like. As I argued in the introduction, consciousness is today lived out in the virtual world somewhat like the body experiencing a ghost limb. We are wired to embody responses and reactions to a lived, real world; when that world—even it its presentation of mortality as "eternal negation"—gets subcontracted out to the virtual, consciousness still requires the hit of the real that this virtual draws from. Without it, we are left staring down at a body that is no longer there wondering when and how I can ever throw off the feelings this ghost body gives me. Derrida regards the age of the "domination of technology" as producing a new kind of individualism:

> Technological civilization produces a heightening or mobilization of the orgiastic, with the familiar accompanying effects of aestheticism and individualism, but only to the extent that it also produces boredom, for it "levels" or neutralizes the mysterious or irreplaceable uniqueness of the responsible self. The individualism of technological civilization relies precisely on a misunderstanding of the unique self. It is the individualism of a *role* and not of a *person*... The alternatives are confused: individualism becomes socialism or collectivism, it stimulates an ethics or politics of singularity; liberalism joins socialism, democracy joins totalitarianism.[74]

However, if we are losing the encounter with the virtual "eternal negation," as Nishida and Derrida suggest, we are also losing the means to describe and formulate its self-expression. Therefore, even the language of phenomenology and of philosophers such as Nishida creates a zone of representation built on embodied self-reflexivity that is no longer accessible to many young people. Our act of describing and encountering the representation of self-reflexivity has migrated online and yet sometimes we need to have verbalized to us what we are experiencing. Society is no less needy in relation to self-expression and what it means for consciousness but today it has less patience with philosophies of self-expression and auto-affection. Ultimately, it may well mean that when the subject, as Nishida describes, then experiences those moments, moments very often today realized through feelings of loneliness, when "the sorrow of human life is reflected on at a profound level," we frequently do not have the language to describe or perceive the "problems of philosophy" that arise, especially since in this secular age we also may not see the experience as one where "the problem of religion [also] arises."[75] Loneliness then as a key modern motivation for allowing us to engage with "the sorrow of human life" is set adrift from these early formulations of mortality, self-negation, and even of "the problems of philosophy" and we become—in our narcissistic and self-centered selves—too prone to blame ourselves for the sorrow, lacking the concepts and language to persuade ourselves that the feelings are simply part and parcel of existence. As Nishida writes: "[t]here is no life when there is no death."[76]

Nishida's philosophy is, of course, a philosophy of the self as non-self that relies heavily on religious accounts of being and also nothingness. It is a ground-breaking work in terms of its cross-cultural East–West fusion of religious notions of being. However, in the context of a secular loneliness, the most engaging idea we can take from Nishida is the idea that the "fundamental ground of the self" is the "contradictory identity of transcendence and immanence"[77] that realizes itself in the self and that exists only in that "it knows of its own death. It knows that it is born to die eternally" or that "we live by dying."[78] For today's young people this idea might be better summed up by the recent Lana Del Rey song "I was born to die." In the absence of any acceptance of the kind of conceptual plane that allows for phenomenological and onto-theological discourses of self-reflexivity and self-awareness, the online virtual, second life, or human–computer interface experience itself becomes a new field for playing out this "contradictory identity of transcendence and immanence." However, in making the virtual the real, in a manner not dissimilar to how Hegel, for Marx, makes the Real the new Ideal, the Information Age reverses the relation of transcendence and immanence. Whereas previously the self was regarded as the expression of the world's being, today, the virtual space, the cyber sphere, is the mediation of the self. To argue then that the self only knows itself through how it knows its own death as "eternal death" is to preach a gospel of nothingness that can take on frightening proportions today. The challenge of death for young people hooked to the virtual world loses none of its appeal today despite the fact that they do not have the armory of self-reflexive vocabulary detailing religious and philosophical states that Nishida relies on. In states of loneliness—or when "the sorrow of human life is reflected on at a profound level"—death as absolute can assume transcendental proportions as the ultimate challenge, especially when it is confronted stripped of the somewhat comforting discourse of religious and spiritual self-awareness that Nishida casts it in. Death can then appear as an ultimate challenge that will help them realize themselves and help them feel they are alive; it can appear to offer them, or so they believe, the feeling of embodied immanence they crave. Nishida writes that "[e]very person has this religious mind. But many do not realize it."[79] This kind of "religious mind," for Nishida, is one that employs "active intuition" to see things from a standpoint transcending that of the preconceived conscious self. This is the "creative world in the very depths of the active self."[80] Even if lonely young people who are indeed religious understand existence in this way, it is much of the time mediated to them through a virtual experience. The human–computer interface embodies much of the contradictions that Nishida either assigned to a purely self-reflective state or to an encounter between the self and another as object. Nishida's philosophy therefore describes a state of emptiness and nothingness that in depending on a discourse of self-reflexivity that reads existence chiefly in terms of the acceptance of death, offers little for the lonely Internet junkie feeling empty and alone. As an atheist, how can the lonely convenience store worker, whose breaks are spent online, connect with the feeling of "eternal death" that Nishida assigns to all of us? To explore this further, I will now move to a reading of some Japanese literary works on loneliness in light of the work of Doi, Soseki, and Nishida.

Loneliness in the work of Soseki, Murakami and Murata

Haruki Murakami's introduction to Soseki's novel *Sanshiro* reveals some interesting contrasts between the Japanese novel and the European or "Western novel." The reader of *Sanshiro*, as Murakami suggests, is struck by the somewhat noncommittal attitude of Sanshiro: "that arms-folded, lukewarm life stance of Sanshiro's that wraps logical and ethical complications in the softest possible emotional cloak" disturbs any easy plotting of cause and effect in the novel.[81] In many ways, the novel might seem to prefigure the postmodern or existential characters of Camus or John Barth. This is, of course, an attitude that many of Murakami's own characters manifest even in speaking of loneliness. His recent collection *Men Without Women* introduces us to a group of male characters who are "without women"; ensnared by loneliness their experiences are still recounted with what feels like an "arms-folded, lukewarm life stance." For example, when Hibara in "Scheherazade" loses his own Scheherazade he thinks of lampreys, of "jawless lampreys fastened to rocks, hiding among the waterweeds, swaying back and forth in the current" and he imagines himself waiting for the trout that never passes.[82] The protagonist of "Men Without Women" even opines on the day each man becomes "Men Without Women" as if it is some universally acknowledged state. It can happen unexpectedly to any man, a state that is "[a]lways a relentlessly frigid plural."[83] He then falls to imagining the unicorn, with its single "sharp horn," as the "symbol of Men Without Women, of the loneliness we carry as our burden." It is almost as if Murakami describes the phallus as speaking for loneliness today; it is the proper end of men and masculinity; it describes a dystopian future for men who feel they would rather remain isolated than suffer the consequences of closeness. Murakami writes: "Perhaps we should sew unicorn badges on our breast pockets and hats, and quietly parade down streets all over the world."[84] Once a man, for it is always a man, enters this state

> loneliness seeps down inside your body, like a red-wine stain on a pastel carpet ... The stain might fade a bit over time, but it will still remain, as a stain, until the day you draw your final breath ... And you are left to live the rest of your life with the gradual spread of that colour, with that ambiguous outline."[85]

Murakami's presentation of loneliness is then very different to that of David Foster Wallace or even of Richard Yates. There are no grand theories of loneliness woven into the dialogues of the characters as with Wallace's Shane Drinion and Meredith Rand. Loneliness is more like a mythic state reserved for men only who for any number of reasons will one day be visited by the unicorn of loneliness. With Murakami's protagonists possessing the same "arms-folded, lukewarm life stance" that he admires in Soseki, loneliness visits rather like inclement weather and the trick is only to find some symbol for it and honor it as a rite of passage.

However, Murakami's work also hides a more profound message beneath its seeming nonchalance, what might itself have something to do with a uniquely Japanese tendency that manifests itself as an unwillingness to labor the point when it comes to discussing painful emotional states in public. Murakami's presentation of loneliness in terms of the solitary lamprey or the solitary unicorn might also be saying something about the retreat and redundancy of a certain kind of masculinity today that Japanese society and other societies too have been slow to acknowledge despite the prevalence of directionless, wallowing lampreys running aground on our shores.

Murakami's reading of Soseki also reveals how important the historical context is for understanding the representation of loneliness. Murakami locates Soseki's unique style of characterization in the context of his times; Japan did not experience "the maturation of a middle-class citizenry" because, for Murakami, it "slipped sideways from a feudal system into the authoritarian emperor system that held sway until the Second World War" thereby producing a readership that does not possess any "strong expectation" that Sanshiro will, or should, eventually enter into society as a "mature citizen."[86] Murakami also notes that *Sanshiro* only contains the "palest hint of mythical elements."[87] It was published in 1909 and Soseki's work is therefore contemporary with that of Joyce. While *Portrait of the Artist as a Young Man* also does not give us a clear impression that Stephen Dedalus has evolved into a "mature citizen," not to mention an artist, Joyce does still rely on myth in his later work *Ulysses*, while also lampooning notions of the citizen through his portrayal of "The Citizen" in the "Cyclops" chapter. Soseki does not feel he needs to use any mythic model and he also does not inhabit the same nationalist world that Joyce grew up in and that Joyce criticizes for reducing citizenship to nationhood and blinkered patriotism. Therefore, Soseki employs a "Western framework," as Murakami notes, but he jumbles the metaphysical and physical together and employs an authorial voice that is free of obvious satire, metafictional self-consciousness, or even ribald humor; he leaves us with the sense that "affirmation and negation are clearly indistinguishable at times."[88] Yet Murakami admits that Soseki does present us with many of the "forms and functions of the Japanese psyche" transplanting them "[i]nto the format of the modern Western novel."[89] With these differences in mind, differences that are themselves only framed here in order to pursue cross-cultural discussion of the novel, we can then ask how does loneliness appear in the novels of Soseki? How does it appear alongside the loneliness we have read in James, Yates, O'Connor, McCullers, and Wallace?

Sanshiro is one of the young elites of Japanese society attending the Tokyo Imperial University. He has just entered the university and his mother sends him a letter telling him the cousin of a family friend is also studying there and directing Sanshiro to call on him. Nonomiya is a science student and he spends his days in a dark cellar when the traffic has stopped conducting an experiment on the pressure exerted by a beam of light.[90] Nonomiya is not a great communicator and he seems obsessed by his science experiment, unable to imagine that Sanshiro might not be interested. When Sanshiro leaves Nonomiya, he experiences a profound sense of loneliness. The narrative leading up to the description of Sanshiro's loneliness alerts us to the fact, through passages of free indirect discourse, that Sanshiro is beginning to realize how university life is cut off from the real world:

> He walked beneath a canopy of black-green leaves, the openings between them dyed red. On the trunk of a large zelkova tree a cicada was singing. Sanshiro came to the edge of the University pond and squatted down.
>
> It was extraordinarily quiet. Not even the noise of the streetcars penetrated this far. One streetcar line was to have run past the Red Gate, but the University had protested and it had gone through Koishikawa instead ... If it refused to let streetcars pass by it, the University must be far removed from society.[91]

Soseki does not use a mythic method here and his descriptions do not possess the ostentatious metafictional experimentation, satirical showboating, or even the ribald humor of other "Western" modernists. However, what Murakami calls "that arms-folded, lukewarm life stance of Sanshiro's that wraps logical and ethical complications in the softest possible emotional cloak" belies a subtle symbolism that runs counter to the seemingly "lukewarm life stance" of Sanshiro. The zelkova tree, the cicada, the Red Gate, and the description of the university buildings and the sky above reveal a raging emotional struggle going on inside Sanshiro. The buildings of the University were "sparkling as if on fire" and the "[p]ale red flames of burning sun swept back from the horizon into the sky's deep clarity," their "fever" rushing "down upon him." Under such an onslaught, Sanshiro "entered the woods, whose back, like his, lay half in darkness."[92] We undoubtedly have modernist echoes here of the notebook entries of Edvard Munch or even of some of the pathetic fallacies of Goethe's *Werther*. The painful, passionate description of the surroundings is focalized through Sanshiro, a young man who has just missed the opportunity—and has been teased for it—of losing his virginity with a woman he met on the train to Tokyo. He feels the sting of the missed opportunity and of the woman's knowing rebuke. He has also just visited the appropriately named Nonomiya (No No Me Yaaa!) whose almost monastic existence in the bowels of the University "removed from society" makes Sanshiro realize all the more the stark opposition between the kind of life the train encounter offered him and the kind the University is beginning to represent for him for the years ahead. The vibrant, pulsating, almost erotic descriptions of the sky and sun and of the zelkova leaves with the "openings between them dyed red" symbolizes the battle within him as a young man eager to encounter life to the full. The cicada, a common leitmotif in Japanese poetry and haikus, often symbolizes the transience of life due to the cicada's brief existence above ground after its subterranean slumber of up to 17 years.[93] Read together then, the raging, passionate natural imagery and the allusion to transience capture the desperate *carpe diem* sense Sanshiro may be riven by at this moment. His visit to Nonomiya in the cellar only brings this sense home to him all the more. The Red Gate of the Tokyo University was one of only two left standing and it was built in 1827 to celebrate the marriage of the Kaga lord Maeda Nariyasu to Yōhime (Lady Yasu) who was the twenty-first daughter of Shogun Tokugawa Ienari. Tokugawa Ienari apparently fathered 75 children and kept a harem of 900 women. Soseki was surely aware of this history, as was Sanshiro. The profligacy and promiscuity of the Shogun, captured forever by this Red Gate, this red threshold to University life, stands out in almost painful contrast against what he has experienced so far in the University. Rather like the young boy watching the wedding dance of the foxes from behind the trees in the first vignette, "Sunshine through the rain," of the Kurosawa classic, *Dreams*, the description of Sanshiro's plight is enriched by this subtle symbolism. In the Kurosawa movie a small boy is warned by his mother not to go into the woods when the rain falls through the sunshine. He then witnesses a fox wedding but is spotted by the foxes. When he returns home his mother tells him a fox has called to the house leaving a knife for him. He is to commit suicide if he does not go into the woods to seek forgiveness from the foxes. To suggest then that Sanshiro does not give us the "palest hint of mythical elements" may only be half the story. The central themes of Kurosawa's rendition of this Japanese folktale or myth about the loss of innocence and about how its passing means we must confront the terrors we have witnessed also applies to Sanshiro. Sanshiro's recollection of espying the girl through the trees near the pond is described by Soseki as being cast in a "tawny, foxlike shade, the translucent color of a lightly toasted rice cake."[94] One might also parallel Sanshiro's vision of the girl and her mother high up on the embankment near the pond in traditional Japanese costumes with the second vignette in Kurosawa's *Dreams*, "The Peach Orchard." Ultimately, Sanshiro rues his "weakness"[95] that had prevented him from being with the woman on the train. He associates the appearance of this woman with the fear that accosted him when he was with the woman in the hotel room. He is filled with a sense of "some terrible contradiction" that he is fast learning is what University life instils in young people where they have to somehow bring together "society" outside the University and the life within. He feels this contradiction now suggests he must immolate himself on the dagger of his shame if he is to mature.

Sanshiro then looks out on the pond that will take its name from him. Squatting by the pond, he begins to reflect on his University experiences so far, what is again given in a partially free indirect style with elements of omniscient narrative voice:

> One thing was clear, however: the scale in the telescope could move all it liked, and it would still have nothing to do with the real world. Perhaps Nonomiya hoped to avoid contact with the real world as long as he lived. A person could come to feel that way quite naturally, no doubt, breathing this quiet atmosphere. And he, too, Sanshiro wondered, perhaps he too ought to lead a life like this, undistracted, unconnected with the living world.
>
> He stared at the surface of the pond. The reflection of many trees seemed to reach to the bottom, and down deeper than the trees, the blue sky. No longer was he thinking of streetcars, or Tokyo, or Japan. A sense of something

far-off and remote had come to take their place. The feeling lasted but a moment, when loneliness began to spread across its surface like a veil of clouds. The solitude was complete, as if he were sitting alone in Nonomiya's cellar. At school in Kumamoto, he had climbed to the top of nearby Tatsuta Mountain, a place still more silent than this; he had lain by himself in the playing field when it was carpeted in evening primrose; he had often felt the pleasure of forgetting all about the world of men. But never before had he known this sense of isolation.[96]

This is a profound sense of loneliness and isolation triggered by his first encounter with the life of an academic researcher in a University environment that can refuse "to let streetcars" and the "real world" pass too close. The reflections in the pond blur with the self-reflection the scene incites in Sanshiro. When we read that the "reflection of many trees seemed to reach to the bottom, and down deeper than the trees" we know that the deliberation on the reflection in the pond's waters is also a profound self-reflection. This commingling of self with such a University environment after having encountered for the first time a life—Nonomiya's—transformed and almost unrecognizable to this boy "from the country" due to its devotion to research, produces the feeling of loneliness that "began to spread across its surface like a veil of clouds." As with Proust, where reflection on an object for the sake of temporal apperception always becomes self-reflection, the loneliness here spreads across both the scene contemplated, the pond's water, and the self contemplating it. The description of loneliness as a feeling that spreads across the "surface" like a "veil of clouds" also suggests that loneliness can act as an obstacle to a more than surface-level moment of self-awareness. And just as in Proust, where the encounter with a natural scene contemplated, such as the spires of Combray, forces you back to an engagement with an earlier self that had contemplated a similar scene, Sanshiro is also thrown back to his childhood in Kumamoto and Tatsuta Mountain. However, whereas the Proustian recollection is likely to foreground resemblance, Sanshiro becomes aware of the stark difference between the emotions unleashed by these seemingly similar encounters with the natural environment. The institutional reality of the University environment with its "Red Gate" and its power to remove itself from "society" means that even the attempt to merge with the natural environment only makes one all the more aware of the contrived nature of existence in this secluded, gated community.

As with Qian Zhongshou's *Fortress Besieged* and Joyce's *A Portrait*, the encounter with the University incites a profound sense of loneliness for the young artist and student that can be too difficult to surmount. In his first days on campus Sanshiro comes face to face with the body of a young woman who has committed suicide by throwing herself under the train: "The train had made a clean tear from the right shoulder, beneath the breast, to the left hip, and it had gone on, leaving this diagonal torso in its path. The face was untouched. It was a young woman."[97] The unsettling encounter with the face of the young woman and the response it engenders from Nonomiya in the University incites a traumatic and vitriolic attack on the world of the critic and the academic. In trying to come to terms with the death, Sanshiro recalls the words of a man he had met on the train who had advised him "You'd better watch out—life can be dangerous."[98] It sparks the following reflection:

> For all his talk of danger, the man was annoyingly self-possessed. Perhaps one could be like that if he stood in a position so free of danger that he could afford to warn others against it. This might be a source of amusement for those men who, while part of the world, watched it from a place apart. Yes, for certain, the man was one of them. It was obvious from the way he ate those peaches, the way he sipped his tea and puffed on his cigarette, looking always right ahead. The man was a critic.[99]

This leads to Sanshiro momentarily wondering whether he too should "live as a critic" but then the "ghastly face of the dead woman" comes back to him; this "ghastly face" becomes a symbol for the kind of life Sanshiro now associates with the University. Sanshiro then meets Nonomiya who regrets having missed the "chance" to view the body of the victim: "'You don't get a chance like that very often. Too bad I wasn't here. They've gotten rid of the body, I suppose. I probably couldn't see anything if I went for a look now."[100] It draws a shocked response from Sanshiro, his words merging with the omniscient voice of Soseki: "He ascribed this insensitivity to the difference between night and day, youthfully unaware that a man who experiments on the pressure of light reveals that characteristic attitude in all situations, even one like this."[101] It is a foretaste of what the University life might do to him. However, still a new student, he has the wherewithal to remind himself that "Time spent with people was real time, while the many days Nonomiya spent experimenting in the cellar should be considered leisure time distant from human life."[102] The description of Nonomiya in "the cellar" in his "leisure time" is a nice description for the life lived online today, time not "spent with people" in "real time." It looks forward to the more dystopian visons of research and academia in Wallace, Bolaño, and Houellebecq.

Loneliness in Sayaka Murata's *Convenience Store Woman*

Sayaka Murata's examination of loneliness in contemporary Japan in *Convenience Store Woman*, a novel published over a century after *Sanshiro*, is one that completely transforms the institutional encounter with loneliness. In a world where we all live in "the cellar," Murata's convenience store worker forgoes a life of companionship for the performance of togetherness the convenience store offers, a life that grants her greater consolation. Murata's Miss Furukura, or Keiko, sees her life in stages; there is no real life before she was "reborn" as a convenience store worker: "The time before I was reborn as a convenience store worker is somewhat unclear in my memory."[103] The fact that the author Murata has herself worked in a convenience store, the lack of obvious dystopian or even magic realist elements in the novel, and the fact that Keiko shares Sanshiro's somewhat carefree, sangfroid attitude to events in possessing what Murakami calls "that arms-folded, lukewarm life stance" all give the novel a realist or even documentary-style feel in depicting modern life in Japan. However, we learn that Keiko is someone who has spent most of her time "alone"; as a child she was unable to understand the wider implications of her violent actions. Having failed to fully understand through the explanations given to her by adults why her actions—which corresponded with what she had seen on TV—were wrong, she retreats into herself and "doggedly refused to say anything more than absolutely necessary."[104] The story is being told by

Keiko in a first-person voice and we detect no sense of self-pity or emotion when she describes her childhood and teenage years alone:

> I didn't make any friends at school, but I wasn't particularly picked on or bullied, and I managed to get myself through elementary and secondary without saying anything uncalled for.
>
> I didn't even change after graduating from high school and going on to university. I basically spent my free time alone, and didn't talk to anyone in private at all.[105]

Keiko's first sighting of the soon-to-be-opened convenience store, the Smile Mart, appears as a kind of revelation in the midst of her lonely environment:

> I can still clearly recall the moment I came across the as-yet-unopened store. I'd been to see a Noh performance as part of my coursework and, not having any friends, was making my way home alone when I took a wrong turn and found myself in a completely unfamiliar office district, totally lost.
>
> It occurred to me all of a sudden that the place was deserted. I was alone in a world of graceful white buildings, an artificial scene of paper models. It was Sunday afternoon, and there was no sign of anyone other than me in the street. It was like a ghost town.
>
> … At last I saw a sign and, relieved, was running toward it when I came across the ground floor of a pure white building converted into what looked like an aquarium.[106]

Keiko realizes she is "part of the machine of society" with a great deal of excitement and a sense of self-discovery; it is like being *"reborn"* (19). After she has worked there for 18 years, she speaks of herself as two persons. There is the "I" who is 36 and the "convenience-store-worker-me" who is 18. She realizes she is a "cog in society" but this is the "only way I can be a normal person."[107] However, she has literally been recreated by the store as her "body is entirely made up of food from the store."[108] Not only this, she sees herself as being made up of her colleagues; she is "infected" by them and thus her actions are imitations of their actions: "[i]nfecting each other like this is how we maintain ourselves as human is what I think."[109] It's a dystopian view of human interaction but one shared by many young people I teach. A recent M.Phil. thesis I read in Hong Kong wrote of the need to see youth and youthfulness as a state of dysfunction that is suffered temporarily by society, quite like "madness" for the student, before we are conditioned to grow out of it and thus contribute to society. The "dependable, normal world" of the convenience store is all that makes Keiko feel normal, the morning rituals of shouting "Irasshaimase!" together with her coworkers give her the feeling that "'morning' itself is being loaded into me."[110] Rather like some of today's incels and asexuals, Keiko also admits to herself that she had "never experienced sex" and "never even had any particular awareness of my own sexuality."[111] She cannot understand why her friends think she must be miserable because of this and why they jump to unfounded conclusions about her being "abused" as a child. In the end, she felt it wearying "why everyone felt such a need for reassurance."[112] She longs for the convenience store and the normality it offers and this leads her to reflect on her life: "The sensation that the world is slowly dying feels good,"[113] Death and dying are imagined as good as it is the throng of life about her in the shape of her sometime-friends that makes her feel so awkward; she calls it a "cast-off-cicada-shell world."[114] True humanity is found not in virtue, charity, or filial piety, the staples of Western humanism and also of Confucianism, but in finding validation through the recognition that the "world is dying" and in the stare that greets you when you confront condescending attitudes:

> When you work in a convenience store, people often look down on you for working there. I find this fascinating and I like to look them in the face when they do this to me. And as I do so I always think: that's what a human is …
>
> I find the shape of people's eyes particularly interesting when they're being condescending. I see a wariness or a fear of being contradicted or sometimes a belligerent spark ready to jump on any attack. And if they're unaware of being condescending, their glazedover eyeballs are steeped in a fluid mix of ecstasy and a sense of superiority.[115]

The human is found in this willingness to condescend and then to belligerently defend this stance of superiority. The convenience store, where most workers except Shiraha have prescribed roles and live in a state of "equality," offers Keiko a reprieve from this belligerent competitive world of attack. Speech itself is only a means to produce words that "sounded human when really he wasn't saying anything at all."[116] Her loneliness feeds her sense of longing for the convenience store: "The normal world has no room for exceptions and always quietly eliminates foreign objects. Anyone who is lacking is disposed of. So *that's* why I need to be saved. Unless I'm cured, normal people will expurgate me."[117] The same message comes back to us from secondary school students in Hong Kong who complain of the competition they suffer under. They resign themselves to a life they already see as unsuccessful; in a process of self-stratification they resign themselves to being "disposed of" in the education system, describing themselves similarly as "foreign objects" and as "trash" (see Chapter 8 on secondary school students in Hong Kong). We learn later that it is Shiraha, her co-worker, who has been using the phrase "foreign objects" and that perhaps Keiko has been "infected" by him in using this phrase. Shiraha speaks of how "our society doesn't allow any foreign objects. I've always suffered because of that."[118] In the end, Keiko and Shiraha decide to get married as "a matter of paperwork" so that they can "play the part of the fictitious creature called an 'ordinary person' that everyone has in them in the same way that everyone in the convenience store is playing the part of the fictitious person called 'a store worker.'"[119] Keiko decides to finally go along with what society wants since she admits she does not "have any particular purpose of my own."[120] The only solution then is to "eliminate the parts of your life that others find strange." It is precisely the opposite of the Western humanist ideal that sees the subject finding some validation for an internal sense of self or an Ibsenist notion where the "strongest man in the world is the man who stands alone." Individualism in a lonely world is to be found by being reborn and eliminating the parts of your life that society finds strange; conformism is key. The two lonely individuals who feel hounded by society come together. Shiraha feels the incredible weight of being a man:

> If I go out my life will be violated again. When you're a man, it's all 'go to work' and 'get married.' And once you're married, then it's 'earn more' and 'have children'! You're a slave to the village. Society orders you to work your whole life. Even my testicles are the property of the village! Just by having no sexual experience they treat you as though you're wasting your semen.[121]

He therefore retreats to Keiko's bathtub and stays there wanting to "spend my whole life doing nothing. For my whole life, until I die, I want to just breathe without anyone interfering in my life."[122]

In the end, when word gets back to her coworkers and manager in the store that she is living with Shiraha, they start to criticize Shiraha openly, hoping he will come out for a drink so they can say it to his face. Keiko hears their words only as a "strange atmosphere" where they are "fast reverting to ordinary males and females."[123] She has become so conditioned by her job that she only hears their rebukes as noise that interferes with her life as store worker. In the end, she looks to the customers for a reminder of who she is: "Now only the customers still allowed me to be just a convenience store worker."[124] Individuals become so cut off from anything even resembling authenticity or a connection with what might be conducive to "normal" social interaction outside work that they seek validation from those they serve in the day job. When her sister calls to the apartment and meets Shiraha, she advises Keiko to see a "counselor." We then momentarily get the outsider perspective in the novel, the perspective of someone who sees Keiko's approach to life as potentially harmful.

A similar device is employed in Gail Honeymoon's *Eleanor Oliphant Is Completely Fine* where Eleanor's split personality is only discovered near the end when the feelings for Raymond allow her to see through to the abnormality of her previous behavior and she decides to change. Late in the novel we learn how Eleanor's history of abuse and mental illness has marked her in profound ways that the novel keeps at bay right to the end by chiefly giving us Eleanor's perspective on everything. However, once Eleanor begins to discover what care and love is through Raymond's kindness, we also begin to get a somewhat omniscient perspective that alerts us to the harmful nature of some of Eleanor's actions. So, for example, when Eleanor is rejected by a man she stalks and builds up a fantasy relationship around, it is the kindness of Raymond that literally sustains her; she realizes that "No one was supposed to live like this. The problem was that I simply didn't know how to make it right … But no one had ever shown me the right way to live a life, and although I'd tried my best over the years, I simply didn't know how to make things better."[125] In a similar way, Keiko also begins to discover that she simply does not know what is best for her. A life seemingly lacking in caring relationships and full of people attacking her, telling her who she should be, and acting condescendingly towards her has left her finding consolation in the machines of industry to the extent that she sees herself as an animal channeling their message. As Eleanor Oliphant also tells herself, before she has opened up to help through Raymond's kindness, loneliness is "liberating": "Some people, weak people, fear solitude. What they fail to understand is that there's something very liberating about it; once you realize that you don't need anyone, you can take care of yourself. That's the thing: it's *best* just to take care of yourself. You can't protect other people, however hard you try. You try, and you fail, and your world collapses around you, burns down to ashes."[126] We learn only later that this negative understanding of helping others comes from a traumatic childhood experience that Eleanor has suppressed. Her mother had set fire to their house when they were children with Eleanor and her sister inside. Eleanor had tried to save her sister but failed. As readers, we learn very late that the mother she speaks to every week also died in the fire. The picture Eleanor presents of solitude and loneliness and complete self-reliance as "liberating" even after traumatic events is one that our competitive society keeps pushing on us by way of cloneliness. It is also one the social network model requires so that we will keep feeding the online beast that liquidates true friendship and true care.

However, Keiko has not found someone like Raymond who is generous and open; instead she has accepted Shiraha into her life who is abusive and parasitical on her generosity. She does not have the emotional strength and the loving relationships through which to know what is best for her and so she needs to be instructed on what to do: "So, will I be saved if I leave the convenience store? Or am I better staying working there? And should I kick Shiraha out? Or am I better with him here? Look, I'll do whatever you say. I don't mind either way, so please just instruct me in specific terms."[127] This can be read as a sad indictment of a society where social conditions ensure people are made to feel content with only a semblance of relationships. When impersonal, virtual, or in-store relationships become the acceptable norm and we see all human interaction in terms of "infection" or "imitation" then we lose track of who we are. However, the problem is that society has become so competitive that many choose to opt out of the only life narratives regarded as acceptable. As Keiko realizes when Shiraha lies to her sister about their relationship: "now that she thinks he's 'one of us' she can lecture him. She's far happier thinking her sister is normal, even if she has a lot of problems, than she is having an abnormal sister for whom everything is fine."[128] Normality becomes the mask we wear to hide the abnormality we prefer inhabiting. Keiko finally decides to leave the store and she doesn't know what do with herself: "My body had belonged to the convenience store even when I wasn't at work. Having been liberated from this, I didn't know what to do with myself."[129] She no longer knows "what standard to live by" (148). With no friends and no lovers she now "spent all day and night in my bed inside the closet, only coming out when I felt hungry."[130] She is suffering from feelings of depression and aimlessness:

> I had judged everything on the basis of whether it was the sensible thing to do for the convenience store, but now I'd lost that standard. There was nothing to guide me over whether an action was rational or not. Before I became a store worker, I must have been following some kind of logic in my judgments, but I'd forgotten whatever guiding principles I'd followed back then.[131]

In the end, she finds her way back to a convenience store after only a month. On the way to an interview, she steps into a convenience store and she is overwhelmed by how the store and the reaction of the customers speaks to her: "I couldn't stop hearing the store telling me the way it wanted to be, what it needed. It was all flowing into me. It wasn't me speaking. It was the store. I was just channeling its revelations from on high."[132] She realizes that "the voice of the convenience store won't stop flowing through me. I was born to hear this voice."[133]

Shiraha realizes his plan to have Keiko work to keep him is falling apart: "You'll just be persecuted by everyone and live a lonely life. You'd be far better off working to support me. That way everyone'll breathe easier."[134] She comes to the realization that she is an "animal" in the sense that she "can't betray my instinct."[135] The "human me" is too bound up with roles she is expected to play that leave her destitute and unsure of herself because they lead to such a barrage of abuse built on the survival of games of competition such as when Shiraha's sister replies in response to an enquiry about whether she should have children: "Keep those rotten genes to yourself for the course of your lifetime and take them to heaven with you when you die without leaving even a trace of them here on earth."[136] The final scene is once again one of rebirth; she sees herself as her newborn nephew unleashing a newborn cry of birth on the unsuspecting viewer: "I thought of the window in the hospital where I first saw my newborn nephew. Through the reflection a bright voice resembling mine rang out. I could distinctly feel all my cells stirring within my skin as they responded in unison to the music reverberating on the other side of the glass."[137] This is a curious replaying of a primal scene; one recognizes oneself in the mirror as an ideal self only here the ideal is to be reborn knowing with every fiber you were born for this world and no other. Murata's novel is of course a stinging commentary on the acerbic, competitive, and spiteful world of everyday life roles. However, it also offers a somewhat tragic yet strangely life-affirming account of the life of a lonely store worker who finds this competitive world too much for her. The only direction she can find is in the prescribed role of the store worker; unlike Richard Yates's depiction of barmen and retired soldiers or Sartre's depiction of bad faith, Keiko does not even realize she is lonely. She only knows that life falls apart when she is not following the orders of a manager and responding to convenience store jingles and clocks; there is not even the suggestion that friendship or affection was ever known to be missed. Keiko has leapfrogged loneliness to a state that finds comfort away from societal roles and expectations in the solitary life of a wholly committed store worker who never leaves the job even at home. Keiko is the perfect invention for capitalism; eternally starved of fellow feeling in a world obsessed with competition and expectation she finds herself as an "animal" hooked up to the routines of labor. Not only has she lost ownership and control over the means of production, she finds that seeing herself purely as the means of production and as "a cog" channeling the flows and jingles of industry is the only way to find comfort and a semblance of meaning. As I argued at the beginning of this book, this is the kind of subjectivity the virtual world demands of us; with friendship liquidated and fellow feeling reduced to competitive like games, the shallow high and hit of the information stream is all we can channel in wading in ever deeper until we become nodes unable to live outside its virtual connectivity, not knowing there was ever an offline community to miss or feel part of.

Radical Loneliness and Shintoism
by Raphael Wung Cheong Chim

What is loneliness? One is tempted to explicate its meaning in terms of preexisting texts of the Kyoto school, but the inadequacy of the Kyoto school and its methodologies in covering the entirety of a "Japanese" phenomenon is as evident as their dependence on Buddhist traditions, in particular the overarching theme of "absolute nothingness." It is necessary, if only for the sake of completeness, to seek out the other "religion" decisive of Japanese worldviews—Shinto—and investigate the meaning of loneliness therein.

One word for loneliness in Japanese is *hitori*. In one of the two Shinto scriptures, *Kojiki*, this word might be found in the portrayal of the first three gods:

These three Deities were all Deities born alone, and hid their persons.[138]

此三柱神者。並獨神成坐而。隱身也。

Hitori is as an "adjective," attached to *kami* (god); an alternative translation of *hitorigami* is "solitary, lonely gods" (獨神), "lonely" being used in a peculiar sense. What does it mean for a god to be "lonely"? We might take as our clue then the "verb" (隱身) accompanying the "subject" (獨神), translated as "hid their persons." A god is lonely insofar as she hid herself away. This appears simple enough, but it is in truth complicated by the fact that a "hidden world" (隱世) would have the meaning of an underworld.[139] The first chapter of *Kojiki* must have been written in profoundly ill humor: the first three gods to appear in the entire mythology perish as soon as they are born; and perish not by means of murder, but by hiding *themselves* away, of their own volition: by *suicide*. It suffices to say for the moment that the hiding decisive of loneliness is not a gesture that might be explicated with ease. Rather than settling immediately for one or multiple significations, we must first look further in *Kojiki* for other references to hiding.

Two instances stand out within the first volume of *Kojiki*: the hiding away of Amaterasu and that of Okuninushi. In the first we find the sun-goddess has fled to a cave frightened by her brother's outburst and the consequent death of a priestess of hers. The first appearance of the Kanji for "hiding"

(隠) is found in her enquiry regarding the commotion beyond the cave, "Methought that owing to my retirement the Plain of Heaven would be dark, and likewise the Central Land of Reed-Plains would all be dark,"[140] "hiding" being here translated as "retirement." We might see here and in the preceding lines "eternal night prevailed," that the hiding away of Amaterasu inconvenienced the other gods; the sun that refuses to shine might be said indeed to be a retirement, *from one's obligation*. Does it mean then that to hide away one's body is to have retired from the community of humans/gods or one's obligations therein?

Tetsuro Watsuji of the Kyoto school would perhaps agree that it is very much so; his hermeneutic efforts in outlining a Japanese ethics are, though laced with Buddhist undertones like the writings of his colleagues, deserving of some consideration. He noted in his seminal treatise on ethics, *Rinrigaku*, that for an individual to be an individual, "it negates the totality so as to become an individual," and that the same goes for when the individual becomes a member of a communal totality—that this "dual character of a human being" might be called an "absolute negation."[141] Herein lies Amaterasu's obligation to the communal totality, to remain in the heavens as the sun, regardless of her fears; fleeing to the cave and lingering therein is then to betray communal interests, to negate its totality, and assert her own individuality. What is hidden away here is her radiance, her instrumental merit or capacity to contribute, the communal obligation of shining upon the fields, nurturing the rice fields, and holding at bay "the myriad portents of woe" every night;[142] but does not this call reduce Amaterasu then to a mere lightbulb in the greenhouse, a searchlight in the dark? One shines and must shine until the last hint of warmth has departed and rigor mortis sets in.[143] Loneliness as hiding away would then be a negation of, a resistance against, a communal totality that calls for endless exploitation and nothing less than the extinguishment of one's life. One might compare this quite rewardingly with the character of Keiko in *Convenience Store Woman*. To not hide is, in this context, no different from terminating one's own life by communal hands; to hide is to seek a death on one's own terms. Loneliness that is constituted by hiding away would become a plea for (individualistic) dignity, answered by itself, in a self-hiding.

The second instance of hiding away might be found in the episode dedicated to the abdication of Okuninushi and the land of Izumo to the heavenly deities. Here we find the Kanji 隠 deployed for the first time in the first volume of *Kojiki*, unaccompanied by any other noun or verb. We might first consider the translation of this unique moment in the *Kojiki*, in a monologue delivered by Okuninushi prior to his hiding away,

> In accordance with the [heavenly] command, I will at once yield up this Central Land of Reed-Plains. But as to my place of residence, if ye will make stout the temple pillars on the nethermost rock-bottom, and make high the cross-beams to the Plain of High Heaven like the rich and perfect august nest where the august child of the Heavenly Deities rules the succession of Heaven's sun, and will deign to establish me, I will hide in the eighty (less than a hundred) road-windings, and wait on him ... Having thus spoken he hid himself. So in accordance with his word, they built a heavenly august abode on the shore of Tagishi in the land of Idzumo.[144]

At the time of this monologue, both his sons have taken their leave, and Okuninushi, deprived of his two closest allies, is confronted by the heavenly deities to abdicate. This is not, however, a repetition of a previous hiding away premised upon a powerlessness before a destiny sketched out by the community that consists only of "'fortune' and circumstances which 'come its way' or are the result of 'the cruelty of accidents.'"[145]

This monologue is on the contrary a demand, a law and its legislation, the force of which might only be diluted in retrospect to "negotiation." This is evident from how Okuninushi did not wait for the heavenly deities to respond to his demand; he anticipated only that they shall comply. What is made plain here too is that we are quite mistaken in presupposing that hiding away is here organized around what might be regarded as *negative* movements *away* from either the individual or community. Hinted at already by the fact that Amaterasu did indeed leave the cave, it is now made explicit by the fact that Okuninushi did not hide away *to evade his exploitation by a communal totality*. In hiding away, he did not choose to "die by his own terms," to commit suicide to preserve one's individuality; instead Okuninushi demanded a shrine to be built, "like the rich and perfect august nest" of the very gods who "bested" him. Taking this as our clue, we must now review our earlier interpretations: who among the gods who hid themselves away, is without power? The three *hitorigami* who hid themselves away are the forerunners and founders of the pantheon to come. Amaterasu, even prior to her exaltation under the imperial cult, is easily one of the most prominent deities of the pantheon. Okuninushi is the ruler of Izumo who in being defeated, triumphed over all the gods. It was not demand, but *supplication*, that drew out these gods from their hiding: even in the case of Amaterasu who appears to have gained little but a fate of servitude for the sake of the communal totality, the gods did not, dared not, call to her, and instead organized an entire festival in her honor.[146] Hiding-away is not a gesture one is forced into; it is not born of powerlessness before the community. Loneliness constituted by this hiding away is then not a signifier of marginalization, but of godly dignity. The hidden in departing from her loneliness is not so much negated by the community that "demands" her to depart. On the contrary, it is the lonely (god) who commands the community, *for the interests of this community is contingent upon her individuality not being negated*. This is clear in the way Amaterasu would not retaliate by dimming her radiance and in the way Okuninushi would not muster a coup d'état after his abdication.

One might argue that the narratives concerning Amaterasu and Okuninushi differ fundamentally in that the former concerns a movement away from hiding away and the latter a movement into hiding away; but this is to neglect one obvious fact. In the case of Amaterasu, her departure is in truth, only a movement into another hiding away: Amaterasu in leaving the cave illuminates the world once more, but in so doing she merely transits from one solitude (in the cave) to another (on the heavens); whereas Okuninushi in hiding away, enters into a contract with the heavenly gods and thus ceases to hide himself away. It is never a straightforward question of affirmation *or* negation; but it suffices for the purpose of this chapter to say that *loneliness is never negated even as it departs from itself into a community: loneliness only repeats, that is to say, affirms itself.*

The repetition of loneliness might also speak for the critique Watsuji posed in regard to Western logic that "granted ... priority to the individual *qua* individual."[147] where the logic of individualism is premised upon the very repetition of the identity of an individual. For Watsuji, given that "social consciousness is at the same time individual consciousness," this very repetition, as the affirmation of individuality, must come in the form of a negation of community.[148]

In our defense, we must invoke the logic of absolute mediation formulated by the late Hajime Tanabe, another member of the Kyoto school, in *Philosophy as Metanoetics*. While Watsuji denoted "the independence of an individual" that hides herself away from community, as merely "badness,"[149] Tanabe would have chosen "radical evil" instead.[150] The overcoming of this radical evil is not "a matter of natural necessity—that is, something within my control."[151] To become communal one cannot merely empty oneself, "regardless of how this emptying is performed":[152] the tendency towards hiding away is such that insofar as it is performed by the individual, it already becomes an act of "continually extending the self," that is, of the individual repeating itself in a self-assertion, or a hiding away into loneliness.[153] In truth, the radical nature of this "badness" is merely something Watsuji neglected to speak of. Writing predominantly of the movement from "goodness" to "badness" (rebellion), and then of the return of "badness" to "goodness" (sacrifice), *he did not write of the subsequent fall of "goodness" back to "badness."* This fall might be identified both neutrally, as a rebellion, and chronologically, as a *relapse*. Without the term "relapse" a human being would be no more than a perpetual motion machine capable only of 1 and 0, and it is only if one considers the "third" movement from "badness" to "goodness" as a relapse that this movement becomes something "sensible," something that the human machine is not merely *programmed* to do, for obviously, one does not simply begin rebelling *again* without an object or cause. It goes without saying too that this "third" movement of relapse is what guarantees the possibility of the fourth movement back to "goodness"; and thus relapse is just as integral to Watsuji's conception of human relations as rebellion and sacrifice. This essential tendency towards relapse is precisely what Tanabe referred to as "radical evil," and what Watsuji, without ever explicitly naming it, has already inscribed deep within his ethics.

Casting aside the derogatory terminologies of Watsuji and Tanabe, we might speak of hiding away and loneliness not as "badness" or "radical evil," but as a radical tendency of human beings to assert themselves as individuals away from community. It is so radical and deeply entrenched in human relations that even in the midst of a community, a human being might maintain itself as individual, that is to say, it hides itself away in loneliness. Indeed, to invoke the cliché: is it not precisely in the thickest crowd that one might feel the most profound loneliness? This tendency to hide oneself away, to be lonely, might well be termed "radical loneliness."

We come now then to perhaps the most pertinent question on loneliness: if loneliness is radical, does it not mean that the individual shall never be fully "integrated" into a community and total communal solidarity never attainable? That as Derrida would say, an economy of war in which the individual and community might only attempt "the most peaceful" and never "*absolutely peaceful*" gesture in relation to one another? We are confronted here perhaps with the myth of how a community might be impaired by antisociality, isolation, and loneliness; but as we have hoped we have demonstrated through our readings of the myths of Amaterasu and Okuninushi, the myth against loneliness is even more of a myth than the narratives in *Kojiki*, and the talk of an individual losing as much from her loneliness as the community is a myth of no less proportion. In cases of a loneliness that hides away, the community in not supplicating in truth stands to lose far more than the individual, for the community consists of individuals, as much as individuals are born into and molded by the community. Indeed, even Watsuji would agree that "individuals are basically different from society and yet dissolve themselves into society,"[154] and that because of the radical loneliness "communal existence contains the danger of extinction on each and every occasion."[155] It is by virtue of his negligence of *radical* loneliness that he underestimated the exact extent of this threat of extinction, and the extent of the community's dependence upon the individual. The community exists mediated by the revolt, sacrifice, and relapse of the individual, and all such movements hinge upon the radical loneliness or "individuality" (the repeated identity of individual-qua-individual) of this very individual; the individual is mediated by the reciprocations from community. To quench, eliminate, or completely satisfy one's loneliness would be to quench the individual and with it shatter the fundamental structure of a community. So often this would entail the tragic conclusion that the individual and community are caught forever in a series of proxy wars, ever fearful of taking one step too far and annihilating the other side and with it its own side as well; and yet as we have seen in the myth of Amaterasu and Okuninushi, there is an alternative for enshrining loneliness and hiding away, to host for them a festival of their own. It is in the midst of that festival that the individual shall like the sun emerge only to hide away again.

7

Filial Piety and Loneliness in a Selection of Chinese Novels: Cao Xueqin, Mo Yan, Dai Sijie, Ha Jin, and Yiyun Li

If, as Franco Moretti argues in *Distant Reading*, narratives and novels are like "species" then how might these different species be reliant on their different environments and how might their species-identity align with their national identity? At a time when eco-criticism and the criticism and writing of the Anthropocene is also asking us to examine the objects of a post-human age, how might we also be able to examine novels and narratives as objects that prefigure endangered aspects of our shared humanity such as our means of representing self-reflection, self-awareness, and individualism? In reading novels after the fact can we track back to those early signs where a way of representing interiority and individualism began to feel endangered? And, if we regard narratives in terms of experientiality, radical embodied cognitive loneliness, and universal cognitive schemas that communities of readers bring to texts in narrativizing them, as Monica Fludernik suggests, and not so much as "qualities adhering to texts," how are the narratives of a community also revealing of its privileged schemas? Such a framing of narrative works not so much to privilege intrinsic narratability as something akin to a language acquisition device but to foreground the relationship between community and narrative. Obviously, one must be wary in treating narratives as "species"; cross-cultural readings of narratives must avoid any hint of speciesism and they must also be careful to speak for the unique context of the "local." As Longxi Zhang reminds us, in response to the "world-systems" approach of Moretti:

Drawing on Immanuel Wallerstein's "world-systems" theory, which is in itself based on European historical experience, Franco Moretti argues that the modern novel develops from European centers of metropolitan culture to non-European peripheries, a kind of a radiation of influence from European centers to non-European receptacles. Such a model largely ignores the local tradition and its resilience, the counter-influence of a local form that often plays a significant role in the transformation of the traditional novel into a new and modern incarnation.[1]

Franco Moretti's world literature canon almost completely ignores Chinese novels. In this chapter, I will therefore give a brief reading of a selection of Chinese novels—written in Chinese, English, and French—alongside the more well-known claims for Western modernist works belonging to Moretti's canon of world literature, works I have discussed earlier in reading and touching on the work of James, Joyce, O'Connor, Yates, Mansfield, McCullers, and others. Moretti also looks to what he calls "allopatric speciation" as a means whereby a homeland elsewhere is assigned to European narratives that are asked to assume all kinds of national literatures and cultures in a kind of archipelago of texts. It is about time we added to this mix the homeland elsewhere of non-European texts. Moretti's "total reliance" then on the "canon of European masterpieces" offers us a vision of individualism in world literature that is one-sided and that can benefit from the insights of such experts in the Chinese canon as Longxi Zhang. Moretti privileges European literature's formal inventiveness that makes it unique. And yet when I read these novels today in my classes in Hong Kong my students often question why this genre of narrative so suited this European psyche. In what often feels like a post-European age, in the sense that Europe's communitarian post-war dream of bureaucratic and business integration has never been so challenged, the classics of the genre that Moretti has a "total reliance" on, those long, introspective narratives of European modernist interiority, look back to a European spirit of individualism that must have prefigured its own sense of being endangered. The high modernist narrative style of complex self-reflection and self-representation has now long been endangered; it influenced notions of self-reflection and individualism in general and, in turn, notions of solitude and loneliness. In an age when such self-reflective narratives are endangered, how might we then look to the narrative traditions of other regions for signs of a very different understanding of individualism and hence loneliness? Today, we read the old canonical narratives of European introspection to ourselves nostalgically, all the time furthering their legacy of isolation and individualism. We cannot transpose even the reading style we apply to Joyce or Proust onto Chinese novels since students in our classes respond "you are reading too deeply" or "but the author says this in the introduction" when we try to do so. Moretti acknowledges that the "unity" of the European project after twenty centuries is threatened as never before. With this in mind, this chapter explores how a selection of Chinese narratives that very often present filial piety as a kind of first philosophy, offer a communal ethic sensitive to environment that was perhaps never so easily given up as it was in the European modernist tradition. The Chinese novels are read in light of the questions posed already in regard to individualism, self-reflection and loneliness.

The questions Zhang raises in regard to comparative research are important considerations for any exploration of narrative from a comparative or cross-cultural perspective. And in a spirit of fairness, it is also good to remind ourselves of how Asian writers have also indulged occasionally in dualistic thinking in East–West comparative readings:

> Modern Asian writers have also been more or less complacent (or defensive) in their own sweeping contrasts between Asia and Europe, between Eastern and Western thought and culture. We have, for example, Liang Ch'i-ch'ao's contrast between Eastern wisdom and Western learning, Kitaro Nishida's distinction between the rule of the intellect in European culture and the stress on feeling in Eastern culture, Kitayama's opposition of "space" and "time" cultures, and Nagayo's emphasis on the difference between "soul training" and "mental culture." Okakura held that Christian Europe never ascended above a human godhead to the Eastern vision of the universal in its "eternal search for unity in variety."[2]

This chapter explores then, in being mindful of Zhang's warning to those involved in comparative analysis, one aspect of the resilient "local tradition" of Chinese philosophy and narrative. It examines how loneliness and individualism in a selection of Chinese novels may sometimes appear to the Western reader to become submerged under a privileging of what is often regarded as "filial piety" *xiao* (孝) or filial affection and responsibility (*qin qin* 親親); in other words, any sense of what Frank O'Connor describes as the "submerged population group" in narratives, what is for him, an integral component of the short story because it speaks of loneliness, may often appear less submerged in some of these Chinese narratives. Some of the insights for this chapter come from an M.A. course on comparative approaches to literary studies that I taught for Hong Kong and Mainland China students at the Chinese University of Hong Kong in 2017. Narrative as species may offer a zone of reflection whereby such cross-cultural questions can be explored creatively and in discussion. Another question the class raised was whether the long, sprawling, highly self-reflective narratives of Western modernism and postmodernism (e.g., *Ulysses, À la recherche, Infinite Jest*) might be endangered forms of narrative in a "Chinese century" and in an online age in the sense that they have been dying forms of narrative for some time and hence also dying forms of thinking about individualism and loneliness.

If there are narrative forms that enhance the representation of interiority and individualism such as interior monologue and stream of consciousness, are there narrative forms more suited to the representation of a communitarian ethos and a collectivist practice? Many scholars note how important filial piety is for Chinese philosophy: Chenyang Li notes that "[u]nlike in the West, where filial morality is rarely a philosophical topic, in China it has long been at the center of philosophical discourse."[3] Li reminds us that "[r]enowned scholars like Chien Mu and Hsieh Yu-wei have described Chinese culture as 'the culture of filial morality' (*xiao de wenhua*)" and that "[o]ne cannot understand traditional Chinese culture without understanding the role of filial morality."[4] Joseph Chan, however, argues in *Confucian Perfectionism* that there is a "strong internal reason to reform and revise the traditional understanding of filial piety"[5] so that it can include a sense of "personal autonomy." Traditional Confucianism endorses a hierarchical system of familial and social relationships and this system is supported by an "elaborate ethics of filial piety."[6] Chan also reminds us that it was precisely this feature of Confucianism that May Fourth thinkers argued was "responsible for the suppression of personal freedom and individuality."[7] It is generally agreed that modernization chiefly came to China in the twentieth century (and we must recall here Bruno Latour's question about whether the 'West' has ever been modern) and modern Chinese society would thus be slow to absorb any changes to a familial society rooted in filial piety. This chapter might then be regarded as contributing to the discussion on how the old Confucian order, for the May Fourth thinkers, suppressed "personal freedom and individuality" and with it any profound engagement with such related concepts as individualism and loneliness.

Other traditions of Chinese thought besides Confucianism also, of course, influence the representation of individualism in Chinese novels. Daoism and Chan Buddhism may be even more important in this regard. Zhaoming Qian translates the Dao as "the Alone" in a reading of Wallace Stevens's "Six Significant Landscapes."[8] It is a "verse panel" by Stevens that "exemplifies Southern Song landscape painting" in an ekphrastic manner.[9] The poem describes an "old man" in a painting who "sits/ In the shadow of a pine tree / In China." Later in the poem, his role shifts "from that of a passive model to that of an active observer/seeing artist";[10] the "viewer *in* the landscape has metamorphosed into the viewer *of* the landscape." For Qian, this makes us "question our own identity as the reader/observer/artist" until finally in the last four meditative lines "all the distinctions among art, artist, model and observer disappear and everything in and beyond the poem … becomes one, moving along with the motion of the great 'cosmic rhythm.'"[11] This then is the "perfect experience of the Dao or 'the Alone,'" a state that cannot be represented. However, Qian's reading clearly demonstrates that if the original Chinese philosophy—Daoism—is all about getting the reader or viewer to experience such a state, a dynamic state of aloneness that is yet in sync with the cosmic rhythm, then the notion of a state of loneliness divorced from such unity runs counter to what much Chinese art strives to achieve. Experiencing "the Alone" is all about giving the readers the opportunity to "feel the breathing of nature and to become one with it."[12] Qian reminds us that Daoism and Confucianism are also expected to be "mutually complementary" philosophies[13] that together, in the words of Li Zehou, do yet foster practices of isolated individualism in Zhuangzi: "Confucius's respect for the individuality of the members of a clan … led directly to Zhuangzi's idea of independent individuals who abandon the world and isolate themselves from secular concerns."[14] With its preference for "forgetting self," Qian is still able to write in 2003 that the "Daoist aesthetic cannot be fully appreciated by Western readers."[15] Qian is clear that with its instinct "for expressing meaning impersonally" Chinese artists "disciplined by Daoist notions would not allow personal identity to be revealed."[16] This does of course pose problems for examining the representation of loneliness. With this rich philosophical and artistic tradition in mind, I read extracts on family, language, and personal identity from a classic eighteenth century novel alongside extracts from twentieth and twenty-first century novelists. While only a beginning, the intention is to gesture towards how such modern works of art respond to the political climate of their times in detailing the unravelling of such traditions as dynastic rule and the emergence of impersonality in the novel.

The obvious feature of the Western modernist novel as encountered in Joyce, Proust, Woolf, and Richardson is its exploration of different forms for representing what might be described as a radical individualism. Such motivation in fiction often had political connotations but some recent criticism on Chinese narratives of the twentieth century explains how these forms were slow to take in China. Ban Wang in "The People in the Modern Chinese Novel" describes how "individualism" was often a taboo subject for the socialist humanism taught by the likes of Zhou Libo in the Lu Xun Academy in China in the late 1930s.[17] However, it was not only Chinese scholars who objected to the deeply self-reflective experiments in the European novel. European scholars such as Georg Lukács also questioned the value of such subjectivity in the novel. Lukács writes that "specific individuality cannot be separated from the context in which they were created."[18] Lukács was, of course, adopting a Marxist or cultural materialist approach. Today in the Chinese university system, a system that is expected to be "guided by Marxism," there is a very different sense of "specific individuality" being promoted by the Xi Jinping Thought strand of Marxist thought. The meaning of socialist humanism and revolutionary subjectivity has changed a great deal in the Marxist context since Lukács's day. This transformation also affects the representation of individualism. So, for example, how do we read in Hong Kong and in China today older European Marxist notions of the "people," "shared victimhood," and the reaction against traditional romantic notions that see historical communities in terms of an organic *longue durée* and as deeply embedded in time-honored national traditions? Ban Wang also seems to champion a vision of Chinese neo-Marxist democracy in his reading of narrative.[19] Wang finishes his reading of the Modern Chinese novel with a quote from Mao on the "world communist movement." However, Wang tells us that the word Mao chose for communist in the essay was *datong*, which can also mean "great community of the world"; Wang then relates this usage to a book by the Chinese philosopher Kang Youwei, *Datong Shu* or "book of world community," which allows Wang to finish this essay by arguing that any such use of the word *datong* "envisions a forum of cultural exchange in humanist knowledge between East and West."[20] We are back then with yet another strident claim for the value of cross-cultural humanities.

However, despite these differences perhaps we can agree cross-culturally that we are living in an age where people are described as "interconnected loners" because we are experiencing an "epidemic of loneliness"; as Yiyun Li writes: "[w]e now live in an ever-connected world, allocated only the wishful thinking of privacy and solitude."[21] The means of recording such isolation, examined thus far in terms of "essential loneliness," "existential loneliness," "sentimental loneliness," and the "lonely voice" of the submerged populations, is often very different in Chinese novels. If one of the most enduring European textual vehicles for the contemplation and exploration of individuality and for the representation of solitude, aloneness, and loneliness is no longer capable of captivating or capturing loneliness today for our young readers, where has the high art of loneliness and introspection shifted? What might it mean in an age of "connected loners" and a "loneliness epidemic," when 9 million in the UK alone report feeling lonely much of the time, for there no longer to be this narrative vehicle?

The philosopher Wang Yangming sees the practice of filial piety as the prime example for the unity of ethical knowledge and action in Chinese writing.[22] In such novels as the *The Story of the Stone* and the twentieth-century novels *Waiting*, *Balzac and the Little Chinese Seamstress*, and *Red Sorghum*, novels that are either firmly entrenched in the dynastic order or are looking back to a time when society was being ravaged in making the transition to modernity, family is often all there is. One might argue that the rites and claims of family seem to intrude more into the actions and exchanges of the characters in their environments than in many of the Western works from the same period. For example, Cao Xueqin's contemporaries—Swift, Sterne, and Goldsmith—were

Irish expat writers who moved to London and sometimes back again in exploring issues of identity that even then seem less anchored to family values. These writers were writing from a position of expatriate isolation; their writing then mediates this either through assuming masks—often orientalist masks—as foreigners from cultures they knew little about or, in the case of Swift, by creating explorers who appear ever eager to fly the nets of family. While many key Chinese novels of the twentieth century explore the playful negation of traditional family expectations much of the action is still grounded on an awareness and observance of these familial expectations. For example, even though Mo Yan's *Red Sorghum* brutalizes and ravages family in a novel depicting the Civil War and the Sino-Japanese war, the novel still allows family to provide the narrator with the last zone of identity in a war-torn community. How many family members, cousins, and ancestors do we meet in these novels? In such European masterpieces as *Ulysses* family often seems absent or simply a placeholder for the free play of individualism; there are only the two Blooms really, Molly and Leopold, and in *À la recherche* Marcel only briefly relays encounters with parents as a catalyst for extensive personal self-reflection.

In comparing narratives cross-culturally and in recalling Moretti's terminology that reads narratives as species, can we argue that such analogies are implicitly enabling of the generative and familial reading of narrative? If narratives embody a species-identity, can they embody a living for generation or a generational imperative? Stephen C. Angle reminds us, in referring to the work of one of the earliest Neo-Confucians, Zhang Zai (1020–77), that filial piety forms a central concern of much Chinese philosophy and it leads to an outlook where "[a]ll people are my brothers and sisters." Even the dynastic ruling system and the emperor himself are to be regarded in this Neo-Confucian philosophy in terms of family: "The great ruler [i.e., emperor] is the eldest son of my parents [i.e. Heaven and Earth] … Even those who are tired, infirm, crippled, or sick; those who have no brothers or children, wives or husbands; all are my brothers who are in distress and have no one to turn to."[23] The ideal also for Confucianism, as expressed in the *Mencius*, is that even in the most desperate circumstances where his father is trying to kill him, that the sage-king Shun is still able to feel "filial love, and act accordingly" towards such a father.[24] Of course, the end of the Imperial Order brought dramatic shifts and civil wars ravaged family life in ways that would have been inconceivable for such Confucian scholars. However, despite the ravaging of family life due to civil wars and the cultural revolution that is depicted in the following Chinese novels, one still discerns a key regard for filial piety and a traumatic and haunting sense of guilt at its disturbance that overwhelms individualism in ways that is rarely so apparent in the twentieth-century Western works we have read.

Filial piety, family, and our connection with the idea of the "virtue of ancestors implanted in us"[25] is, as Jia Zheng says in *The Story of the Stone*, mirrored through our representation of our relationship with nature. Zheng writes that we must find this virtue in the "careful analysis of nature" that then enables us "to find characters"[26] that reconnect one with family. The novel speaks for an environmental awareness that is badly needed today. Bao-yu's father, Jia Zheng reminds us, "But without large hills and ravines in one's breast (liberal capacities), how could one attain such imagination!"[27] However, the Chinese characters chosen to describe the landscape and gardens and the family's place in them are all chosen so as to fulfil the "principles of etiquette" considered appropriate for an Imperial Dynasty consort's "visit to her parents."[28] The family code extends to the representation of the relationship between its members and their environment. This is very different from the contemporary destruction of the landscape that Cao's Western contemporaries such as Oliver Goldsmith lament in their work. In Goldsmith's long narrative poem "The Deserted Village" the speaker similarly laments a drastic change coming to society but it is, for this expatriate writer, more about the loss of a sense of community associated with village life than about the loss of a family order. The reason the description of the individual's place in the environment and hence the grounding in a philosophy of filial piety and dynastic succession is so different in Cao Xueqin might lie in the close relationship between filial piety and a filiality or faithfulness with regard to how the person integrates written characters with the natural landscapes that surround them. This is the filiality of the proper representation triggered by the careful analysis of nature. This idea is, one might argue, already being framed by inauthenticity in Goldsmith by way of his mask of Englishness. In looking again more closely at the remarks on filial piety in *The Story of the Stone*, we can explore this connection with regard to the emperor:

In the whole there is (in his opinion), no more essential thing than filial piety; maintaining that the feelings of the father, mother, son and daughter are indiscriminately subject to one principle, without any distinction between honourable and mean. The present Emperor himself day and night waits upon their majesties his Father and the Empress Dowager, and yet cannot, in the least degree, carry out to the full his ideal of filial piety. The secondary consorts, meritorious persons, and other inmates of the Palace, he remembered, had entered within its precincts many years back, casting aside fathers and mothers, so how could they not help thinking of them? Besides, the fathers and mothers, who remain at home must long for their daughter of whom they cannot get even so much as a glimpse, and if, through this solicitude, they were to contract any illness, the harmony of heaven would also be seriously impaired, so for this reason he memorialised the Emperor, his father, and the Empress Dowager that every month, on the recurrence of the second and sixth days, permission should be accorded to the relatives of the Imperial consorts to enter the palace and make application to see their daughters. The Emperor, his father, and Empress Dowager were, forthwith, much delighted by this representation, and eulogised in high terms, the piety and generosity of the present Emperor, his regard for the will of heaven and his research into the nature of things. Both their sacred Majesties consequently also issued a decree to the effect: that the entrance of the relatives of the Imperial consorts into the Palace could not but interfere with the dignity of the state, and the rules of conventional rites, but that as the mothers and daughters could not gratify the wishes of their hearts, their Majesties would, after all, show a high proof of expedient grace, and issue a special command [...] by virtue of which the worthy relations of the imperial consorts could enter the palace on the second day and sixth days, any family, having extensive accommodation and separate courts suitable for the cantonment of the imperial bodyguard, could, without any detriment, make application to the Inner Palace, for the entrance of the Imperial chair into the private residences, to the end that the personal feelings of relations might be gratified, and that they should collectively enjoy the bliss of a family reunion.[29]

This is a remarkable passage in terms of what it says about the removal of the "sacred" majesties to the actual homes of the families whose daughters and consorts work for the emperor. Rites are to be bent to observe the demands of filial piety to the extent that families can even "make application to the Inner Palace, for the entrance of the Imperial chair into the private residences." This is so that "the personal feelings of relations might be gratified, and that they should collectively enjoy the bliss of a family reunion." It is suggestive of great generosity on the part of the emperor for the service of filial piety. However, the very fact that the relationship with the landscape and how it is encapsulated in written characters works also for the service of this "ideal of filial piety" demonstrates the inherent connection between the "harmony of heaven" and the representation of this harmony between humanity and its environment as realized in the "ideal of filial piety." Jia Zheng also realizes, before the arrival of his imperial consort daughter, that the "points of beauty" of the landscape cannot be fully appreciated if the landscape is not accompanied by characters literally "harmonizing" with the landscape by being pitched on it:

> Were now, for the time being, two, three, or four characters fixed upon, harmonizing with the scenery, to carry out, for form's sake, the idea, and were they provisionally utilized as mottoes for the lanterns, tablets, and scrolls, and hung up, pending the arrival of her highness ... when she could be requested to decide upon the devices, would not two exigencies be met with satisfactorily?[30]

The lovers of the novel, Daiyu and Baoyu, are also beautifully described in terms of how they differ in relation to partaking in company. We learn that Daiyu is someone who avoids "social gatherings" so she will not feel the resulting "loneliness" when the party breaks up:

> Lin Daiyu had a natural predilection for retirement. She did not care for social gatherings. Her notions, however, were not entirely devoid of reason. She maintained that people who gathered together must soon part; that when they came together, they were full of rejoicing, but did they not feel lonely when they broke up? That since this sense of loneliness gave rise to chagrin, it was consequently preferable not to have any gatherings. That flowers afforded an apt example. When they opened, they won people's admiration; but when they faded, they added to the feeling of vexation; so that better were it if they did not blossom at all! To this cause therefore must be assigned the fact that when other people were glad, she, on the contrary, felt unhappy.[31]

Since we learn next that Baoyu "simply yearned for frequent gatherings" and wished for flowers to "bloom repeatedly" and was "haunted with the dread of their dying in a little time" it seems that the novel prefigures here the tendency for Daiyu and Baoyu's love to be grounded on a difference of perspective, one that speaks for the time-bound value of narrative itself and how it must embody this acceptance of difference. Like our current students in the Hong Kong schools we quizzed, Baoyu also feels school is all about competition, dishonesty, and "worming themselves into a job"[32] This leads him to feel immense loneliness in school:

> He reflected on their exceptionally boorish appearance, and the face of Qin Zhong came suddenly into his mind. Since the death of his friend there had been no one to keep him company in his studies, no one to share his innermost thoughts. He was overwhelmed with a sense of grief and loneliness, and sat silently staring at his books."[33]

The Story of the Stone is a novel where family dynamics encompass any relationship with the environment. A generational narrative of family can never be a narrative of individualist introspection; the novel's somewhat painful description of the decline of one family within a larger dynastic order that was also moving towards its end is a powerful commentary on community and environmentalism and of the necessity for both to work in harmony.

In moving forward 200 years to the end of the Imperial Order and with it the notion of a "sacred" familial order overseeing the Great Void, after the long Chinese civil war, and the Sino-Japanese war, and after the practical usurpation of the State over the familial order in the one-child policy, we still have key Chinese novels of nation centered around family. However, family here is very often treated by way of its graphic destruction and desecration; an older family order is being torn apart. Mo Yan's *Red Sorghum* gives us a detailed, graphic depiction of the destruction of family order in China in the twentieth century; it is so meticulously described and so harrowing that one comes to read it as a metaphor for China's painful self-extraction from the legacies of rule under a dynastic order. Mo Yan's novel, told from the perspective of a son who sees life and understands life solely through the suffering of his father, mother, grandparents, and great-grandparents, gives us possibly the most

Filial Piety and Loneliness 163

painful rendering in modern narrative of the death of the mother—a macabre Madonna and child portrait—with the son cradling the bleeding breast of his mother, which is riddled with shotgun wounds:

> Father falls to his knees, drapes her arms around his neck, then stands up with difficulty, lifting her off the ground. Fresh blood quickly soaks his neck and assails his nose with the aroma of sorghum wine. His legs tremble under the weight of her body, he staggers into the sorghum field as bullets whizz overhead ... He strains to crawl out from under her, and after he lays her out on her back, she looks up, breathes a long sigh, and smiles weakly. Unfathomable mystery is embedded in that smile, an iron that burns a horseshoe brand into his memory.[34]

The novel describes the brutal civil wars and the Sino-Japanese wars of the 1930s. The protagonist relives the events through recounting them as experienced by his parents and grandparents. He struggles to find an individual voice separate from that of a family he has seen, if only in his mind's eye, savaged and also guilty of carnage. Towards the end of the novel, we expect to find him emerging from behind his ancestors only for the guilt of remembrance and commemoration to become too strong. He returns from the city after ten years to his family's village in Northeast Gaomi Township, a village that had been massacred by the Japanese in 1939. Even now he can't find an authentic individual response since he becomes aware of how he stands before his Second Grandma's grave "affecting the hypocritical display of affection I had learned from high society."[35] He becomes aware of the incommensurable gap between the new urban life and the old life of savagery, civil war, and barbarism: "There are, it appears, two separate human races, each evolving in accordance with its own value system."[36] He becomes conscious of how difficult it is to speak for what his family has experienced: "I have begun to utter the words that others have spoken, themselves repeating the words of still others. Have I no voice of my own?"[37] As he stares at the land and at the red sorghum, he hears the land speaking to him and once again, when we thought we would hear his own individual voice, he becomes smothered by the voices of his family:

> Then a desolate sound comes from the heart of the land. It is both familiar and strange, like my grandad's voice, yet also like my father's voice, and

like Uncle Arhut's voice, and like the resonant singing voices of Grandma, Second Grandma, and Third Grandma, the woman Liu. The ghosts of my family are sending me a message to point the way out of this labyrinth:

You pitiable, frail, suspicious, stubbornly biased child, whose soul has been spellbound by poisonous wine, go down to the Black Water River and soak in its waters for three days and three nights … Then you can return to your real world. Besides the yang of White Horse Mountain and the yin of the Black Water River, there is also a stalk of pure-red sorghum which you must sacrifice everything, if necessary, to find. When you have found it, wield it high as you re-enter a world of dense brambles and wild predators. It is your talisman, as well as our family's glorious totem and a symbol of the heroic spirit of Northeast Gaomi Township.[38]

The trauma of a family experience that has not yet been fully recounted, one you cannot fully bear witness to, one that cannot fully be represented requires the sacrifice of everything, if necessary. In speaking for the family, the protagonist will find his own voice, one that has been tainted by the ten years in the city. It is almost impossible to feel a sense of isolation in the protagonist or to ever catch him deliberating on loneliness; the relationship with the family is all-consuming.

Dai Sijie is a Chinese novelist who writes in French and whose works celebrate their allegiance to the tradition of the European novel. *Balzac and the Little Chinese Seamstress* is a novel that describes how a chance encounter with a suitcase of banned western novels alerts two young Chinese teenagers sent down to a remote village for re-education under the Chinese Communist Party to a new sense of individualism, a sense of individualism that will bring them to play out in their own lives versions of the tragic denouements and passion-fueled affairs that only a heightened appreciation of individualism can incite, what the heroes and heroines of the European novels they read embody for them in the face of family disapproval and local customs. At one point the protagonist reflects on how Romain Rolland's novel *Jean-Christophe* changed his life: "But Jean-Christophe, with his fierce individualism utterly untainted by malice, was a salutary revelation. Without him I would never have understood the splendor of taking free and independent action as an individual. Up until this stolen encounter with Romain Rolland's hero, my poor educated and re-educated brains had been incapable of grasping the notion of one man standing up against the whole world".[39] However, it leads to the very kind of "possessive individualism that Pang Laikwan argues in *The Art of Cloning* is a unique aspect of western culture very different to the kind of self-copying or cloning that she argues was essential to the work of both intellectuals and villagers during the cultural revolution. The protagonist of the novel recalls how "[m]y passion for *Jean-Christophe* was so great that, for the first time in my life, I wanted something to be my very own rather than a possession I shared with Luo".[40] The form of the novel shifts to convey this heightened awareness of individualism gleaned from western novels with each chapter in the second half of the novel being presented from the perspective of a different character. We learn that the heroine of the novel, the Chinese seamstress, also learns about the performance of identity from how they act out together different scenes from the novels: "It was a totally new experience for me. Before, I had no idea that you could take on the role of a completely different person, actually become that person – a rich lady, for example – and still be your own self."[41] Sijie's description of these lessons in the practice of individualism and performance through the characters' retellings of the stories from the western novels is also a metaphor for his own exploration of authorial identity and creative practice in becoming an author. In the end, however, even this book describing the value of Western narratives to two young Chinese teenagers ends with them burning the stash of Western books:

> And Luo wouldn't be able to marry the Little Seamstress for several years, given that marriage under the age of twenty-five was illegal. The situation was hopeless. There was nowhere for them to go, for there was no conceivable place where a Romeo and his pregnant Juliet might elude the long arm of the law, nor indeed where they might live the life of Robinson Crusoe attended by a secret agent turned Man Friday. Every nook and cranny of the land came under the all-seeing eye of the dictatorship of the proletariat, which had cast its gigantic, fine-meshed net over the whole of China.[42]

Sijie's next novel *Once on a Moonless Night* continues this exploration of creative practice by a young Chinese artist eager to learn from the encounter with artworks from beyond the pale of Chinese propaganda works. In the more autobiographical sections from the novel, Sijie recalls how, the protagonist, an alter ego, liked to make "Western coffee" and to play "cassettes of French songs" while a student in Beijing at the university with the "best reputation in all China".[43] However, he is an isolated and lonely figure there:

> In my isolation, the only thing I learnt in class by way of literature were the words of Mao [...] Lying in bed in the mornings I would often picture myself at death's door, struck down by some fatal illness, and I would start composing my own obituary under the title *A Revolutionary Parrot Beneath the Peking Sun*. At night, locked in my room, I would sleep for ten hours, sometimes more, as there were no nightclubs anywhere, or concert halls or cinemas screening anything other than propaganda films…There was a great wall covered in weeds and moss between China and me.[44]

Once again, an author's recounting of a moment of intense isolation and loneliness is described as the ground from which creative individualism took seed. Ironically, however, it is only by leaving China and following the trail of a French Sinologist named Paul d'Ampere in a Borgesian search for a lost segment of an ancient scroll that the protagonist becomes acquainted with the profound depths of his Chinese culture, a scholarly quest that takes him back once again to a lengthy investigation into the archives of the imperial dynasty and the work of three of its emperors to preserve this archive. In the end, it seems that loneliness is the defining feature of the young protagonist but also a means through which he finds a creative voice beyond re-education, propaganda and a scholarly reverence to an old dynastic order that gives him the courage to write about his own experiences and to make the young artist his "only protagonist" over and over again: "Ma had other friends besides me. Lots of friends. He always did, wherever he went. People being re-educated, locals, prisoners, thieves, tramps, girls, boys, young, old. I didn't. I'm lonely as a red-haired horse. My life, no, let's say the chapter on friendship, began with Ma and he's still the only protagonist."[45]

Another novel that clearly depicts social transformations with regard to familial expectations in the move to modernization in Chinese society is Ha Jin's *Waiting*. The novel spans approximately 20 years from 1963 to the mid-1980s. Lin Kong, a doctor living away from his wife and child, has been seeking a divorce for 17 years so he can marry his new love Manna Wu. Every summer he travels back to his home village to ask his wife for a divorce. At first, she agrees only to back out when confronted by the authorities. The novel is then an exploration of longing and loneliness in a Communist China struggling to transition from a feudal past into one where family composition is defined by Party diktat. However, the novel also presents us with regions in China, the rural and the urban, that experience these changes at different paces; the villagers in the home where his wife and child live understand completely why he must wait 17 years for a divorce whereas the urban environment associated with the much younger Manna Wu and her fiancé can no longer understand how such familial strictures stunt the progress of personal autonomy. At the end of the novel, Lin Kong realizes that his own family upbringing, one built on arranged marriages, family connections, and such old traditions as foot binding, has denied him the opportunity to love and that "emotionally he hadn't grown up."[46] Even at the end he is wracked by guilt over his duty to his family: "he knew he would have been weighed down with remorse if he had abandoned his family to seek his own happiness."[47] Despite their 17 years of waiting and longing to be married, both Lin and Manna end up lonely in their new life: "Isn't Manna a lonely woman herself? Did she imply that she didn't feel as lonely as Shuyu because she had a family intact?"[48] And Manna too recognizes during her final illness that Shuyu, Lin's first wife is also lonely: "She must be lonely, no family around except Hua."[49] Ha Jin also examines how Maoist philosophy can serve not to uphold traditional Confucian values but to enable people to snap out of their feelings of indebtedness to the Confucian familial inheritance. His roommate in the army camp advises him:

> "Forgive me for my candid words," Geng Yang said. "We're army men and shouldn't talk and think too much about a decision that has already been made. If you've decided to divorce your wife, you must carry it out by hook or by crook. What's the good of being a good man? You can't be nice to everybody, can you? In this case, damage is unavoidable. You have to choose which one of them to hurt."
>
> "I can't."
>
> "You're always afraid that people will call you a bad man. You strive to have a good heart. But what is a heart? Just a chunk of flesh that a dog can eat. . . .

"Yes. You know so much, but you can't act decisively." He closed his eyes and recited another quotation. "'Materialist dialectics holds that external causes are merely the condition of change whereas internal causes are the basis of change.' Who said that?"

"Chairman Mao in On Contradiction."

"See, you know everything, but nothing can make you steel yourself. If you really have the will to change, you can create the condition for change." "My case is not so simple." "Chairman Mao also said, 'If you want to know the taste of a pear, you must change the pear by eating it yourself.' Trust me, my friend, sleep with Manna. If you find her good in bed, you'll be more determined to get a divorce."[50]

Maoist materialist dialectics suggest Lin should pursue divorce; one system of dogma replaces another and yet not able to give himself up wholly to anything, not able to "love passionately," Lin only acts when it is too late and when the waiting itself has become what is longed for. In some ways then, the process of waiting becomes a metaphor for the "Chinese Dream," the dream of progress and modernization that will lead to a better life for all, a "Chinese Dream" where "all beautiful things can be created."[51] It is a Chinese Dream that marches endlessly "towards the future" and that will be achieved only if we wait and "close ranks" so that the "wisdom and strength of our 1.3 billion people [is turned] into an invincible force."[52]

It is worth recalling, at this point, how Western philosophers eager to privilege a "care of the self" have spoken of family. Foucault long ago acknowledged that care of the self, of the self he respected, "must completely reverse the system of values conveyed and laid down by the family."[53] He recalls Epictetus who advises that the ideal Cynic has no family because his family is mankind.[54] The responsibility for the "universal family is what prevents the Cynic from devoting himself to a particular household."[55] He also gives us a way of understanding self-examination and this glorification of the "care of the self"—a move he traces back to Socrates, Epictetus, etc. and others that then of course spearheads individualism in the Western narrative. He reminds us of both Socrates's notion of the examined life but also of Epictetus who advises that we all stand as "night watchmen" in relation to ourselves, like those who "checks the entries at the gate of cities or houses."[56] One must exercise on oneself the functions of a "tester of coinage," an "assayer," one of those moneychangers who won't accept any coin without having made sure of its worth."⁵⁷ Unlike Socrates, for Foucault, Epictetus "deals with representations, that aim to 'test' them, to 'distinguish' (*diakrinein*) one from another and thus to prevent one from accepting the 'first arrival.'"⁵⁸ He asks, in a way that recalls the words of the imperial consort when she visits the Jia family's gardens and lands in *The Story of the Stone*: "Do you have your token from nature, the one which every representation which is to be accepted must have?"⁵⁹ Foucault argues that "[w]hen a representation enters the mind, the work of discrimination, of *diakrisis*, will consist in applying to it the famous Stoic canon that marks the division between that which does not depend on us and that which does."⁶⁰ Obviously, when a narrative tradition bends to the generational imperative there are certain named dependents and the filial piety is presumed. For Epictetus, one inspects so that "one will not become attached to that which does not come under our control."⁶¹ But how does this pan out when the object is family?

> To keep constant watch over one's representation, or to verify their marks the way one authenticates a currency, is not to inquire (as will be done later in Christianity) concerning the deep origin of the idea that presents itself; it is not to try and decipher a meaning hidden beneath the visible representation; it is to assess the relationship between oneself and that which is represented, so as to accept in the relation to the self only that which can depend on the subject's free and rational choice.⁶²

Is Foucault suggesting that narrative and storytelling in the Western tradition must then also act as a kind of "night watchman" or a medium through which our self-analysis works? Are we only to allow certain representations to pass through; narrative is, of course, also that which can sway our understanding of what is free and rational.

Monica Fludernik's natural narratology is also useful for a cross-cultural reading of narrative. The idea of narrative as grounded on "universal cognitive schemas"⁶³ and not as "a quality adhering to a text"⁶⁴ but instead as an "attribute imposed on the text by the reader who interprets the text *as narrative*, thus *narrativizing* the text" can usefully explain differences in narrative traditions. In *Narrative Politics* Frederick Mayer also argues that our capacity for narrative is a key factor in explaining collective action since it explains internalization, emotional attachment, engrossment, and identity-making. Narrative politics and natural narratology can then explain collective action; the narratives we produce also internally explain our narrativization of the texts we read. Fludernik describes the importance of narrative in terms of its "*experientiality*"[65] and this suggests that the feelings and emotions narratives elicit are central. These issues also raise the question of a private language and a public language at the individual level. Yes, narratives explain collective action and readers narrativize texts in line with traditions of collective action in different cultures, but for the writer, the producer of narrative, there is also the daily battle with this collective action in narrative and this is one aspect of individualism that I now wish to examine in the Chinese writer Yiyun Li.

Yiyun Li and the Lack of a "Private Language"

Yiyun Li's *Dear Friend from My Life I Write to You in Your Life* is a contemporary and more experimental Chinese narrative that foregrounds the individual voice over and above any sense of filial piety or dynastic order. Yiyun Li's *Dear Friend* (from Mansfield) is essentially a contemplation of the loneliness of the writer, a writer recently discharged from an institution for those needing fulltime psychological care after a suicide attempt. Yiyun Li's memoir is a rich intertext built on the reading experiences of a lifetime and on how these influenced her own writing. Li covers many of the great writers in delving into their diaries and letters to each other to discover how agents and events such as overpowering mothers, tactful fathers, and lives lived in solitude with books influence the readers and writers we become. It is a deeply emotional book and Li is battling with the demons that led her to seek hospitalisation. There is careful reading and extended commentary on so many European and American writers, spirit guides during a lifetime of reading. She looks into every detail of what she can garner about their personal lives in order to find sustenance for her own behaviours and the person they suggest to her. She discusses many of the great Russian writers

(Turgenev, Dostoevsky, Tolstoy), Irish writers (Bowen, McGahern, William Trevor especially), English writers (Hardy, Lawrence, Larkin). We find long extended pieces on the American authors Marilyn Moore and Hemingway and on the European novelist Stefan Zweig; there are pieces on Mansfield and MacPherson. And yet in this emotional journey of this Chinese writer contemplating growing up in China and then becoming an international author there is very little, if any, references made to Chinese authors. The only novelist briefly mentioned is Chen Duansheng, an eighteenth-century novelist who wrote a novel in verse—*The Tale of Renewed Connections*—that Yiyun Li tells us she can't finish. Li also tells us that at one point in her writing career she made a list of Chinese poets with the same surname as her and tried to read them all. She completes the short few lines on this episode by saying "What attracted me to their work, I now realize, was their unreadableness."[66] There is then not a single work of Chinese narrative—apart from a late reference to *The Story of the Stone*—that Li appeals to in recovering from a life and death situation through the meticulous exploration of narratives that have been important to her in giving her some understanding of the writing life. How might this relate then to what Frank O'Connor describes in *The Lonely Voice* as the "submerged populations" that are necessary for a treatment of loneliness?

Li also relates the writer's urge for narrative to the distinction between what she describes as a public and a private language. Li always wrote in English choosing not to write in Chinese and she calls English her private language. What she is describing here is the idea, one feels, that one has the ability to employ a form of communication that allows one room for reflection and deliberation and that these moments of communication are quite distinct from the kinds of communication one takes up in society, in work, and in politics. She found that Chinese could not be a private language for her. She asks can "one's intelligence rely entirely on the public language; can one form a precise thought, recall an accurate memory, or even feel a genuine feeling, with only the public language?"[67] Yiyun Li writes that the idea that "one could reach a point where the border between public and private language no longer matters is frightening";[68] she writes that much of what one does to seek happiness and stay healthy is to "keep a space for one's private language." The "automatic participation in life, however, can turn that space into a secured tomb." She argues that "loneliness is the inability to speak with another in one's private language."[69]

It is Li's treatment of experientiality that suggests different cultural experiences might produce different narratives in different cultures not because of the texts themselves but because the readers have traditionally brought different expectations, narrativize differently, and thus produce a different kind of experientiality. The background of the generational imperative, so strong for narratives such as those of Cao Xueqin, written within a dynastic order, is not always there in more contemporary Chinese texts written in English, French, and Chinese. The twentieth century was a turbulent time for Chinese authors and artists, as Pang Laikwan and others have demonstrated, and many resorted to a saving "art of cloning." Whether this also resulted in the kind of cloneliness we are witnessing today is difficult to know. Loneliness, then, and its related conditions of introspection, isolation and aloneness with its potential for allowing us to find a private language enables us to rise out of debilitating loneliness, very often in creative ways, so that we can "speak with another in one's private language".

8

"I Am Trash": How Student Stress and Student Self-Stratification Is Creating a Generation of "Interconnected Loners" [with Flora Ka Yu Mak]

Introduction

This chapter examines how extreme levels of competition are affecting young people in secondary schools in Hong Kong and leading them to regard their peers as competitors rather than classmates. This situation is not, of course, unique to Hong Kong; many recent studies have documented similar situations elsewhere.[1] The intense competition heightens stress levels among students that leads to students self-stratifying themselves; the school system therefore contributes to their feelings of isolation, factors that push students further towards the state of "interconnected loners." Research into student mental health and the recent rise in full-time students committing suicide reveals strong correlations between student stress and attempted suicide.[2]

Competition for places at public university is intense in Hong Kong. As a result, students highlight the effects of competition in their responses. They also engage in self-stratification that reveals low self-esteem and high levels of stress. The Hong Kong government has implemented wide-ranging structural changes to the education system in recent years[3] and many of these changes have been made with the intention of alleviating what previous governments and Education Bureau papers have variously referred to as "old elitism"[4] and "inequality."[5] However, studies reveal that inequality,[6] the number of working poor families in Hong Kong,[7] and student stress levels[8] have increased dramatically in recent years in Hong Kong while social mobility[9] and graduate opportunities have declined. Structural educational reforms such as the DSS school system and the "through-road" system have been described as either increasing inequality or leading to a sometimes corrupt[10] and "privatised" school system[11] while increased test-taking (TSA and HKDSSE) has brought parents out onto the streets. We therefore felt it was important to examine the results of this competitive system on students' perceptions of university and on their self-perceptions of their chances of getting a place in university. The competition and stress on young people is a hot topic in local media.[12] It is therefore important to investigate the relationship between stratification, both institutionalized and internalized, and students' perceptions of competition. We believe that the banding system in Hong Kong is a key factor in the education system in Hong Kong. It sustains high levels of competition and stress, it is hugely influential on students in determining whether they will gain a place at a UGC university, and it is also enabling of government policy that continues to maintain a relatively low participation rate in degree courses at UGC universities. We also argue that our research findings reveal how students from lower band schools and from family backgrounds where one parent, or both parents, did not attend university have internalized the "success narrative" of a competitive and unequal education system.

Student Stress and the Competitive Education Environment in Hong Kong

Studies argue that stress is the result of an individual's perception that they do not have the resources to cope with a perceived situation from the past, present, or future.[13] Competition is strongly associated with stress. Studies reveal that stress is caused by something that appears as a threat or a task.[14] Paul Verhaeghe explains how even our understanding of identity is rooted in notions of equality; he reminds us that identity and identification have the same etymology, deriving from *idem*, Latin for "equal";[15] therefore, identity is strongly motivated by feelings that we *should* be equal to some peer group or even to some elite group. Tests and admission examinations can be the first life experiences that alert us to perceived inequalities in society.

The Hong Kong education pathway is riddled with admissions tests, intelligence tests, and academic tests. This results in self-perceptions and self-stratifications whereby gaining a place at a UGC Hong Kong university is often experienced as an impossible task. Stress levels therefore increase as students progress towards their HKDSE exams.[16] The local population is deeply concerned about the issue. This year, at least three surveys have been conducted by different social organizations on the stress levels of HKDSE students: the Hong Kong Federation of Youth Groups, Hong Kong Sheng Kung Hui Welfare Council, Education 2.1. All three surveys report high levels of stress among students at different stages of HKDSE. For example, the Hong Kong Federation of Youth Groups survey reached over 850 exam candidates through surveys and phone interviews. Over 50.1 percent of the respondents report a stress level of 7–10 on a scale of 10. The organization also has a record of over 1,300 cases asking for emotional help two months before the release of the public exam results. Other studies reveal that stress levels of students are also strongly affected by competition and by having to work part-time and even full-time jobs while taking their degrees.[17] However, the tragedy is that the students are not aware of the fact that they are stressed. They see it as the norm. In seeing such stress levels as the norm, they are completely unprepared both physically and mentally for the psychological, emotional, and physical symptoms such stress levels undoubtedly bring on. Their coping mechanisms atrophy because they see slowing down and reflecting on the symptoms of stress and the resulting feelings and emotions as a bar to further achievement in academic and career goals.

Studies in Europe and the United States reveal that some students experience significant levels of stress[18] and that students are increasingly suffering mental health problems. However, a majority of studies of stress seem to focus on "Western" academic environments and many on medical and nursing students.[19] Ka-hung Leung has written a 1994 MA dissertation on stress amongst Hong Kong secondary school students that compares and contrasts stress levels and depression across two classes. Leung's study reveals that the key stressors were tests and examinations and Leung finds that this correlates with the only other study found on Hong Kong students at the time.[20] Other international studies also reveal that students suffered disturbing feelings due to such factors as highly competitive academic environment, doubts about personal worth, and loneliness and fear of failing.[21] We argue in this essay that the students we questioned also describe the same fears and feelings with regard to loneliness and self-worth. Doubts about personal worth seem to have evolved to become engrained practices of self-stratification whereby students accept in an almost resigned fashion their place in an institutionally sanctioned pecking order.

Robotham also argues that the majority of previous studies on student stress has focused on a "quantitative approach where participants complete a self-report inventory that claims to measure stress, well-being or stressors."[22] Not only are these stress assessor instruments then unsuited to assess the social, institutional and emotional context of stress among Hong Kong students, but they are also quantitative in nature. As Robotham argues, there is an assumption, in using such tests, that "stress is a concept that can be measured through what he calls "quasi-quantitative measures" and that quantifying the level of stress experienced may "intimidate the subjects".[23] This lack of a qualitative approach to stress levels in Hong Kong can only be remedied by research that focuses more on the subjective explanations students give indirectly for what appear as symptoms of stress since they are often unaware of the fact that they are suffering from stress. This book has therefore focused on the representation of loneliness in literature and philosophy; in this chapter we employ open-ended questions to enable students to reveal how competition and parental and societal expectations affect their self-perception and self-stratification.

School Banding in Hong Kong

School banding in Hong Kong is an integral part, if not the cornerstone, of the competitive education system in Hong Kong. Studies reveal that parents' ambitions for their sons and daughters, not ranking rubrics, educational globalization, or credentialization is the key motivating factor for greater competition and ultimately greater inequality in education today.[24] This is nowhere more pronounced than in Hong Kong where an "old elitism" associated with colonialism, race. and rank has been replaced by a meritocratic "new elitism" that has been championed by former chief executives[25] and that has paralleled Hong Kong's rising GINI coefficient that sees it being described as the developed city with the highest GINI coefficient in the world. Anita Poon argues that in this "highly competitive examination-oriented education system, both students and parents experience enormous pressure. A few lucky ones are able to stand out and succeed while the rest are losers."[26] This harsh meritocratic system is now reified by the government's adoption of such language in their policy documents and it has also been taken up by students and the media. An unproblematized and unchallenged use of the term "loser" in Hong Kong society suggests that there is an unwillingness to get at the roots of a societal practice that marks out young people as inadequate before they have even started school. Competition is so intense that one recent news story caused a stir when a local parent advised all families to start planning from the "moment of ejaculation."[27] A survey by the Hong Kong Institute of Asia-Pacific Studies this August shows that 90 percent of respondents perceive "winning from the starting line" as a common social ideology.[28] Education Bureau documents themselves employ the language of winners and losers in exhibiting a very limited psychological awareness of how such descriptors can take root in a society. The Education Commission Document of 1999 reads: "Our education system appears to have stagnated in the industrial age. The system still caters to a selected few, while disadvantaging the majority and creating a large number of 'losers.'"[29] The result is that there is very often no middle ground. Psychologist Paul Verhaeghe's prognosis for deeply meritocratic systems that "reward the most intelligent and industrious" and "punishes the rest" is that they soon "becomes toxic to its citizens."[30] He argues that in societies where the focus is entirely about "separation and individualism," which is precisely what highly meritocratic and competitive societies promote through their testocratic practices, "group forming suffers, leading to competition, social isolation, and loneliness".[31] This chapter aims to explore firsthand how a highly competitive schools and university system in Hong Kong demonstrates such a tendency with students internalizing the results of the testocratic system resulting in self-stratification, low self-esteem and feelings of being resigned to a fate outside elite universities. Highly competitive and test-based school systems teach students to see each other as competitors for limited places thereby privileging an individualist outlook embodied in self-stratification that works against "group forming" and community building. Students seldom look beyond the forms of classification and credentialization granted by universities in assessing their emotional and social needs for the future and loneliness and social isolation are likely to result when the students feel they are inadequate or performing badly in regard to standards laid down by their society.

Students' Awareness and Internalization of School Banding

School banding is described in research papers as "confidential"[32] and by students who have gone through the system as an "open-secret." Studies describe it as creating a "stable stratification system."[33] However, school banding marks Hong Kong students for life. As Melissa Benn writes with regard to the banding process in UK schools, "the damaging labels endured, throughout our school lives and beyond."[34] School banding has changed in recent years in Hong Kong with the stated intention of tackling "inequality"[35] and nurturing a new "meritocratic" system. However, Hong Kong society has become more unequal and more elitist. While previously there were five different bands of school in Hong Kong, now there are only three. Band 1 schools are the best performing in terms of student entry scores and Band 3 have the lowest student entry scores. The allocation system for secondary schools has also changed in recent years. The new "through-road" system reduces the percentage of principal-selected students from 65 percent to at most 20 percent and increases that of the centrally allocated students from 35 percent to 50 percent with up to 30 percent being "automatic" admissions for the siblings of the current students and the children of the staff in the schools.[36] However, it is important to recall that school banding is a misnomer. In reality, it is not the school that is receiving a "grade" or a "score," but the pupil. Teachers in Hong Kong speak openly of their schools having, for example, approximately 80 percent Band 1 pupils. Teachers know that it is the students who carry the band with them. Before the pupils enter secondary school, they are given a grade and score based on their performance in tests usually conducted over the final two years of their studies in primary school. Students then choose up to twenty secondary schools in order of preference. They are assigned to secondary schools based on their grades by the Education Bureau. The top school will be the school with the most first-preference selections from students with the highest scores. The large majority of government school places are filled in this way. The students' individual scores before they enter secondary school are kept by the Education Bureau in Hong Kong. These scores are confidential. However, parents are well aware of the "bands" of schools despite the fact that the bands are officially confidential. It's a case of the Emperor's New Clothes; everyone knows the reality of the situation but no one is willing to openly discuss the situation for fear that the hierarchical order will fall down about them and take their children with it.

The choice of school and the school a student is assigned has a direct result on their performance 6 years later in the HKDSE exams that decide their university place. Obtaining C grades in Chinese and English, for example, is essential to gaining admission to university in Hong Kong. About 50 percent of students fail to meet these requirements for both English and Chinese and therefore cannot go on to university. Only the better-equipped schools and the better off schools have the resources to ensure there is adequate training for these exams in English and Chinese.

Social Fixation

Social fixation is then clearly a factor among young people and parents in Hong Kong. It is obvious that, despite the Education Bureau's effort to eliminate the labelling effect, society takes its place to reinforce the concept of meritocracy, which worked well in the colonial past, when university places were inaccessible to the majority of local citizens and when obtaining a degree guaranteed social mobility. The social fixation is mirrored by the presence of secondary school guidebooks and websites. The Book of Schools and Schooland are two notable authentic-looking websites that list the banding of secondary schools, ranging from 1A to 3C, along with comprehensive analysis of their performance in aspects such as exam results, facilities, teacher qualifications, and participation in music and sports.[37] Similarly, guidebooks published by Education Info (HK) claim to reveal details related to confidential school banding.[38]

School Banding and Inequality in Hong Kong

There have been calls for greater measures to deal with educational inequality in Hong Kong. Leo F. Goodstadt writes that "the government made no effort to honour its commitment to ensure that children from low-income families had access to the best schools" and that "the poverty created by Hong Kong's Third World legacy and the current shortfalls in social expenditure could not be dismissed indefinitely. In 2009, the government conceded that individuals had been made vulnerable because they had no access "to essential services and opportunities such as housing, health care, education and employment, etc."[39]

Participation rates in universities are also relatively low although the government is trying to address this through associate degrees, the value and quality of which has been questioned, and through self-funded program.[40] The value and utility of these self-funded programs is also being questioned by university administrators and by students themselves when they gain very little financially from the degrees. The OECD average for entry levels of young people into university-level education in developed OECD countries is 62 percent and Australia, Poland, and New Zealand have figures of 80 percent or above.[41] The Higher Education Initial Participation Rate (HEIPR) for English domiciled first-time entrants to higher education courses in the United Kingdom was 40 percent for 2001–02.[42] In contrast, 15.8 percent of the Hong Kong population aged 15 or above have completed a degree course in 2011.[43] Recent UNESCO publications also reveal that Hong Kong's gross enrollment ratio for Bachelors programs is, even by Asian standards, middling at best and is comparable with the ratio in the Philippines and well behind that of Iran and Thailand.[44]

Research Methodology

In our study, we examined the questionanaire responses of 510 secondary school students in Hong Kong. The questionnaires were in English and Chinese. The secondary school students we examined were attending Forms 5 (ages 16–17) and 6 (ages 17–18) in government Band 1 and Band 2 schools. A small group of them were attending ESF schools and international schools in

Hong Kong. Government schools in Hong Kong are divided into three bands with bands 1 and 2 referring to the highest performing schools. International schools and ESF schools are EMI schools and are generally regarded as the most expensive schools in Hong Kong. They are also generally regarded as having high academic standards and in many of these schools a majority of students will go on to study at elite universities outside Hong Kong. Considering that the total number of students at these levels in Hong Kong government schools is approximately 60–70,000, the sample was representative with a 4 percent margin of error and 95 percent confidence level. However, the questionnaires include both closed-ended and open-ended questions. We chose questionnaires with a good deal of open-ended questions over individual interviews because in a large Hong Kong secondary school population, questionnaires had the advantage of giving us a much larger sample size and thus a degree of representativeness.

The questions cover the curriculum and the kind of subjects students would like to study in school and college, how students perceive their own learning environment and their place in this environment, and more personal questions that ask the students to give some details about their educational and family background; the questionnaire also asked them to reflect through open-ended questions on the place of education and the university in their lives. We believe that these open-ended questions give us an important qualitative look at students' self-perceptions, stresses, feelings of loneliness, and ambitions for the future.

Research Findings

The questionnaires included open-ended and closed-ended questions. The questionnaires cover three key themes: self-perceptions and self-stratification with regard to obtaining a place at a Hong Kong university; reasons for wanting to attend a university or study certain subjects in Hong Kong; educational self-assessment and family background. We believe that students' descriptions of their abilities and performances reveal elements of self-stratification. Their self-assessment of their performances in terms of their educational background and socioeconomic context also reveals they have internalized a dominating "success narrative" in Hong Kong. This success narrative perpetuates a belief that the school you are in largely determines your chances of going to university. Students are also aware that Hong Kong has a high world ranking in university reputation—it was recently ranked in joint third place in the *Times Higher Education* poll of Top University Cities—and this also has an important influence on levels of competition for places in Hong Kong.

Theme 1: Your Perception of Universities in Hong Kong and your Perception of your Chances of Getting a Place

When we asked the students whether they wanted to attend a UGC university 93 percent answered "yes" and only 7 percent answered "no." Considering that only 18–20 percent of young people of university age attend a UGC university, it suggests that competition is intense and that a vast majority of young people will be disappointed when it comes to obtaining a place at a UGC university.

However, when we asked students "why do you think you will not get a place at a UGC university" students gave very practical reasons that suggest that both the entrance requirements for entering university are too difficult and that students have to deal with intense competition that leads them to self-stratify. This leads to negative self-descriptions in terms of ability, which should be a matter of concern for teachers, parents, and education policy makers. The responses from Bands 1 and 2 students to the above question are given in table 8.1.

When we asked students, "why do you want to study at a UGC university?" we received a surprisingly high percentage of responses that focused on financial concerns and that also, in a quite shocking manner, saw students once again defining themselves in negative terms and self-stratifying socioeconomically in an almost resigned manner. Notions of autonomy and individual control appear to have vanished to be replaced by what psychologists and educationalists such as Paul Verhaeghe have described as the internalization of the "quantitative evaluations, performance interviews, and audits" of the neoliberal university.[45] Table 8.2 includes a selection of the responses:

Table 8.1 Why do you think you will not get a place at university?

Responses From Band 1 and Band 2 Students	Question: Why do you think you will not get a place at a UGC university?
Student A	"Even though my results are good, *the competition is too tough for even above average students to get a place* [our emphasis]"
Student B	"*the university place is too competitive* [our emphasis]. Even I am not bad in academic results, but I still can't 100% sure that i can got a university place."
Student C	"Although my school's level is quite good but the university places are really less in Hong Kong, even my result have reach the standard."
Student D	"*The competition for university places in Hong Kong is very intense, i am not sure whether i can get a place in university* [our emphasis]."
Student E	"i am trash"
Student F	"*The competition of getting a university place is too intense* and I did not get a very good academic results [our emphasis]"
Student G	"Although my school is top in this district, my score of some of the subjects are not good. The requirements are higher in these years, we even need to get 5** in our subjects, so we can get into the university"
Student H	"My Chinese is very bad furthermore English vocab is quiet little.at the school exam my English teacher said me can get level 2 in the hkdse. But I think I practice more. I will have little chance get university degree"
Student I	"have to be humble"
Student J	"Apart from English which is my strength, I cant handle subjects like Chinese or Liberal Studies. I'm not confident enough."
Student K	"Chinese is the death of me"

Such responses reflect badly on the levels of competition and self-stratification in society and also on the economization and commodification of education in society in Hong Kong to the extent that students as young as 15 are revealing that it is poverty and financial considerations that are the main concern when they describe their reasons for wanting to study at the eight leading universities in Hong Kong. A total of 499 out of 510 students responded "yes" to the question "Do you think competition for university places in Hong Kong is very intense? 你認為在 香港，大學學位的競爭是否十分激烈？" This approximates to 98 percent of the students surveyed. The stress levels of students with regard to gaining a place, not placing too much of a financial

Table 8.2 Why do you want to study at a UGC university?

Responses From Band 1 and Band 2 Students	Question Why do you want to study at a UGC University?
Student L	"I'd like to lessen my parent's burden"
Student M	"It can reduce the financial burden of the family."
Student N	"I am poor"
Student O	"I am very poor"
Student P	"Poverty"
Student Q	"Cheaper"
Student R	"Family burden"

burden on their parents, and achieving what society and parents expect are thus very high. The responses also reveal how many students are aware of their families' limited economic means and view all life choices in terms of their limited means at a very young age.

Theme 2: The Impact Getting a Place at University Has on Your Future Career

We gave students the following open question: "Going to university means a higher chance to achieve my dream career?" Most students agreed that going to university would improve their chances of landing their dream career. The most popular dream jobs or ideal jobs reported by students all require a degree qualification: doctor (7.5 percent), lawyer (7.5 percent), engineer (5.9 percent), accountant (5.1 percent), and teacher (3.8 percent). Failing to secure a university place in Hong Kong will mean that the career aspirations of many of these students will not be realized. We should not dismiss the institutional force behind these students' experience of life's first major disappointment. And to make matters worse, the statistics from the first HKDSE in 2012 reveal that approximately 10,000 students who have actually attained the minimum university entrance requirements still failed to get one of the 17,000 publicly funded degree places available every year (Table 8.3), a figure that has increased only slightly since then. To some of our respondents the failure will also mean they have lost the major means to improve the less-than-well-off financial condition of their families.

Table 8.3 Statistics showing the intense competition for university places in Hong Kong

Admission year	Number of students with minimum university entrance requirement (Core subjects at 3322 or better)	Number of students enrolled to FYFD places of UGC-funded programs Full-time equivalent	Ratio of students eligible for a FYFD place and students who obtained a FYFD place
2012/2013	26552	16760	1.63:1
2013/2014	28418	17089	1.66:1
2014/2015	27943	17309	1.6:1
2015/2016	25740	17410	1.47:1

Source: University Grants Committee, "Student Enrolment of First-Year-First-Degree (FYFD) Places of UGC-Funded Programmes, 1965/66 to 2015/16," 2016; Hong Kong Diploma of Secondary Education (HKDSE) Examination Results Released," 2012–15, http://www.hkeaa.edu.hk/DocLibrary/Media/PR/20120719_HKDSE_Results_ENG_FULL.pdf HKEAA 2012–2015.

While the participants of our survey are mostly students from Band 1 schools with a small proportion from Band 2 schools, it can be speculated that students from Band 3 schools either suffer from worse levels of anxiety towards university entrance applications or from the unfavorable social label attached to those regarded as "mediocre" in Hong Kong society. The expansion of the private associate degree market and the low social recognition of such degrees fail to reassure students about their abilities or relieve their stresses.

Responses to Open-Ended Questions

The students gave their most in-depth answers in response to the question: "Going to a university often means you have a higher chance of achieving your own dream career." Do you agree? Explain your answer briefly. 「就讀大學代表有更高機會實現我的夢想職業。」你贊同嗎？請簡短地解釋你的答案。 The responses to this question allowed us to get some deeper understanding of the reasons for the students' responses about university. Table 8.4 compiles a selection of their responses to this question.

There was then a strong tendency among students to speak of competition and money when considering the relationship between university and a "dream career." Students speak of the benefits of university in terms of "competitive power" and "competitiveness." Only 1 student out of the 510 personalized the

Table 8.4 Selection of questions and responses

Question	Responses
"Going to a university often means you have a higher chance of achieving your own dream career." Do you agree? Explain your answer briefly.	
Student R	"Yes because graduating from university means getting a ticket to society."
Student S	"Yes it is easier to get a job and earn money. no matter what my own dream career is, the very first important thing is money."
Student T	"Yes. HK has attracted many elites all over the world, so graduating from uni ensure a certain of competitiveness."
Student U	"Agree, because then one has higher competitive power."
Student V	"YES … because the certificate of graduation allows me to have higher bargaining power, a better job, and a higher income."

response to the extent that s/he related education in university to her/his "own needs and goals." This student responded: "I disagree because my dream job does not require university qualification. But if I can attend university, I can learn better about my own needs and goals. I don't go to university because of higher chance to achieve my own dream career." Only two other students related the experience of going to university to personal "goals" and one student did reply that going to university can "broaden your horizons." On the whole, however, there was a strong tendency for students to perceive the experience of going to university in terms of money and getting ahead in a competitive society.

Conclusion

This essay examines the relationship between student stress and self-stratification among secondary school students in Hong Kong. It reveals that students are aware of the competitive nature of the admissions process in

Hong Kong. Many students appear to be doing their very best and yet they are still not able to obtain a place and, more importantly, they view themselves at a young age as being incapable of obtaining a place at a university in Hong Kong. The study also reveals that the competitive system in Hong Kong with low admission and participation rates at university (both private and public) has a clear influence on students' perceptions of their own abilities. We believe that such levels of competition describe a society where as Paul Verhaeghe the "focus is entirely about separation and individualism" which in turn leads to a situation where "group forming suffers, leading to competition, social isolation, and loneliness". Students appear to be very downbeat about their chances of going on to study at university and therefore about their general academic abilities with all the knock-on effects this has in terms of self-esteem, ambition, and stress. Students also appear to be far more likely and far more confident about going on to study at a university if they have attended 1 of the 21 expensive fee-paying ESF schools in Hong Kong. A principal interviewed with regard to the current state of education and the competitive admissions systems at both secondary school and university believes that schools must simply give students the kind of opportunities their parents expect for them. One principal replied: "you must remember that meritocracy does push the envelope." The study also revealed that students face unnecessary stressful decisions about having to place financial burdens on their parents by opting to study abroad if they do not get the place they desire at a UGC university in Hong Kong. We believe this study demonstrates firsthand the affects of intense levels of competition and stress on students personal well-being and their sense of worth. The virtual world offers some solace to young people who feel they are being left behind by a society that values only the winners. Social isolation and loneliness can be exacerbated by a highly testocratic society that ends up having its students describes themselves as worthless, not up to the mark and no better than "trash". Stress at the top of the education system in the undergraduate and postgraduate levels can be alleviated by opening up more public places at UGC universities. In saying this, there is also a long-term need in this university city plagued with inequality[46] to recognize the worth and talent of its young people beyond the measure of university degrees and academic qualifications.[47]

9

An Erotics of Loneliness

Research tells us that feelings of loneliness can lead to increased use of what are called "arousal-oriented online sexual activities" (OSAs) and extensive use of OSAs can, in turn, exacerbate loneliness when efforts to reach out to people for affection, love, and physical relationships offline are found to be more unpredictable. Technology has advanced the cause of an erotics of loneliness. The internet gives us an array of OSAs, described as "any activities on the Internet that involve sexually explicit and/or sexually arousing stimuli." These activities can be solitary-arousal activities, requiring only one person, or they can be "partnered-arousal activities that involve at least two people interacting."[1] One study from 2013 on the self-appraisal of people on their "arousal-oriented online sexual activities" finds that "for most people, participating in solitary- and partnered-arousal OSAs has little impact on them." However, another study of Israeli adolescents finds that "engagement in online sexual activities and use of pornography were high among anxiously attached individuals regardless of the extent of their loneliness" but that loneliness was found "to increase the use of online sexual activities and pornography" among "secure and anxiously avoidant individuals."[2] Since, the study tells us, secure and anxiously avoidant types typically make up about 80 percent of control groups, loneliness can then be found to increase the use of OSAs for a majority of those using them. Anxiety about attachment to significant others can lead to the perception that one is "socially isolated" and this coupled with a sense of loneliness, what John and Sarah Cacioppo describe as "a discrepancy between what you want in terms of social relationships and what you have," can lead to a greater reliance on OSAs. John and Sarah Cacioppo also suggest that the perception that you are socially isolated "means that you are on the social perimeter—a dangerous place for a social animal, because you don't have the same mutual aid and protection you have when you have salutary connections with those in your social environment."[3] However, we cannot presume that OSAs are the cause of increased loneliness; Nicola M. Döring reminds us that "[c]aution is advisable not merely regarding the attribution of causality, but also in the assessment of the presumed consequences."[4] It may very well be, she argues, that "sexually insecure adolescents turn more frequently to pornography rather than becoming insecure because of it." Fisher and Barak also note that "encounters with pornography [that] may foster sexual liberalism or dis-satisfaction with one's own sex life may not be negative per se, but might stimulate constructive personal development."[5] However, Jean M. Twenge's extensive studies lead her to argue that, yes, "[i]t's possible that loneliness causes smartphone use instead of smartphone use causing loneliness, but the abrupt increase in loneliness makes this alternative much less likely ... It seems much more likely that smartphones became popular, screen time increased, and thus loneliness increased."[6]

However, it is not only OSAs that are changing desire; information itself and "keeping up" become not only a distraction from pre-online sexual encounters and practices but objects and shapers of desire themselves. Our understanding of desire is changed by the advent of biopolitics and the infosphere. Michel Foucault ends *The Order of Things* with a look to the future. He speculates on what a future age might look like where for the first time in "Western culture" "the being of man and the being of language" could "coexist" and "articulate themselves one upon the other."[7] Writing in 1966, he asks whether the "task ahead" is to "advance towards a mode of thought, unknown hitherto in our culture, that will make it possible to reflect at the same time, without discontinuity or contradiction, upon man's being and the being of language."[8] Today's infosphere where subjects live out and are shaped by new forms of virtual being and "self-ing" through online "written" codes and algorithms marks such a coming together of the ontologies of language and being. It is the major biopolitical event of our time. Foucault is, of course, the father of biopolitics and the biopolitical event that he looked forward to, what should be a "source of innovation" and a "new production of subjectivity,"[9] may very well be the emergence and incorporation of the infosphere into our subjectivities. However, this new incorporation of subjectivity into the infosphere also requires a new description of subjectivity, desire, and its values. Information theorists such as Luciano Floridi give us these new definitions; Floridi reminds us that in today's infosphere the "least, most general common set of attributes that characterizes something as intrinsically valuable, and hence worthy of some moral respect" is a minimal condition of possibility of an "entity's least intrinsic value" and that this is to be "identified with its ontological status as an informational entity."[10] Therefore, the minimal moral value of today's "entities"—what describe Foucault's future subjectivities—are to be gauged according to their ontological status as informational entities; it is then a new biopolitical system of values. The archaeology of knowledge has evolved to bring together representation as information and being in the infosphere. And since information is the basis of this system of values and its entities, it also shapes and molds desire as never before. Information becomes both a ground for determining value and for understanding desire. This evolution from Foucault's early prognosis for a biopolitcal future to today's infosphere is one possible route for understanding the turn to the screen and the interface in terms of desire. It is a modern-day love story. It also suggests that loneliness today without solitude may well be a kind of lingering embodied excess experienced by bodies that have not yet fully adapted to this new relation with desire by way of the infosphere.

Losing the Desire for Solitude and our "Loneliest Loneliness"

It is once again about perceptions; loneliness might not *feel* so bad so long as you are not perceiving yourself as "socially isolated." The sense is that if you can only weather the general sense of loneliness on your own then you might be okay and might learn to live successfully with it. However, loneliness as social isolation is today regarded as something to be escaped from. This is very different, as we have seen, to the sense of loneliness we get in such writers as Friedrich Nietzsche and Thomas Merton. As John Kaag reminds us, Nietzsche writes of a supreme moment of self-enquiry that hits only in our "loneliest loneliness" when we must come to what we value on our own: "the answer cannot be given by consensus or on behalf of some impersonal institutions."[11] Whatever we do, we must do it because we chose it and can own up to it: "[i]n the story of our lives, these choices are ours and ours alone, and this is what gives things, all things, value."[12] And of course desire is a key aspect of value; learning what we desire and how we desire is one of the most important aspects of understanding value for young people.

However, in a society dominated by an online world, as I argue in this book, we are often denied the chance to really commune with our loneliness, not to mention our "loneliest loneliness." If our general sense of loneliness is coupled with a sense that we are, or are perceived as, "socially isolated," it becomes harder to live with loneliness. There is a subtle distinction here in this newer research between feelings of loneliness and feelings of being anxiously attached to significant others. Moretti and Peled describe how teenagers displaying "anxious-avoidant" characteristics may have parents who were themselves very often unavailable and who were unable to communicate affection in an appropriate manner: "parental unavailability and harsh rejection is associated with insecure anxious-avoidant attachment. These children view themselves as unlovable and unable to attract care from their parents, and they view others as punitive and disinterested in them. Anxious-avoidant children are reluctant to approach their parents even when distressed, because they fear their overtures for comfort will be rejected or punished."[13] The chief concern for those who are looking out for people suffering from loneliness is then this anxiety about being perceived as "socially isolated" that is rooted in an anxiety about attachment to significant others. This is also highlighted by Stefanie Marsh in her discussions with teenagers on the role of parents as significant others. The teenagers she spoke with reveal that what really bothers other teenagers who are lonely is the tendency of parents not to connect with them, to ask clichéd questions, and to put them in a box marked "alien." Therefore, it is not only loneliness that might be responsible for greater use of OSAs but loneliness coupled with a feeling of being anxious about your attachment to significant others.

However, the link between young people experiencing loneliness and the use of OSAs does raise the question of how desire is changing for young people and how they are navigating what they perceive as an integral connection between desire and identity. Jonathan Dollimore reminds us that "it's one of the delusions of identity politics to think that our desire comfortably coexists with our identity, a belief which has to do more with consumerism than desire. I've come to feel that sexuality might at different times express different aspects of one's self, a situation further complicated by the fact that the self changes."[14] He reminds us that "desire is always potentially dangerous because you never quite know when it is going to subvert selfhood, reveal it as the fiction or fabrication that it is; 'fabrication' because it is a construct susceptible to unravelling, coming to pieces."[15] One might argue that for young people who perceive themselves as "socially isolated" and who are described as anxious avoidant, loneliness drives them to OSAs that help them to define who they are according to where desire takes them. However, in the absence of a much-needed closeness to significant others, loneliness might also leave them lost amidst the cacophony of desires offered by OSAs, lost in the funhouse, lost in the sense that they no longer know which version of selfhood is a fabrication and which *feels* right for them. It comes back to our concern about whether we are aware that we are becoming disconnected from our emotional lives.

Teenage abbreviations and slang also reveal a greater awareness of the connection between time alone with technology and desire. Recent slang abbreviations include: WTTP—Want to trade photos; LMIRL—Let's meet in real life; GNOC—Get naked on camera; NIFOC—Naked in front of the computer. These are of course activities and means of being aroused that were unthinkable to the characters of O'Connor and Yates; even Wallace did not delve into how such an erotics of loneliness might play out in terms of desire. The characters of Gail Honeymoon and John Boyne from novels on loneliness published in the last few years also rely more on face-to-face encounters than on virtual relationships. Studies also reveal how shared sexual online activities are imitated by teenagers out of peer pressure. Series such as *13 Reasons Why* reveal how isolation in schools around the sharing of sexual experiences can lead to public shaming and even suicide. Jean M. Twenge argues that the decrease in the number of young people dating or having sex is due to both the reluctance to get involved in a pervasive "hook-up" culture that sells "emotionless or meaningless sex"[16] and a belief that relationships involving too much time, emotion, and sex might leave you with "catching feelings."[17]

The iGen is so concerned about an individualism co-created and mediated online that they "fear losing their identity through relationships"[18] (215) or "being too influenced by someone else at a critical time."[19] The teenagers Twenge interviewed reveal a lack of curiosity about "actual sex" because they've "seen so much of it" online on porn sites;[20] "porn is enough and real sex seems unnecessary" for many whom she interviews in the United States.[21] The training in cloneliness is almost complete; the individualism concocted through the interface and through screen time in displaying yet higher levels of loneliness than previous generations is content to persevere as it grows fearful of how relationships it is unprepared for might infect or destroy that hard-won individualism. Desire, its feeding and its sustaining, is one of the strongest bulwarks of this individualism as cloneliness. However, not all teenagers even see OSAs as that important to them. Teenagers who have established blogs to help others with mental health issues say, "Porn is more like background noise to people in their teens now. Saying that the net causes loneliness is like saying that television caused teenage loneliness in the 1960s."[22]

Loneliness as Erotic

There are now more ways than ever before to simulate sex with the online presence of others and to achieve self-arousal online while being physically alone. It is perhaps hard for young people who regularly use OSAs to imagine how the lonely crowds of Riesman, Glazer, and Denney or the submerged population groups of O'Connor in the 1950s and 1960s coped with desire and self-arousal. Joyce's *Ulysses* demonstrates how pornography and public arousal was important for the turn-of-the-century middle-aged man whose marriage was struggling. Wallace reminds us of the extent we go to to repress desires in our day jobs. However, loneliness even then was less open to the range of erotic technological aids, VIRP aids[23] (virtual intercourse with real people), sex robot research creations (covered by the wonderful word, teledildonics), and haptic technology afforded by today's internet. Does the proliferation of pornography, various OSAs, and teledildonics grant to loneliness today an erotic image it did not possess before? The very nature of spending time alone has altered dramatically since the 1950s and 1960s because today we also see it as time spent alone with others online. However, this works two ways. Thanks to the proliferation of these opportunities for arousal through technology, not only has the image of loneliness altered but so has the image of desire and sexuality. Young people very often prefer to get aroused online alone. Alone but online one only has oneself to please; in virtual reality there might not be the same kind of desire to please the other as one might experience when touching another in close physical proximity. Online users might also find the experience is less hassle: one does not have to deal with another person's sweat and secretions and one may feel less guilt about having to hang around when you have sated your desire.

What then do philosophers of desire tell us? Slavoj Žižek argues that in Deleuze drive replaces desire since it is no longer about subjectivity based on lack but about loss itself as the object; the repetition of this process of loss ends up giving most enjoyment. Perhaps desire in the virtual reality age plays out well according to such a model; the virtual is premised on loss perhaps more than lack and this loss sustains the drive as the need to keep returning to the self or to the original desiring-machine. However, because Deleuze's descriptions of machine and of virtuality call for so much more fine-tuning in an age when machines and their mode of incorporation of the human have advanced so much, it is difficult to prevent Deleuze's descriptions of desire and of desiring-machines spreading out to encompass everything and nothing. As Fredric Jameson writes of Deleuze, if "everything is libidinal investment, everything is desire [there is] nothing outside desire."[24] Deleuze's own reading of immanence in "Immanence: A Life" is also revealing of the difference his notion of virtuality sets up between how the "singularities," or free flowing aspects of becoming, "of *a* life," connect and how "individuals connect."[25] He writes that the "singularities and the events that constitute *a* life coexist with the accidents of *the* life that corresponds to it, but they ... connect with one another in a manner entirely different from how individuals connect."[26] For Deleuze, the all-encompassing life that swirls about us and that "is everywhere" is very much his focus above and beyond any "events or singularities that are *merely* [my emphasis] actualized in subjects and objects."[27] It is very much "*a* life" over "the life" together with its "accidents" that is celebrated. Is this a classic case of not wanting to get your hands dirty? At any rate, virtual reality and OSAs constitute a whole new world of virtuality today and therefore it is difficult to know precisely how Deleuze's immanent life maps onto how "individuals connect" in this world. Moreover, loneliness is a feeling and an experience that must be reflected on not by focusing only on universal life flows but rather on the "accidents" that causes life in its individuality to feel the way it does for a unique person.

Two of the most influential theories of desire and sexuality—Freudian psychoanalysis and Deleuze and Guattari's schizoanalysis—are challenged by the new erotics of loneliness. Deleuze and Guattari, in rejecting the object-oriented sexuality of Freud, still admit that the libido "does not come to consciousness except in relation to a given body, a given person that it takes as its object." However, Deleuze and Guattari define this "object choice" as a "conjunction of flows of life and of society that this body and this person intercept, receive, and transmit, always within a biological, social and historical field where we are equally immersed or with which we communicate."[28] How does this communication extend beyond the purely biological in virtual reality and online? They argue that, in contrast to Freud's theory, sexuality and desiring-machines are "one and the same" and are "operating in the social machines."[29] They sum up their schizoanalytic argument by saying it is "simple": "desire is a machine, a synthesis of machines, a machinic arrangement-desiring machines."[30] "The order of desire is the order of *production*; all production is at once desiring-production and social production."[31] They reproach psychoanalysis for having "shunted" this "order of production" "into *representation*."[32] The old psychoanalysis only believes; it no longer produces. The old psychoanalysis is trapped then by the myths and by belief *as* representation of the family. One might expect that loneliness is one manner of breaking out of this dominant familial conscription of desire; loneliness mitigated through machines as online technological arousal aids may well lead to desiring machines attaching to social production by way of other purely capitalistic desiring-machines. In one sense then, these online flows can be regarded as breaking down the constraints of desire as exclusively bound up with familial representation and as restricted to the desiring-machine of Deleuze and Guattari. The question, however, is whether the conglomeration of desiring-machines we have today with OSAs within social production results in the kind of desiring production Deleuze and Guattari describe for their schizoanalysis? As Deleuze and Guattari argue: "[t]he truth is that sexuality is everywhere: the way a bureaucrat fondles his records, a judge administers justice, a businessman causes money to circulate; the way the bourgeoisie fucks the proletariat ... [a] revolutionary machine is nothing if it does not acquire at least as much force as these coercive machines have for producing breaks and mobilizing flows."[33] The question to be asked of this model in the virtual age is whether subjects as desiring-machines know how to tell the "revolutionary" machines from the "coercive" ones in contributing to social production, and, in turn, how the new manner of contributing to social production in the online world affects the force of their own personal desiring-machines? When the larger social production machine that all desiring-machines contribute to is already running according to algorithms designed to harness as much desire as possible for capital accumulation, how does this change desire and its force? As Deleuze and Guattari say of the movement away from myth and representation in an earlier stage of capitalism, "capitalism is constructed on the ruins of the territorial and the despotic, the mythic and the tragic representations, but it re-establishes them in its own service and in another form, as images of capital."[34] In a virtual age, an age of algorithms, even the somewhat salvific sense assigned to the recognition of desire as working through desiring-machines as bodies without organs is lost since we now yearn to be more machine than ever before; if desire is replaced by drive as loss then we should not be getting what we want so easily. However, there is also a real yearning for what the organic and the natural affords us; desire today feels as constrained by the old story of seeing itself as a desiring-machine—even if failed—as it did, for Deleuze and Guattari, when it was reduced to myths and representation.

In an age when we are never "off machines"—in a manner Deleuze and Guattari might not have predicted—how revolutionary is it for us to tell young people that they are desiring-machines? When they are yearning for experiences beyond screen time how can they be reminded that they are "other" to machines? Loneliness is, after all, one of the first qualities a "politics of desire" based on schizoanalysis and desiring-production was supposed to do away with. Mark Seem writes in his introduction to the English edition of the book in 2004: "A politics of desire would see loneliness and depression as the first things to go. Such is the anti-oedipal strategy: if man is connected to the machines of the universe, if he is in tune with his desires, if he is 'anchored,' 'he ceases to worry about the fitness of things, about the behaviour of his fellow-men, about right and wrong or justice and injustice.'"[35] One question this raises today in the age of the fourth industrial revolution is what is the nature of the "machines of the universe" that Deleuze and Guattari had in mind long before anyone was hooked up 24/7 to the machines of cyberspace? Now that people have given themselves up to the "machines of the universe" like never before, why is there an "epidemic of loneliness"? Are we connected to the wrong kinds of machines? And, if so, how are we ever to know what the right kind of machines are if we see our own embodied desires themselves as desiring-machines? Clearly something has gone wrong in terms of the politics of desire and the clarity the connection to machines was to offer us. Have we presumed that the new machines we are hooked up to are extensions of, or are unproblematically complementary to, our own desiring-machines? Deleuzian theory talks about being "hooked up" to the right machine, but now that young people are truly "hooked up" in ways Deleuze and Guattari did not wholly envisage, the question might not be so much about bodies without organs and desiring-machines but about machines *with* organs and, in the age of the Anthropocene, about a nostalgia for desiring-bodies. The nature of the machines we are hooked up to is never clarified in Deleuze and Guattari and it can therefore expand to cover all aspects of what Giorgio Agamben calls the "anthropological machine." In the same way that Agamben describes how man has fenced off the animal inside, so have we now fenced off the human in our rush to both accommodate the machine and a human environment under threat as never before by machines? Agamben reads anthropological theories as defining man as a "machine or device for producing the recognition of the human." For Agamben this "anthropological machine of humanism" holds man "suspended between a celestial and a terrestrial nature." As man has reached what Agamben calls his "historical telos" in the age of the Anthropocene, Agamben argues that it is the "taking on of biological life itself" that is now the supreme political task. This unresolved tension in Deleuze and Guattari between the human and the machine must also face up to this environmental reality and to the resulting sense of loss that an engagement with ourselves as desiring-machines fosters. Loneliness is a lingering response to loss that may very well be one of the most enduring voicings of our shared humanity; it may only be when loneliness is so pervasive as to be unrecognizable that we might begin to see ourselves completely as desiring-machines. Cloneliness shapes and molds users with the machines and algorithms of surveillance capitalism into the interconnected loners it needs; when each one of us finds the "incommunicable personality" that only loneliness reveals, we might then feel truly connected.

Notes

1 Introduction: Radical Embodied Cognitive Loneliness

1. P. Verhaeghe, *What about Me? The Struggle for Identity in a Market-Based Society* (London: Scribe Books, 2104), p. 206.
2. Will Storr, *Selfie: How the West Became Self-Obsessed* (London: Picador, 2018), p. 146.
3. Johann Hari, *Lost Connections: Uncovering the Real Causes of Depression—and the Unexpected Solutions* (London: Bloomsbury, 2018), p. 82.
4. Ibid.
5. Brian A. Primack, Ariel Shensa, Jaime E. Sidani, Erin O. Whaite, Liu yi Lin, Daniel Rosen, Jason B. Colditz, Ana Radovic, and Elizabeth Miller, "Social Media Use and Perceived Social Isolation Among Young Adults in the U.S.," *American Journal of Preventive Medicine* 53, no. 1 (2017): 1–8. Available online: http://www.sciencedirect.com/science/article/pii/S0749379717300168.
6. Erin O. Whaite, Ariel Shensa, Jaime E. Sidani, Jason B. Colditz, and Brian A. Primack, "Social Media Use, Personality Characteristics, and Social Isolation among Young Adults in the United States," *Personality and Individual Differences* 124 (2018): 45–50. Available online: http://www.sciencedirect.com/science/article/pii/S0191886917306360.
7. Curtis Silver, "Patents Reveal How Facebook Wants to Capture your Emotions, Facial Expressions and Mood," available online: https://www.forbes.com/sites/curtissilver/2017/06/08/how-facebook-wants-to-capture-your-emotions-facial-expressions-and-mood/#6c39b2256014.
8. Hari, *Lost Connections*, p. 89.
9. Zygmunt Bauman, *Stangers at Our Door* (London: Polity, 2016), pp. 105–6.
10. Ibid., p. 105.
11. Ibid.
12. Ibid., p. 107.
13. Ibid., p. 110.
14. Ibid.
15. Olivia Sagan and Eric D. Miller, eds., *Narratives of Loneliness: Multidisciplinary Perspectives from the 21st Century* (London: Routledge, 2018), p. 13.

16 J. T. Cacioppo and P. Williams, *Loneliness: Human Nature and the Need for Social Connection* (New York, NY: W.W. Norton, 2009), p. 12. Sagan and Miller, *Narratives of Loneliness*, p. 13.
17 Julianne Holt-Lunstad, Timothy B. Smith, and J. Bradley Layton, "Social Relationships and Mortality Risk: A Meta-analytic Review," *PLoS Med* 7, no. 7 (2010): e1000316. Available online: https://doi.org/10.1371/journal.pmed.1000316.
18 W. J. T. Mitchell, *Cloning Terror: The War of Images, 9/11 to the Present* (Chicago: University of Chicago Press, 2011), p. 42.
19 Ibid., p. 31.
20 Ibid., p. 30.
21 Ibid., p. 37.
22 See https://www.gov.uk/government/news/pm-commits-to-government-wide-drive-to-tackle-loneliness.
23 Combatting loneliness one conversation at a time. See: https://www.jocoxloneliness.org/pdf/a_call_to_action.pdf.
24 "Loneliness Epidemic Costs UK Businesses 2.5 Billion a Year," February 20, 2017. Available online: https://www.co-operative.coop/media/news-releases/loneliness-epidemic-costs-uk-businesses-gbp2-5-billion-a-year.
25 Jean M. Twenge, *iGen: Why Today's Supe-Connected Kinds Are Growing Up Less. Rebellious, More Tolerant, Less Happy- and Completely Unprepared for Adulthood* (New York, NY: Simon & Schuster, 2017), p. 97.
26 Hong Kong is experiencing a high number of student suicides. See: http://www.scmp.com/topics/youth-suicide-hong-kong.
27 Vivek Murthy, "Work and the Loneliness Epidemic: Reducing Isolation at Work Is Good for Business," *Harvard Business Review*, September 28, 2017. Available online: https://hbr.org/cover-story/2017/09/work-and-the-loneliness-epidemic.
28 Michael O'Sullivan, *Academic Barbarism, Universities and Inequality* (London: Palgrave, 2016).
29 Richard Thaler, *Misbehaving: The Making of Behavioral Economics* (New York, NY: W.W. Norton, 2015).
30 Jean-Paul Sartre, *Nausea* (New York, NY: New Directions, 1969), p. 17.
31 Ibid.
32 Ibid.
33 Ibid., p. 18.
34 Ibid.
35 Ibid., p. 122.
36 Ibid.

37 Ibid., p. 123.
38 John Kaag, *Hiking with Nietzsche: On Becoming Who You Are* (New York, NY: Farrar, Strauss & Giroux, 2018).
39 Ibid., p. 74.
40 Ibid.
41 Ibid., p. 246.
42 Ibid., pp. 246–7.
43 Michel De Montaigne, *On Solitude*, Great Ideas (London: Penguin, 2009), p. 3.
44 Ibid., p. 6.
45 Ibid., p. 7.
46 Ibid., p. 19.
47 Ibid.
48 Anthony Chemero, *Radical Embodied Cognitive Science*, A Bradford Book (Cambridge, MA: The MIT Press, 2009), p. x.
49 Ibid., p. 19.
50 Ibid., p. 31.
51 Ibid.
52 Ibid.
53 Allen E. Buchanan, *Beyond Humanity? The Ethics of Biomedical Enhancement*, (Oxford: Oxford University Press, 2013). Luciano Floridi, *The Ethics of Information* (Oxford: Oxford University Press, 2015). Wendell Wallach and Colin Allen, *Moral Machines: Teaching Robots Right from Wrong* (Oxford: Oxford University Press, 2009).
54 Michael Hardt and Antonio Negri, *Commonwealth* (Cambridge, MA: Belknap, 2009).
55 Laikwan Pang, *The Art of Cloning* (London: Verso, 2017); Kelly Oliver. *Technologies of Life and Death: From Cloning to Capital Punishment* (New York: Fordham University Press, 2013).
56 Ben Lazare Mijuskovic, *Loneliness in Philosophy, Psychology and Literature*, 3rd ed. (New York, NY: Universe, 2012).
57 David Riesman, Nathan Glazer, and Reuel Denney, *The Lonely Crowd: A Study of the Changing American Character*, abridged rev. ed. (New Haven, CT: Yale University Press, 2001), p. xii.
58 Ibid.
59 Ibid.
60 Ibid., pp. xlii–xliii.
61 Clark E. Moustakas, *Loneliness* (New York, NY: Prentice-Hall, 1961), p. 221.

62 There is a whole section of the main English language newspaper in Hong Kong devoted to the recent upsurge in student suicides. See Paul Wong and Monica Borschel, "Why talking to depress Hong Kong teens is a matter of life and death" http://www.scmp.com/comment/insight-opinion/article/2083737/why-talking-depressed-hong-kong-teens-matter-life-and-death
63 Pang, *Art of Cloning*.
64 O'Sullivan, *Academic Barbarism*. Lani Guinier, *The Tyranny of the Meritocracy: Democratizing Higher Education in America* (Boston, MA: Beacon Press, 2015). Suzanne Mettler, *Degrees of Inequality: How the Politics of Higher Education Sabotaged the American Dream* (New York, NY: Basic Books, 2014).
65 Pang, *Art of Cloning*, p. 238.
66 Ibid.
67 Ed Finn, *What Algorithms Want: Imagination in the Age of Computing* (Cambridge, MA: The MIT Press, 2018), p. 192.
68 Ibid.
69 Ibid., p. 190.
70 Ibid.
71 Ibid., p. 16.
72 Ibid., p. 2.
73 Ibid., p. 147.
74 Ibid., p. 148.
75 Tom Sparrow, *The End of Phenomenology: Metaphysics and the New Realism* (Edinburgh: Edinburgh University Press, 2014).
76 All translations from the French are mine.
77 Daniel Cohen, *"Il Faut Dire Que Les Temps Ont Changé…": Chronique (Fiévreuse) D'une Mutation Qui Inquiéte* (Paris: Albin Michel, 2018), p. 173.
78 Ibid., p. 185.
79 Ibid., p. 186.
80 Ibid., p. 184.
81 Ibid., p. 186.
82 Bauman, *Strangers*, p. 108.
83 Simone Weil in Zygmunt Bauman and Ezio Mauro, *Babel* (London: Polity, 2016), p. 146.
84 Daniel Zagury, *La Barbarie des Hommes Ordinaires: Ces criminels qui pourraient être nous* (Paris: Éditions de l'Observatoire/Humensis, 2018).
85 Ibid., p. 193.
86 Ibid., p. 192.
87 Ibid., p. 73.

88 Ibid., p. 74.
89 Ibid., p. 198.
90 Ibid., p. 193.
91 The rest of the song reads:

> When all I want and all I know
> Is time spent looking at my phone
> Find me when the lights go down
> Signing in and signing out

92 Cohen, "*Il Faut Dire Que Les Temps Ont Changé*," p. 210.
93 Storr, *Selfie*, p. 154.
94 Cohen, "*Il Faut Dire Que Les Temps Ont Changé*," p. 210.
95 Ibid., p. 194.
96 Ibid., p. 196.
97 In ibid.
98 Ibid.
99 Ibid., p. 200.
100 Ibid.
101 Twenge, *iGen*, p. 211.
102 Cohen, "*Il Faut Dire Que Les Temps Ont Changé*," p. 202.
103 Ibid., p. 203.
104 E. Kross, P. Verduyn, E. Demiralp, J. Park, D. S. Lee, N. Lin et al., "Facebook Use Predicts Declines in Subjective Well-Being in Young Adults," *PLoS ONE* 8 no. 8 (2013): e69841. Available online: https://doi.org/10.1371/journal.pone.0069841.
105 Sabina Lissitsa and Svetlana Chachashvili-Bolotin, "Life Satisfaction in the Internet Age—Changes in the Past Decade," *Computers in Human Behavior* 54 (2016): 197–206. Available online: http://www.sciencedirect.com/science/article/pii/S0747563215300790.
106 P. DiMaggio, E. Hargittai, C. Celeste, and S. Shafer, "Digital Inequality: From Unequal Access to Differentiated Use," in *Social Inequality*, ed. K. M. Neckerman (New York, NY: Russell Sage Foundation, 2004), pp. 355–400; E. Hargittai and A. Hinnant. "Digital Inequality: Differences in Young Adults' Use of the Internet," *Communication Research* 35 (2008): 602–62.
107 S. Hu and L. Leung, "Effects of Expectancy-Value, Attitudes, and Use of the Internet on Psychological Empowerment Experienced by Chinese Women at the Workplace," *Telematics and Informatics* 20 no. 4 (2003): 365–82.
108 Hari, *Lost Connections*, p. 83.
109 Ibid. p. 76.

110 World Happiness Report Update 2016, eds. John Helliwell, Richard Layard, and Jeffrey Sachs,p. 204. Available online: http://worldhappiness.report/wp-content/uploads/sites/2/2016/03/HR-V1_web.pdf.
111 Cohen, "*Il Faut Dire Que Les Temps Ont Changé*," p. 212.
112 Ibid.
113 Ibid., p. 212.
114 Ibid., pp. 212–13.
115 Ibid., p. 213.
116 Ibid., p. 214.
117 Ibid., p. 215.
118 Ibid.
119 Ibid., p. 216.
120 Ibid., p. 220.
121 Ibid.
122 Ibid., pp. 220–1.
123 Ibid., p. 221.
124 Ibid., p. 228.
125 In ibid., p. 230.
126 Floridi, *Ethics of Information*, p. 98.
127 Ibid., p. 99.
128 Ibid., p. 260.
129 Matthew D. Lieberman, *Social: Why Our Brains Are Wired to Connect* (New York, NY: Crown, 2013), p. 37.
130 Moustakis, *Loneliness*, p. 5.
131 Lars Svendsen, *A Philosophy of Loneliness* (London: Reaktion Books, 2017), p. 142, n.4.
132 Ibid.
133 Ibid.; Mijuskovic, *Loneliness*, p. 82.
134 Ibid., pp. 142–3; ibid., pp. 13, 20.
135 Ibid., p. 143, n.4.
136 Ibid., pp. 135–6.
137 Ibid., p. 125.
138 Ibid., p. 119.
139 Ibid., p. 127.
140 Ibid., p. 51.
141 Ibid., p. 126.
142 Olivia Laing, *The Lonely City: Adventures in the Art of Being Alone* (London: Canongate, 2016), p. 65.
143 Svendsen, *Philosophy of Loneliness*, p. 135.

2 Loneliness as Method: Henry James and the "Essential Loneliness" of Artistic Practice

An earlier version of this chapter appeared in *Textual Practice*: Michael O'Sullivan, "Loneliness as Method: Henry James, Individualism and the 'More Intimate Education,'" *Textual Practice* (2018), DOI: 10.1080/0950236X.2018.1508492.

1 Michael D. Higgins, President of Ireland, Opening Address at the European University Association Conference, Galway, 2016.
2 Henry James, *The Portrait of a Lady* (New York, NY: Random House, 2007), p. 362.
3 Ibid., p. 374.
4 Ibid., p. 311.
5 Ibid., p. vii.
6 Ibid., p. xx.
7 Ibid., p. xix.
8 Michael Roth, *Beyond the University: Why Liberal Education Matters* (New Haven, CT: Yale University Press, 2015).
9 Louis Menand, *The Metaphysical Club: A Story of Ideas in America* (New York, NY: Farrar, Strauss and Giroux, 2001).
10 Ibid., p. 108.
11 Ibid., p. 156.
12 Jacques Derrida, *Speech and Phenomena, and Other Essays on Husserl's Theory of Signs* (Evanston, IL: Northwestern University Press, 1973), p. 16.
13 Henry James, *Autobiography: A Small Boy and Others – Notes of a Son and Brother – The Middle Years*, Ed. and Intro. Frederick W. Dupee (New York, NY: Criterion Books, 1956).
14 Ibid., p. 19.
15 Ibid., p. 20.
16 Ibid., pp. 58–9.
17 Ibid., p. 65.
18 Ibid., pp. 89–90.
19 Ibid., p. 95.
20 Megan Quigley, *Modernist Fiction and Vagueness: Philosophy, Form, and Language* (Cambridge: Cambridge University Press, 2015), p. 57.
21 James, *Autobiography*, p. 105.
22 Richard Yates's *Eleven Kinds of Loneliness* is a wonderful description of loneliness in the American context and O' Connor's more pugnacious critical reading of the lonely voice in the short story form as a kind of medium for speaking en masse

for different submerged groups in society offers a new reading of loneliness. See Frank O'Connor, *The Lonely Voice: A Study of the Short Story* (New York, NY: Melville House Publishing, 2004) and Richard Yates, *Eleven Kinds of Loneliness* (New York, NY: Vintage Classics, 2008).

23 Leon Edel, *Henry James: A Life* (New York, NY: Harper & Row, 1985), p. 511.
24 Ibid., p. 646.
25 Henry James, *The Letters of Henry James*, Vol. IV: 1895–1916, ed. Leon Edel (Cambridge, MA: The Belknap Press of Harvard University Press, 1984), p. 170.
26 Hong Kong is experiencing a high number of student suicides. See: http://www.scmp.com/topics/youth-suicide-hong-kong.
27 This was advice given to a large group of department Heads in our university by our University Provost.
28 Alexander Lawrie, *The Beginnings of University English: Extramural Study 1885–1910* (London: Palgrave Macmillan, 2014), p. 150.
29 Ibid.
30 Henry James, *Literary Criticism*, ed. Leon Edel, Vol. I. *Essays on Literature, American Writers, English Writers* (New York, NY: The Library of America, 1984), p. 97.
31 Ibid., p. 617.
32 Edel, *Henry James*, p. 583.
33 Adrian Poole, *Henry James*, Harvester New Readings (Hempstead: Harvester, 1991), p. 1.
34 Henry James, *The Ambassadors*, Intro. Harry Levin (London: Penguin Classics, 1986), p. 20.
35 Ibid., pp. 24–5.
36 William James, "The Ph.D. Octupus" *The Heart of William James*, ed. and intro. Robert Richardson (Cambridge, MA.: Harvard University Press, 2010).
37 John Dewey, *Individualism, Old and New* (New York, NY: Capricorn Books, 1962), p. 15.
38 See Lawrie, *The Beginnings*, p. 112.
39 Ibid., p. 95.
40 Ibid., p. 118.
41 James, *Literary Criticism*, Vol. I, p. 124.
42 Ibid., p. 125.
43 Ibid.
44 Ibid.
45 Ibid., p. 126.
46 Menand, *Metaphysical Club*, 108.

47 Ralph Waldo Emerson, "The American Scholar: An Oration before the Phi Beta Kappa Society, at Cambridge, August 31, 1837," *Emerson: Essays and Lectures* (New York, NY: The Library of America, 1983), pp. 51–72, 59.
48 In Quigley, *Modernist Fiction*, p. 52.
49 Fred Kaplan, *Henry James: The Imagination of Genius, A Biography* (Baltimore, MD: Johns Hopkins University Press, 1999), p. 216.
50 Quigley, *Modernist Fiction*, p. 53.
51 Ibid.
52 Henry James, *The Sacred Fount*, Intro. John Lyon (London: Penguin Classics, 1994), p. 105.
53 J. C. Friedrich Schiller, "Letters Upon the Aesthetic Education of Man," *Literary and Philosophical Essays*, The Harvard Classics 1909–14. www.bartleby.com.
54 Ibid., Letter IX.
55 Ibid., Letter II.
56 Ibid., Letter III.
57 Meghan Marie Hammond, "Into Other Minds: William and Henry James," *Empathy and the Psychology of Literary Modernism* (Edinburgh: Edinburgh University Press, 2014), pp. 32–59, 55.
58 Ibid., p. 50.
59 Ibid..
60 Henry James, *Autobiography*, p. 454.
61 Ibid., pp. 454–5.
62 Henry James, *The Tragic Muse*, Intro. Philip Horne (London: Penguin Classics, 1995), p. 394.
63 Ibid., p. 441.
64 Ibid., p. 475.
65 Ibid., p. 490.
66 Larry Siedentop, *Inventing the Individual: The Origins of Western Liberalism*, (Cambridge, MA: Harvard University Press, 2014).

3 The "Lonely Voice" and "Submerged Population" in O'Connor, Joyce, and Mansfield: How Can We Live "Alone Together"?

An earlier version of this chapter appeared as "Loneliness and the Submerged Population: Frank O'Connor's The Lonely Voice and Joyce's "The Dead"". The Irish Short Story. Eds. Elke D'Hoker and Stephanie Eggermont. Oxford: Peter Lang, 2015, pp. 105–20.

1. O'Connor, *The Lonely Voice*, p. 19.
2. Ibid., p. 14.
3. Ibid., p. 15.
4. Ibid., p. 20.
5. Ibid., p. 107.
6. Ibid.
7. Ibid.
8. Ibid., p. 108.
9. Ibid., p. 109.
10. Michael O'Sullivan, "Loneliness as Method: Henry James, Individualism and the 'More Intimate Education.'" *Textual Practice*. 2018.
11. Hari, *Lost Connections*, p. 83.
12. O'Connor, *The Lonely Voice*, p. 221.
13. Ibid., p. 138.
14. Paul De Man, "Autobiography as De-facement," *MLN* 94, no. 5 (1979): 78.
15. O'Connor, *The Lonely Voice*, p. 137.
16. Paul Ricoeur, *Living Up To Death*. Trans. David Pellauer (Chicago: University of Chicago Press, 2009), p. 20.
17. Ibid., pp. 31–2.
18. Ibid., p. 20.
19. Peter S. Druckner, "The Age of Social Transformation," *The Atlantic Monthly*, November 1994, p. 68.
20. O'Connor, *The Lonely Voice*, p. 17.
21. Ibid.
22. Ibid., p. 18.
23. Ibid., p. 158.
24. Ibid., p. 107.
25. Ibid., p. 126.
26. Ibid., p. 132.
27. Ibid., p. 127.
28. Ibid.
29. Ibid.
30. Ibid., p. 138.
31. Ibid., p. 19.
32. Ibid., p. 20.
33. Sean O'Faolain, The Irish: A Character Study (New York, NY: Devin-Adair Co, 1947), p. 40.
34. Ibid.
35. Riesman et al., *The Lonely Crowd*, p. 163.

36 Ibid., p. 164.
37 James Joyce, *Dubliners* (London: Penguin, 1992), p. 221.
38 Ibid., p. 138.
39 De Man, "Autobiography as De-facement," p. 928.
40 Paul de Man, "Shelley Disfigured," *The Rhetoric of Romanticism* (New York, NY: Columbia University Press, 1984), p. 122.
41 De Man, "Autobiography as De-facement," p. 922.
42 Walter Benjamin, "The Work of Art in the Age of Its Technological Reproducibility: Third Version," *Selected Writings, Volume 4, 1938–1940*, ed. Howard Eiland and Michael W. Jennings, (Cambridge, MA: The Belknap Press of Harvard University, 2006), p. 269.
43 De Man, "Autobiography as De-facement," p. 928.
44 O'Connor, *The Lonely Voice*, p. 225.
45 Ibid., p. 123.
46 Elizabeth Bowen, *People, Places, Things: Essays By Elizabeth Bowen*, ed. Allan Hepburn (Edinburgh: Edinburgh University Press, 2008), p. 239.
47 Ibid., p. 239.
48 Joyce, *Dubliners*, p. 160.

4 Loneliness Is Part of the Job: "Sentimental Loneliness" in Carson McCullers and Richard Yates

1 Some of the recent blogs that discuss loneliness among young people include: https://sosasharon.com/2017/04/06/the-key-to-beating-loneliness-as-a-young-adult/; https://www.refinery29.com/en-gb/2018/05/198255/loneliness-young-people-millennials; https://tinybuddha.com/blog/how-to-overcome-loneliness/.
2 https://www.fanfiction.net/book/Thirteen-Reasons-Why/
3 Riesman et al., *The Lonely Crowd*, p. 149.
4 Ibid.
5 Ibid., p. 155.
6 Ibid.
7 Ibid., p. 307.
8 Ibid.
9 Carson McCullers, *The Heart Is a Lonely Hunter* (Boston, MA: Houghton Miflin, 1940), p. 60.
10 Ibid., p. 137.

11 Ibid., 137–8.
12 Ibid., p. 138.
13 Laing, *Lonely City*, p. 44.
14 Ibid.
15 McCullers, *Heart Is a Lonely Hunter*, p. 183.
16 Ibid., p. 187.
17 Marina Keegan, *The Opposite of Loneliness: Essays and Stories* (New York, NY: Simon Schuster, 2014), p. 1.
18 McCullers, *Heart Is a Lonely Hunter*, p. 312.
19 Ibid.
20 Ibid., p. 122.
21 Laing, *Lonely City*, p. 43.
22 Moustakas, *Loneliness*, p. 22.
23 Yates, *Eleven Kinds of Loneliness*, p. 171.
24 Ibid., p. 62.
25 Ibid., p. 131.
26 Yates, *Revolutionary Road*, p. 304.
27 Ibid.
28 Ibid., pp. 304–5.
29 Ibid., p. 20.
30 Ibid., p. 60.
31 Ibid.
32 Ibid.
33 Ibid., p. 23.
34 Ibid.
35 Ibid., p. 75.

5 Beating University Loneliness and Workplace Boredom: David Foster Wallace on "How to Keep Yourself Open to A Moment of the Most Supernal Beauty"

An earlier version of this chapter appeared in Literature Compass: "David Foster Wallace, Loneliness, and the "Pretty Much Nothing" the University Teaches," Literature Compass, 5 July, 2017, https://doi.org/10.1111/lic3.12396

1 D. T. Max, *Every Love Story Is a Ghost Story: A Life of David Foster Wallace* (London: Granta, 2012), p. 221.
2 Ibid., p. 257.

3 Ibid., p. 164.
4 Ibid., p. 257.
5 Ibid., p. 258.
6 Ibid.
7 Ibid.
8 Ibid., p. 285.
9 Ibid.
10 Ibid., p. 286.
11 Ibid., pp. 298–9
12 Ibid., p. 257.
13 Ibid.
14 Ibid., p. 295.
15 Takeo Doi, *The Anatomy of Dependence* (Tokyo: Kadansha International, 2001), p. 83.
16 Ibid., p. 84.
17 Max, *Every Love Story*, p. 287.
18 Ibid.
19 Ibid., p. 289.
20 Ibid., p. 286.
21 Ibid., p. 287.
22 Ibid., p. 218.
23 http://ijas.iaas.ie/index.php/artIbicle-david-foster-wallace-the-death-of-the-author-and-the-birth-of-adiscipline/.
24 http://www.thehowlingfantods.com/dfw/.
25 See Nathan Ballantyne and Justin Tosi, "David Foster Wallace on the Good Life," *Freedom and the Self: Essays on the Philosophy of David Foster Wallace* (New York, NY: Columbia University Press, 2015) and Bloomsbury Academic's Andrew Bennett, "Inside David Foster Wallace's Head: Attention, Loneliness, Suicide, and the Other Side of Boredom," in *Gesturing Towards Reality: David Foster Wallace and Philosophy*, ed. Roger Goldber and Scott Kolb (London: Bloomsbury, 2014).
26 Ibid., p. 214.
27 Ibid. p. 236.
28 Maria Bustillos, "Philosophy, Self-Help, and the Death of David Foster Wallace," in *Gesturing Towards Reality: David Foster Wallace and Philosophy*, ed. Roger Goldber and Scott Kolb (London: Bloomsbury, 2014), p. xx.
29 Jeffrey Severs, *David Foster Wallace's Balancing Books: Fictions of Value* (New York, NY: Columbia University Press, 2017), p. 4.

30 David Foster Wallace, *Infinite Jest* (New York, NY: Back Bay Books, 1996), p. 515.
31 David Foster Wallace, *The Pale King: An Unfinished Novel* (London: Hamish Hamilton, 2011), p. 406.
32 Boswell in Jennifer Howard, "The Afterlife of David Foster Wallace," *The Chronicle of Higher Education. Chronicle Review*, July 6, 2011.
33 Mark McGurl, "The Institution of Nothing: David Foster Wallace in the Program," *boundary 2* 41, no. 3 (2014): 31.
34 Ibid., p. 32.
35 Ibid., p. 34.
36 Ibid.
37 Samuel Beckett, *Collected Poems* (London: John Calder, 1999), p. 59.
38 McGurl, "The Institution of Nothing," p. 46.
39 http://chronicle.com/article/The-Afterlife-of-David-Foster/125823
40 Marshall Boswell's *Understanding David Foster Wallace* (Columbia, SC: University of South Carolina Press, 2009) and Stephen Burn's *David Foster Wallace's Infinite Jest: A Reader's Guide* (London: Continuum, 2003) have become key works for reading Wallace in college courses. This expansion of the field of Wallace Studies continues today.
41 This is from the story "The Suffering Channel" from his Wallace's collection *Oblivion*, p. 284.
42 Adam Kelly, "David Foster Wallace: The Death of the Author and the Birth of a Discipline," *Irish Journal of American Studies*, April 2010. Available online: http://ijas.iaas.ie/index.php/article-david-foster-wallace-the-death-of-the-author-andthe-birth-of-a-discipline/.
43 In Howard, "The Afterlife of David Foster Wallace,"
44 Nathan Ballantyne and Justin Tosi, "David Foster Wallace on the Good Life," *Freedom and the Self: Essays on the Philosophy of David Foster Wallace* (New York, NY: Columbia University Press, 2015), p. 125.
45 Ibid., p. 127.
46 Ibid., p. 125.
47 Ibid.
48 Mortenson, p. 23.
49 Thomas Piketty, *Capital in the Twenty-First Century* (Cambridge, MA: Belknap Press, 2014), p. 486.
50 Wallace, *Infinite Jest*, p. 185.
51 Ibid., p. 156.
52 Ibid., p. 694.
53 Ibid.

54 Ibid., pp. 694–5.
55 Ibid., p. 694.
56 Ibid.
57 Ibid.
58 Ibid.
59 Ibid.
60 Ibid., p. 132.
61 Ibid., p. 125.
62 Ibid., p. 130.
63 Ibid., p. 133.
64 Ibid., p. 134.
65 David Foster Wallace, *The Broom of the System* (London: Penguin, 1987), p. 206.
66 Ibid.
67 Ibid., pp. 206–7.
68 Wallace "remembered how ECT had damaged his short-term memory in 1988"; from Max, *Every Love Story*, p. 300.
69 Ibid.
70 Wallace, *The Pale King*, p. 502.
71 Ibid., p. 486.
72 Ibid., p. 485.
73 Ibid., p. 486.
74 Ibid., p. 497.
75 Ibid., p. 498.
76 Ibid., p. 438.
77 David Foster Wallace, *Oblivion: Stories* (London: Abacus, 2004), p. 284.
78 Ibid., p. 169.

6 Loneliness in a Selection of Japanese Philosophy and Fiction: Doi, Sōseki, Nishida, Murakami, Murata

1 Doi, *Anatomy of Dependence*, p. 42.
2 Siedentop, *Inventing the Individual*, p. 190.
3 Ibid., p. 184.
4 Ibid., p. 190.
5 Ibid., p. 191.
6 Bruno Latour, *An Inquiry into Modes of Existence: An Anthropology of the Moderns* (Cambridge, MA: Harvard University Press, 2013), p. 14.

7 Ibid.
8 Ibid., p. 52.
9 Ibid.
10 Storr, *Selfie*, p. 80.
11 Ibid., p. 72.
12 Ibid., p. 75.
13 Doi, *Anatomy of Dependence*, p. 74.
14 Ibid., p. 86.
15 Ibid., p. 113.
16 Ibid.
17 Ibid., pp. 113–14.
18 Ibid., p. 114.
19 Ibid., p. 115.
20 Ibid., p. 117.
21 Ibid.
22 Ibid., p. 118.
23 Ibid., p. 119.
24 Ibid., p. 120.
25 Ibid., p. 121.
26 Natsume Soseki, *Kokoro*, trans. Meredith McKinney, Penguin Classics (London: Penguin, 2010), p. 229.
27 Ibid.
28 Ibid., p. 230.
29 Natsume Soseki, *My Individualism and The Philosophical Foundations of Literature*, trans. Sammy I. Tsunematsu, intro. Inger Brodey (Boston, MA: Tuttle, 2004), p. 11.
30 Ibid., p. 43.
31 Ibid., pp. 34–5.
32 Ibid., p. 35.
33 Ibid.
34 Ibid., p. 36.
35 Ibid.
36 Ibid. p. 37.
37 Ibid., p. 38.
38 Ibid., p. 40.
39 Ibid.
40 Ibid., p. 43.
41 Ibid., p. 46.
42 Ibid., p. 48.

43 Storr, *Selfie*, p. 126.
44 Soseki, *My Individualism*, p. 48.
45 Ibid.
46 Ibid., p. 50.
47 Ibid., p. 51.
48 Ibid.
49 Ibid., p. 53.
50 Ibid., p. 54.
51 Ibid., p. 56.
52 Ibid., p. 65.
53 Ibid., pp. 134–5.
54 Ibid., p. 136.
55 Ibid., p. 137.
56 Ibid.
57 Ibid.
58 Ibid., p. 140.
59 Ibid., p. 141.
60 Ibid.
61 Ibid.
62 See Michael O'Sullivan, *Michel Henry: Incarnation, barbarism, and belief* (Oxford: Peter Lang), 2006.
63 Kitarō Nishida, *Last Writings: Nothingness and the Religious Worldview*, trans. David A. Dilworth (Honolulu, HI: University of Hawaii Press, 1993), p. 61.
64 Ibid., p. 62.
65 Ibid..
66 Ibid., p. 63.
67 Ibid., p. 66.
68 Ibid.
69 Ibid., p. 67.
70 Ibid.
71 Derrida, *The Gift*, p. 38.
72 Ibid., p. 38.
73 Ibid., p. 17.
74 Ibid., p. 37.
75 Nishida, *Last Writings*, p. 66.
76 Ibid., p. 77.
77 Ibid. p. 98.
78 Ibid. p. 87.
79 Ibid. p. 85.

80 Ibid.
81 Natsume Soseki, *Sanshiro*, Penguin Classics (London: Penguin, 2009), p. 34.
82 Haruki Murakami, *Men Without Women*, trans. Philip Gabriel and Ted Goossen (London: Harvil Secker, 2017), p. 145.
83 Ibid., p. 221.
84 Ibid., p. 223.
85 Ibid., pp. 223–4.
86 Soseki, *Sanshiro*, p. xxxiv.
87 Ibid., p. xxxi.
88 Ibid., p. xxxv.
89 Ibid., p. xxxv.
90 Ibid., p. 20.
91 Ibid., p. 21.
92 Ibid.
93 See Hiroaki Sato, "The Transient Rasping that Captivates the Poets," *The Japan Times*, May 27, 2013. Sato reminds us of the references to cicadas in the poetry of Basho: "Not showing it is soon to die the cicada's voice." Sato also notes that the cicada shell has been used to symbolize the vanity of life in ancient Japanese poetry: "The cicada shell as a symbol of the vanity of life — as in the Biblical 'vanity is vanity'—is expressed well in an anonymous poem in 'Kokinshu,' an anthology from the early 10th century: 'The husks of empty cicadas are left on every tree, but not seeing where their spirits have gone makes me sad.' In the original, 'tree' (ki) also means 'coffin.'"
94 Ibid., p. 27.
95 Ibid., p. 10.
96 Ibid., p. 22.
97 Ibid., p. 44.
98 Ibid., p. 45.
99 Ibid.
100 Ibid., p. 46.
101 Ibid.
102 Ibid.
103 Sayaka Murata, *Convenience Store Woman*, trans. Ginny Tapley Takemori (New York, NY: Grove Press, 2018), p. 6.
104 Ibid., p. 11.
105 Ibid., p. 12.
106 Ibid., pp. 12–13.
107 Ibid., p. 21.
108 Ibid., p. 22.

109 Ibid., p. 26.
110 Ibid., p. 30.
111 Ibid., p. 37.
112 Ibid., p. 329.
113 Ibid. p. 39.
114 Ibid.
115 Ibid., pp. 65–6.
116 Ibid., p. 67.
117 Ibid., pp. 80–1.
118 Ibid., p. 86.
119 Ibid., p. 92.
120 Ibid., p. 93.
121 Ibid., p. 107.
122 Ibid., p. 108.
123 Ibid., p. 128.
124 Ibid.
125 Gail Honeyman, *Eleanor Oliphant Is Completely Fine* (London: HarperCollins, 2017), p. 276.
126 Ibid., p. 159.
127 Murata, *Convenience Store Woman*, pp.131–2.
128 Ibid., p. 133.
129 Ibid., p. 144.
130 Ibid., p. 149.
131 Ibid., p. 150.
132 Ibid., p. 160.
133 Ibid., p. 161.
134 Ibid.
135 Ibid., p. 162.
136 Ibid., p. 153.
137 Ibid., p. 163.
138 O no Yasumaro, "Kojiki," trans. Chamberlain Hall Basil, *Internet Sacred Text Archive*, 2005, www.sacred-texts.com/shi/kj/index.htm, Section I.
139 Further complicating the question, the hidden world is not always held to be the world of the dead, signified in Kojiki as Yomi (黄泉), in the episode of Izanami and Izanagi.
140 Yasumaro, "Kojiki," Section XVI.
141 Tetsuro Watsuji, *Watsuji Tetsuro's Rinrigaku: Ethics in Japan*, trans. Robert Carter and Seisaku Yamamoto (New York, NY: SUNY, 1996), pp. 23–4.
142 Yasumaro, "Kojiki," Section XVI.

143 Watsuji spoke extensively of the human body in the fourth chapter of Rinrigaku, refuting any strictly physiological understanding of human beings; but ultimately made a distinction between a human being and a "material solid," that "a human body transformed into a mere material solid object ... is no longer a person" (*Rinrigaku*, p. 67). One suspects that by "material solid," he meant the deceased. The death of one individual is one such scenario when human connection is "completely destroyed" and the human body becomes material solid or "terminates in absolute emptiness" (p. 68). What is left undiscussed is how this death might be brought about: how for one, it is possible for the individual to become expended in its service to the community, be it on a battlefield in Watsuji's time, or in a workplace in the twenty-first century. Though Watsuji spoke highly of sacrifice performed as a response to trust, one suspects that he would not approve of the mass accelerated expenditure or "sacrifice" of individuals in communal service, be it in war or over work (p. 266).
144 Yasumaro, "Kojiki," Section XXXII.
145 Martin Heidegger, *Being and Time*, trans. John Macquarrie and Edward Robinson, (New York, NY: Harper Perennial, 2008), p. 436.
146 Yasumaro, "Kojiki," Section XVI.
147 Watsuji, *Rinrigaku*, p. 331.
148 Ibid., p. 31.
149 Ibid., p. 134.
150 Hajime Tanabe, *Philosophy as Metanoetics*, trans. Yoshinori Takeuchi and James W. Heisig (Nagoya: Chisokudō, 2016), p. 98.
151 Ibid., p. 88.
152 Watsuji, *Rinrigaku*, p. 117.
153 Tanabe, *Philosophy as Metanoetics*, p. 129.
154 Watsuji, *Rinrigaku*, p. 341.
155 Ibid., p. 12.

7 Filial Piety and Loneliness in a Selection of Chinese Novels: Cao Xueqin, Mo Yan, Dai Sijie, Ha Jin, and Yiyun Li

1 Longxi Zhang, *From Comparison to World Literature* (New York, NY: State University of New York Press, 2016), p. 7.
2 Raghaven Iyer (1965) in ibid., p. 51.
3 Chenyang Li, "Shifting Perspectives: Filial Morality Revisited," *Philosophy East and West* 47, no. 2(April 1997): 218.

4 Ibid., p. 219.
5 Joseph Chan, *Confucian Perfectionism: A Political Philosophy for Modern Times* (Oxford: Princeton University Press, 2014), p. 157.
6 Ibid.
7 Ibid.
8 Zhaoming Qian, *The Modernist Response to Chinese Art: Pound, Moore, Stevens* (Charlottesville, VA: University of Virginia Press, 2012), p. 109.
9 Ibid.
10 Ibid.
11 Ibid.
12 Ibid., p. 101.
13 Ibid., p. 78.
14 Ibid.
15 Ibid., p. 69.
16 Ibid., p. 74.
17 Ban Wang, "The People in the Modern Chinese Novel: Popular Democracy and World Literature," *Novel* 47, no. 1 (2014): 43–56.
18 Georg Lukács, *Realism in Our Time: Literature and the Class Struggle* (New York: Harper & Row, 1971), p. 19.
19 Wang, "The People in the Modern Chinese Novel," p. 50.
20 Ibid., p. 55.
21 Yiyun Li, *Dear Friend, from My Life I Write to You in Your Life* (London: Penguin, 2017), p. 173.
22 Stephen C. Angle, *Sagehood: The Contemporary Significance of Neo-Confucian Philosophy* (Oxford: Oxford University Press, 2012), p. 120.
23 Ibid., p. 68.
24 Ibid., p. 113.
25 Cao Xueqin, *The Dream of the Red Chamber*, trans. H. Bencraft Joly, foreword John Minford, Tuttle Classic (Tuttle: Tokyo, 2010), p. 287.
26 Ibid., p. 260.
27 Ibid., p. 257.
28 Ibid., p. 259.
29 Ibid., pp. 245–6.
30 Ibid., p. 255.
31 Ibid., p. 508.
32 Cao, Xueqin, *The Story of the Stone*, 5 vols., trans. David Hawkes and John Minford, Penguin Classics (London: Penguin, 1982), Vol. IV, p. 56.
33 Ibid., p. 48.

34 Mo Yan, *Red Sorghum*, trans. Howard Goldblatt (New York, NY: Penguin, 1994), p. 67.
35 Ibid., p. 356.
36 Ibid., p. 357.
37 Ibid.
38 Ibid., 369.
39 Dai Sijie, *Balzac and the Little Chinese Seamstress* (London: Vintage, 2002), p. 102.
40 Ibid., p. 103.
41 Ibid., p. 135.
42 Ibid., p. 149.
43 Dai Sijie, *Once on a Moonless Night* (London: Anchor, 2009), p. 74.
44 Ibid., pp. 74–5.
45 Ibid., p. 60.
46 Ha Jin, *Waiting* (London: Vintage, 2000), p. 296.
47 Ibid., p. 299.
48 Ibid.
49 Ibid.
50 Ibid., p. 167.
51 Xi Jinping, *The Governance of China* (Beijing: Foreign Languages Press, 2018), p. 42.
52 Ibid.
53 Michel Foucault, *Hermeneutics of the Subject: Lectures at the Collège de France 1981–1982* (London: Picador, 2005), p. 97.
54 Michel Foucault, *History of Sexuality. Vol. 3. The Care of the Self* (London: Vintage, 1988), p. 158.
55 Ibid.
56 Ibid., p. 63.
57 Ibid.
58 Ibid.
59 Ibid., p. 64.
60 Ibid.
61 Ibid.
62 Ibid.
63 Monica Fludernik, *Towards a "Natural" Narratology* (London: Routledge, 2002), p. 243.
64 Ibid., p. 244.
65 Ibid., p. 245.
66 Li, *Dear Friend*, p. 98.

67 Ibid., p. 147.
68 Ibid., p. 148.
69 Ibid., p. 151.

8 "I Am Trash": How Student Stress and Student Self-Stratification Is Creating a Generation of "Interconnected Loners"

1 See, for example, Lani Guinier, *The Tyranny of the Meritocracy: Democratizing Higher Education in America* (Boston, MA: Beacon Press, 2015); Suzanne Mettler, *Degrees of Inequality: How the Politics of Higher Education Sabotaged the American Dream* (New York: Basic Books, 2014).
2 Jane Zhang, "More Hong Kong students taking their own lives, study by Jockey Club research suicide centre finds." *South China Morning Post*, Sept. 10, 2018.
3 A. Y. K. Poon and Y. C. Wong, "Governance in Education in Hong Kong: A Decentralizing or a Centralizing Path?" in *One Country, Two Systems in Crisis*, ed. Y. C. Wong (Lanham, MD: Lexington Books, 2004); Education and Manpower Bureau, *The New Academic Structure for Senior Secondary Education and Higher Education* (Hong Kong: Government Printer, 2005); C. -H. Tung, *New Elitism*, December 18, 2001, available online: www.info.gov.hk/ce/speech/cest.htm.
4 Poon, "Governance in Education"; Tung, *New Elitism*.
5 Poon, "Governance in Education."
6 Te-Ping Chen, "Hong Kong's Wealth Gap Gets Larger," *Wall Street Journal*, June 19, 2012, available online: http://blogs.wsj. com/chinarealtime/2012/06/19/hong-kongs-wealth-gap-gets-larger/?blog_id=72&post_id=15969&mod=wsj_valettop_email; Gus Lubin, "This City Has by Far the Most Inequality in the Developed World," *Business Insider*, June 26, 2012, available online: http://www.businessinsider.com/inequality-in-hong-kong-2012-6.
7 Jennifer Ngo, "Working Poor Households Increase Alarmingly Despite Hong Kong Government's Attempts to Reduce Poverty Since 2013," *South China Morning Post*, September 30, 2015.
8 Tik Chi Yuen, "Hong Kong Students Need More Options—and Less Stress," *South China Morning Post*, July 15, 2015; *China Daily*, "40% Students Feel Stress: Survey," March 24, 2016.
9 Kim-ming Lee, Hung Wong, and Kam-yee Law, "Social Polarisation and Poverty in the Global City: The Case of Hong Kong," *China Report* 43, no. 1 (2007): 1–30.

10 Leo Goodstadt, *Poverty in the Midst of Affluence: How Hong Kong Mismanaged Its Prosperity* (Hong Kong: Hong Kong University Press, 2013).
11 Poon, "Governance in Education."
12 Jennifer Ngo, "Hong Kong Lawmakers Launch 'Blood-Stained' TSA Paper Protest over Student Suicide Tragedies," *South China Morning Post*, March 16, 2016.
13 R. Lazarus and S. Folkman, *Stress, Appraisal and Coping* (New York, NY: Springer, 1984).
14 Verhaeghe, *What About Me?*
15 Ibid., p. 11.
16 *RTHK*, "40% Interviewed HKDSE Students Found It Difficult to Make Post-Result-Release Choices," July 9, 2016, available online: http://news.rthk.hk/rthk/ch/component/k2/1271641-20160709.htm.
17 David Robotham, "Stress among Higher Education Students: Towards a Reseacrh Agenda," *Higher Education* 56, no. 6 (2008): 735–46; R. J. Manthei, and A. Gilmore (2005), "The Effect of Paid Employment on University Students' Lives," *Education and Training* 47, no. 3 (2005): 202–15; UNITE Student Living Report. UK Government Publication (2004).
18 F. Michie, M. Glachan, and D. Bray, "An Evaluation of Factors Influencing the Academic Self-Concept, Self-Esteem and Academic Stress for Direct and Re-Entry Students in Higher Education," *Educational Psychology* 21, no. 4 (2001): 455–72; M. Brown and S. Ralph, "Using the DYSA Programme to Reduce Stress and Anxiety in First-Year University Students," *Pastoral Care* 17, no. 3 (1999): 8–13; J. S. Bush, M. Thompson and N. Van Tuvergen, "Persona; Assessment of Stress Factors for College Students," *Journal of School Health* 55, no. 9 (1985): 370–5..
19 Pryjmachuk and Richards, "Predicting Stress"; C. Radcliffe and H. Lester, "Perceived Stress During Undergraduate Medical Training: A Qualitative Study," *Medical Education* 37, no. 32 (2007): 32–8; Redwood, 2007.
20 Ka-heung Leung, "The Relationship of Stress & Depression: A Study Among Secondary Students in Hong Kong," M.A. Dissertation, available online: http://hdl.handle.net/10722/65139.
21 D. H. Hepworth, O. W. Farley, and J. K. Griffiths, "Clinical Work with Suicidal Adolescents and Their Families," *Social Casework* 3, no. 3 (1988): 195–203.
22 David Robotham, "Stress among Higher Education Students: Towards a Research Agenda," *Higher Education*, 56 (2008): 735–46.
23 Ibid., p. 737.
24 S. Marginson, "The Worldwide Trend to High Participation in Higher Education: Dynamics of Social Stratification in Inclusive Systems," *Higher Education* 72, no. 413 (2016).

25 Poon, "Governance in Education."
26 Poon, "Governance in Education," p. 36.
27 Alice Wu, "Hothouse Hong Kong Is Spawning a New Breed of Monster Parents," *South China Morning Post*, June 26, 2016.
28 Hong Kong Institute of Asia-Pacific Studies, "60% Respondents Disagree with the Necessity to Win at the Starting Line; 90% Admits that It Is a Common Perception in Hong Kong," August 2016, p. 2, available online: http://www.cuhk.edu.hk/hkiaps/tellab/pdf/telepress/16/SP_Press_Release_20160808.pdf.
29 Poon, "Governance in Education," p. 36.
30 Paul Verhaeghe, *What About Me? The Struggle for Identity in a Market-Based Society* (London: Scribe, 2014), p. 117.
31 Ibid., p. 29.
32 Chau-Kiu Cheung and Elizabeth Rudowicz, "Underachievement and Attributions Among Students Attending Schools Stratified by Student Ability." *Social Psychology of Education* 6 (2003): 303–23.
33 Cheung and Rudowicz, "Underachievement and Attributions among Students Attending Schools Stratified by Student Ability."
34 Melissa Benn, "School Wars by Melissa Benn—Review," *Guardian*, August 8, 2011.
35 Poon, "Governance in Education."
36 Ibid.
37 http://www.bookofschool.com/school/controller/schoolSearch?reporttype=secondaryranking&schoolcategory=2; https://www.schooland.hk/ss/.
38 http://www.hked.org/sspa.htm; Chinese only.
39 Goodstadt, *Poverty in the Midst of Affluence*, p. 162.
40 David Kember, "Opening up the Road to Nowhere: Problems with the Path to Mass Higher Education in Hong Kong," *Higher Education* 59 (2009): 167–79.
41 OECD. 2012. *Education at a Glance 2012: Highlights*. Paris: OECD Publishing. doi: 10.1787/eag_highlights-2012-en.
42 H. Connor, C. Tyers, T. Modood, and J. Hilage. *Why the Difference? A Closer Look at Higher Education Minority Ethnic Students and Graduates*. Nottingham: DfES Publications, 2004.
43 CSDHKSAR, Census and Statistics Department of the Hong Kong Special Administrative Region, *Population Census Summary Results* (Hong Kong: Census and Statistics Department, 2011), p. 45. http://www.statistics.gov.hk/pub/B11200552011XXXXB0100.pdf.
44 UNESCO, *Higher Education in Asia: Expanding Out, Expanding Up: The Rise of Graduate Education and University Research*, 2014, http://www.uis.unesco.org.
45 Verhaeghe, *What About Me?* p. 169.

46 Hong Kong ranks seventy-fifth in the UN's World Happiness Report Update 2016, having dropped from seventy-second in 2015 and sixty-fourth in 2013.
47 World Happiness Report Update, 2016, ed. John Helliwell, Richard Layard, and Jeffrey Sachs, 2016, available online: http://worldhappiness.report/wp-content/uploads/sites/2/2016/03/HR-V1_web.pdf.

9 An Erotics of Loneliness

1 K. Shaughnessy, E. S. Byers, S. L. Clowater, and A. Kalinowski, "Self-Appraisals of Arousal-Oriented Online Sexual Activities in University and Community Samples," *Archives of Sexual Behavior* 43, no. 6 (2014): 1187–97.
2 Yaniv Efrati and Yair Amichai-Hamburger, "The Use of Online Pornography as Compensation for Loneliness and Lack of Social Ties Among Israeli Adolescents," *Psychological Reports*, September 2018.
3 Stefanie Marsh, "Teenagers on Loneliness: We Want to Talk to Our Parents. We Need Their Guidancle," *The Guardian*, April 8, 2017. https://www.theguardian.com/society/2017/apr/08/teenagers-loneliness-social-media-isolation-parents-attention
4 "The Internet's Impact on Sexuality: A Critical Review of 15 Years of Research," *Computers in Human Behavior* 25 (2009): 1089–101.
5 W. A. Fisher and A. Barak, A.,"Internet Pornography: A Social Psychological Perspective on Internet Sexuality," *Journal of Sex Research* 38, no. 4 (2001): 312–23.
6 Twenge, *iGen*, p. 99.
7 Michel Foucault, *Order of Things: An Archaeology of the Human* (London: Vintage, 1994), p. 339.
8 Ibid., p. 338.
9 Hardt and Negri, *Commonwealth*, p. 59
10 Floridi, *The Ethics of Information*, p. 102.
11 Kaag, *Hiking With Nietzsche*, p. 74.
12 Ibid.
13 M. M. Moretti and M. Peled, "Adolescent–Parent Attachment: Bonds that Support Healthy Development," *Paediatric Child Health* 9, no. 8 (2004): 552.
14 Jonathan Dollimore, *Desire: A Memoir* (London: Bloomsbury, 2017), p. 54.
15 Ibid., p. 55.
16 Twenge, *iGen*, p. 213.
17 Ibid., p. 216.

18 Ibid., p. 215.
19 Ibid.
20 Ibid., p. 212.
21 Ibid., p. 213.
22 Marsh, "Teenagers on Loneliness."
23 Of the top three virtual reality sites on the internet, three are for pornography.
24 Slavoj Žižek, *Organs without Bodies On Deleuze and Consequences* (London: Routledge, 2012), p. 71.
25 Gilles Deleuze, *Pure Immanence: Essays on A Life* (New York: Zone Books, 2005), pp. 29–30.
26 Ibid., p. 30.
27 Ibid., p. 29.
28 Gilles Deleuze and Felix Guattari, *Anti-Oedipus: Capitalism and Scizophrenia* (London: Continuum, 2004), p. 323.
29 Ibid., p. 324.
30 Ibid., p. 325.
31 Ibid.
32 Ibid., 326.
33 Ibid., p. 322.
34 Ibid., p. 333.
35 Ibid., p. xxv.

Bibliography

Agamben, Giorgio. *The Open: Man and Animal*. Stanford, CA: Stanford University Press, 2003.

Aherne, D. "Understanding Student Stress: A Qualitative Approach." *The Irish Journal of Psychology* 22, no. 3/4 (2001): 176–87.

Akgun, S. and J. Ciarrochi. "Learned Resourcefulness Moderates the Relationship between Academic Stress and Academic Performance." *Educational Psychology* 23, no. 3 (2003): 287–94.

Alon, Sigal. "The Evolution of Class Inequality in Higher Education: Competition, Exclusion and Adaptation." *American Sociological Review* 74, no. 5 (2009): 731–55.

Andrews, B. and J. M. Wilding. "The Relation of Depression and Anxiety to Life-Stress and Achievement in Students." *British Journal of Psychology* 95 (2004): 509–21.

Ang, R. P. and V. S. Huan. "Relationship between Academic Stress and Suicidal Ideation: Testing for Depression as a Mediator Using Multiple Regression." *Child Psychiatry & Human Development* 37, no. 2 (2006): 133–43.

Angle, Stephen C. *Sagehood: The Contemporary Significance of Neo-Confucian Philosophy*. Oxford: Oxford University Press, 2012.

Ballantyne, Nathan and Justin Tosi. "David Foster Wallace on the Good Life." In *Freedom and the Self: Essays on the Philosophy of David Foster Wallace*. New York: Columbia University Press, 2015, pp. 124–56.

Bauman, Zygmunt. *Stangers at Our Door*. London: Polity, 2016.

Bauman, Zygmunt and Ezio Mauro. *Babel*. London: Polity, 2016.

Beckett, Samuel. *Collected Poems*. London: John Calder, 1999.

Benjamin, Walter. "The Work of Art in the Age of Its Technological Reproducibility: Third Version." In *Walter Benjamin: Selected Writings. Volume 4, 1938–1940*. Ed. Howard Eiland and Michael W. Jennings. Cambridge, MA: The Belknap Press of Harvard University, 2006, pp. 251–83.

Benn, Melissa. "School Wars by Melissa Benn—Review." *The Guardian*. August 8, 2011.

Bennett, Andrew. "Inside David Foster Wallace's Head: Attention, Loneliness, Suicide, and the Other Side of Boredom." In *Gesturing Towards Reality: David Foster Wallace and Philosophy*. London: Bloomsbury, 2014, pp. 202–46.

Bolger, Robert K and Scott Korb. *Gesturing Towards Reality: David Foster Wallace and Philosophy.* London: Bloomsbury, 2014.

Boswell, Marshall. *Understanding David Foster Wallace.* Columbia, SC: University of South Carolina Press, 2003.

Boswell, Marshall. *David Foster Wallace and "The Long Thing": New Essays on the Novels.* London: Bloomsbury, 2014.

Bowen, Elizabeth. *People, Places, Things: Essays by Elizabeth Bowen.* Ed. Allan Hepburn. Edinburgh: Edinburgh University Press, 2008.

Brown, M. and S. Ralph. "Using the DYSA Programme to Reduce Stress and Anxiety in First-Year University Students." *Pastoral Care* 17, no. 3 (1999): 8–13.

Buchanan, Allen E. *Beyond Humanity? The Ethics of Biomedical Enhancement.* Oxford: Oxford University Press, 2013.

Burn, Stephen. *David Foster Wallace's Infinite Jest: A Reader's Guide.* London: Continuum, 2003.

Bush, J. S., M. Thompson, and N. Van Tuvergen. "Persona: Assessment of Stress Factors for College Students." *Journal of School Health* 55, no. 9 (1985): 370–5.

Bustillos, Maria. "Philosophy, Self-Help, and the Death of David Foster Wallace." In *Gesturing Towards Reality: David Foster Wallace and Philosophy.* Ed. Roger Goldber and Scott Kolb. London: Bloomsbury, 2014, pp. 351–403.

Cacioppo, J. T. and P. Williams. *Loneliness: Human Nature and the Need for Social Connection.* New York, NY: W.W. Norton, 2009.

Cahn, Steven M. and Maureen Eckert. *Freedom and the Self: Essays on the Philosophy of David Foster Wallace.* New York: Columbia University Press, 2015.

Camus, Albert. *The Outsider.* Penguin Modern Classics. London: Penguin Random House, 2013.

Cao, Xueqin. *The Story of the Stone.* 5 vols. Trans. David Hawkes and John Minford. Penguin Classics. London: Penguin, 1982.

Cao, Xueqin. *The Dream of the Red Chamber.* Trans. H. Bencraft Joly. Foreword John Minford. Tuttle Classic. Tuttle: Tokyo, 2010.

Carr, Nicholas. *The Shallows: How the Internet Is Changing the Way We Read, Think and Remember.* London: Atlantic Books, 2010.

Chan, Joseph. *Confucian Perfectionism: A Political Philosophy for Modern Times.* Oxford: Princeton University Press, 2014.

Chemero, Anthony. *Radical Embodied Cognitive Science.* A Bradford Book. Cambridge, MA: The MIT Press, 2009.

CSDHKSAR (Census and Statistics Department of the Hong Kong Special Administrative Region). 2011 Population Census Summary Results. Hong

Kong: Census and Statistics Department, 2011. http://www.statistics.gov.hk/pub/B11200552011XXXXB0100.pdf.

Chen, Te-Ping. "Hong Kong's Wealth Gap Gets Larger." *Wall Street Journal*. June 19, 2012. http://blogs.wsj.com/chinarealtime/2012/06/19/hong-kongs-wealth-gap-gets-larger/?blog_id=72&post_id=15969&mod=wsj_valettop_email.

Cheung, Chau-Kiu and Elizabeth Rudowicz, "Underachievement and Attributions among Students Attending Schools Stratified by Student Ability." *Social Psychology of Education* 6 (2003): 303–23.

China Daily. "40% Students Feel Stress: Survey." March 24, 2016.

Chwee, L. C., D. Jiansan, and M. A. Perez, "Validation of the East Asian Student Stress Inventory (EASSI)." *American Journal of Health Studies* 14, no. 3 (1998): 153–61.

Cohen, Daniel. *"Il Faut Dire Que Les Temps Ont Changé ...": Chronique (Fiévreuse) D'une Mutation Qui Inquiéte*. Paris: Albin Michel, 2018.

Connor, H., Tyers, C., Modood, T. and Hilage, J. *Why the Difference? A Closer Look at Higher Education Minority Ethnic Students and Graduates*. Nottingham: DfES Publications, 2004.

Deleuze, Gilles and Guattari, Felix. *Anti-Oedipus: Capitalism and Scizophrenia*. London: Continuum, 2004.

Deleuze Gilles., *Pure Immanence: Essays on A Life*. New York: Zone Books, 2005.

D'Hoker, Elke and Stephanie Eggermont, eds. "Loneliness and the Submerged Population: Frank O'Connor's *The Lonely Voice* and Joyce's 'The Dead.'" In *The Irish Short Story*. Oxford: Peter Lang, 2015.

De Man, Paul. "Autobiography as De-facement." *MLN* 94, no. 5 (1979): 919–30.

De Man, Paul. "Shelley Disfigured." *The Rhetoric of Romanticism*. New York, NY: Columbia University Press, 1984.

De Montaigne, Michel. *On Solitude*. Great Ideas. London: Penguin, 2009.

Derrida, Jacques. *Speech and Phenomena, and Other Essays on Husserl's Theory of Signs*. Evanston, IL: Northwestern University Press, 1973.

Derrida, Jacques. "Violence and Metaphysics". *Writing and Difference*. Trans. Alan Bass. Routledge Classics, 2001.

Derrida, Jacques. *Learning to Live Finally*. Brooklyn, NY: Melville House, 2007.

Derrida, Jacques. *The Gift of Death and Literature in Silence*. 2nd ed. Trans. David Wills. Chicago, IL: University of Chicago Press, 2008.

Dewey, John. *Individualism, Old and New*. New York, NY: Capricorn Books, 1962.

DiMaggio, P., E. Hargittai, C. Celeste, and S. Shafer. "Digital Inequality: From Unequal Access to Differentiated Use." In *Social Inequality*. Ed. K. M. Neckerman. New York, NY: Russell Sage Foundation, 2004.

Doi, Takeo. *The Anatomy of Dependence*. Tokyo: Kadansha International, 2001.

Dollimore, Jonathan. *Desire: A Memoir*. London: Bloomsbury, 2017.

Döring, Nicola M. "The Internet's Impact on Sexuality: A Critical Review of 15 Years of Research." *Computers in Human Behavior* 25 (2009): 1089–101.

Druckner, Peter S. "The Age of Social Transformation." *The Atlantic Monthly*. November 1994: 53–80.

Edel, Leon. *Henry James: A Life*. New York, NY: Harper & Row, 1985.

Education 2.1. "Survey Result on the Stress of HKDSE Exam Release." https://www.edu2point1.hk/survey-result/. 2017.

Education and Manpower Bureau. *The New Academic Structure for Senior Secondary Education and Higher Education*. Hong Kong: Government Printer, 2005.

Efrati, Yaniv and Yair Amichai-Hamburger. "The Use of Online Pornography as Compensation for Loneliness and Lack of Social Ties Among Israeli Adolescents." *Psychological Reports*. September 2018.

Emerson, Ralph Waldo. "The American Scholar: An Oration before the Phi Beta Kappa Society, at Cambridge, August 31, 1837." *Emerson: Essays and Lectures*. New York, NY: The Library of America, 1983.

Finn, Ed. *What Algorithms Want: Imagination in the Age of Computing*. Cambridge, MA: MIT Press, 2018.

Fisher, W. A. and A. Barak. "Internet Pornography: A Social Psychological Perspective on Internet Sexuality." *Journal of Sex Research* 38, no. 4 (2001): 312–23.

Floridi, Luciano. *The Ethics of Information*. Oxford: Oxford University Press, 2015.

Fludernik, Monica. *Towards a "Natural" Narratology*. London: Routledge, 2002.

Foucault, Michel. *History of Sexuality. Vol. 3. The Care of the Self*. London: Vintage, 1988.

Foucault, Michel. *Order of Things: An Archaeology of the Human*. London: Vintage, 1994.

Foucault, Michel. *Hermeneutics of the Subject: Lectures at the Collège de France 1981–1982*. London: Picador, 2005.

Goodstadt, Leo. *Poverty in the Midst of Affluence: How Hong Kong Mismanaged Its Prosperity*. Hong Kong: Hong Kong University Press, 2013.

Guinier, Lani. *The Tyranny of the Meritocracy: Democratizing Higher Education in America*. Boston, MA: Beacon Press, 2015.

Hallam, Susan and Samantha Parsons. "Prevalence of Streaming in UK Primary Schools: Evidence from the Millennium Cohort Study." *British Educational Research Journal* 39, no. 3 (2013): 514–44. DOI: 10.1080/01411926.2012.659721.

Hammond, Meghan Marie. "Into Other Minds: William and Henry James." *Empathy and the Psychology of Literary Modernism*. Edinburgh: Edinburgh University Press, 2014.

Hardt, Michael and Antonio Negri. *Commonwealth*. Cambridge, MA: Belknap Press, 2009.

Hargittai, E. and A. Hinnant. "Digital Inequality: Differences in Young Adults' Use of the Internet." *Communication Research* 35 (2008): 602–62.

Hari, Johann. *Lost Connections: Uncovering the Real Causes of Depression—and the Unexpected Solutions*. London: Bloomsbury, 2018.

Harris, Charles B. *Proofread or Die!: Writings by Former Students & Colleagues of David Foster Wallace*. Gilson, IL: Lit Fest Press, 2016.

Heidegger, Martin. *Being and Time*. Trans. John Macquarrie and Edward Robinson. New York, NY: Harper Perennial, 2008.

Hepworth, D. H., O. W. Farley, and J. K. Griffiths. "Clinical Work with Suicidal Adolescents and Their Families." *Social Casework* 3, no. 3 (1988): 195–203.

Holt-Lunstad, Julianne, Timothy B. Smith, and J. Bradley Layton. "Social Relationships and Mortality Risk: A Meta-analytic Review." *PLoS Med* 7, no. 7 (2010): e1000316. https://doi.org/10.1371/journal.pmed.1000316.

Honeyman, Gail. *Eleanor Oliphant Is Completely Fine*. London: HarperCollins, 2017.

Hong Kong Federation of Youth Groups. "HKDSE Candidates' View about Continuing Studies Survey." July 2016. http://www.hkfyg.org.hk/page.aspx?corpname=hkfyg&i=1887&locale=en-US.

Hong Kong Examinations and Assessment Authority. Press Release. 2012.

Hong Kong Diploma of Secondary Education (HKDSE). "Examination Results Released." 2012. http://www.hkeaa.edu.hk/DocLibrary/Media/PR/20120719_HKDSE_Results_ENG_FULL.pdf.

Hong Kong Diploma of Secondary Education (HKDSE). "Press Release: 2013 Hong Kong Diploma of Secondary Education (HKDSE) Examination Results Released." 2013. http://www.hkeaa.edu.hk/DocLibrary/Media/PR/20130714_HKDSE_Results_ENG_FULL.pdf.

Hong Kong Diploma of Secondary Education (HKDSE). "Press Release: 2014 Hong Kong Diploma of Secondary Education (HKDSE) Examination Results Released." 2014. http://www.hkeaa.edu.hk/DocLibrary/Media/PR/HKDSE_Results_20140713_ENG_FULL.pdf.

Hong Kong Diploma of Secondary Education (HKDSE). "Press Release: 2015 Hong Kong Diploma of Secondary Education (HKDSE) Examination Results Released." 2015. http://www.hkeaa.edu.hk/DocLibrary/Media/PR/20150714_HKDSE_Results_ENG_FULL.pdf.

Hong Kong Institute of Asia-Pacific Studies. "60% Respondents Disagree with the Necessity to Win at the Starting Line; 90% Admits that It Is a Common Perception in Hong Kong." 2016. http://www.cuhk.edu.hk/hkiaps/tellab/pdf/telepress/16/SP_Press_Release_20160808.pdf.

Hong Kong Special Administration Region. "The 2016 Policy Address: Innovate for the Economy Improve Livelihood Foster Harmony Share Prosperity." 2016. http://www.policyaddress.gov.hk/2016/eng/index.html.

Howard, Jennifer. "The Afterlife of David Foster Wallace." *Chronicle Review*. July 6, 2011.

Hu, S. and L. Leung. "Effects of Expectancy-Value, Attitudes, and Use of the Internet on Psychological Empowerment Experienced by Chinese Women at the Workplace." *Telematics and Informatics* 20, no. 4 (2003): 365–82.

Hudd, S. S., J. Dumlao, D. Erdmann-Sager, D. Murray, E. Phan, N. Soukas, and N. Yokozuka. "Stress at College: Effects on Health Habits, Health Status and Self-Esteem." *College Student Journal* 34, no. 2 (2000): 217–27.

Hughes, B. M. "Study, Examinations, and Stress: Blood Pressure Assessments in College Students." *Educational Review* 57, no. 1 (2005).

Kanner, A. D., J. C. Coyne, C. Schaefer, and R. S. Lazarus. "Comparison of Two Modes of Stress Management: Daily Hassles and Uplifts Versus Major Life Events." *Journal of Behavioural Medicine* 4 (1981): 1–39.

Kember, David. "Opening up the Road to Nowhere: Problems with the Path to Mass Higher Education in Hong Kong." *Higher Education* 59 (2009): 167–79. DOI: 10.1007/s10734-009-9241-x.

Koch, Christof. *Consciousness: Confessions of a Romantic Reductionist*. Cambridge, MA: The MIT Press, 2012.

Kross, E., P. Verduyn, E. Demiralp, J. Park, D. S. Lee, N. Lin et al. "Facebook Use Predicts Declines in Subjective Well-Being in Young Adults." *PLoS ONE* 8, no. 8 (2013): e69841. https://doi.org/10.1371/journal.pone.0069841.

James, Henry. *Autobiography: A Small Boy and Others—Notes of a Son and Brother—The Middle Years*. Ed. and Intro. Frederick W. Dupee. New York, NY: Criterion Books, 1956.

James, Henry. *The Letters of Henry James, Volume IV: 1895–1916*. Ed. Leon Edel. Cambridge, MA: Belknap Press, 1984.

James, Henry. "*Literary Criticism*." In *Essays on Literature, American Writers, English Writers*. Ed. Leon Edel, Vol. I. New York, NY: The Library of America, 1984, p. 97.

James, Henry. *The Ambassadors*. Intro. Harry Levin. London: Penguin Classics, 1986.

James, Henry. *The Sacred Fount*. Intro. John Lyon. London: Penguin Classics, 1994.

James, Henry. *The Tragic Muse*. Intro. Philip Horne. London: Penguin Classics, 1995.
James, Henry. *The Portrait of a Lady*. New York, NY: Random House, 2007.
James, William. *"The Ph.D. Octupus" The Heart of William James*. Ed. and Intro. Robert Richardson. Cambridge, MA: Harvard University Press, 2010.
Jin, Ha. *Waiting*. London: Vintage, 2000.
Jinping, Xi. *The Governance of China*. Beijing: Foreign Languages Press, 2018.
Joyce, James. *Dubliners*. London: Penguin, 1992.
Kaag, John. *Hiking with Nietzsche: On Becoming Who You Are*. New York, NY: Farrar, Strauss & Giroux, 2018.
Kaplan, Fred. *Henry James: The Imagination of Genius, A Biography*. Baltimore, MD: Johns Hopkins University Press, 1999.
Keegan, Marina. *The Opposite of Loneliness: Essays and Stories*. New York, NY: Simon Schuster, 2014.
Kelly, Adam. "David Foster Wallace: The Death of the Author and the Birth of a Discipline." *Irish Journal of American Studies*. April 2010. http://ijas.iaas.ie/index.php/article-david-foster-wallace-the-death-of-the-author-andthe-birth-of-a-discipline/.
Kelly, Adam. "David Foster Wallace and the Novel of Ideas." In *David Foster Wallace and "The Long Thing": New Essays on the Novels*. Ed. Marshall Boswell. London: Bloomsbury Academic, 2014, pp. 3–22.
Laing, Olivia. *The Lonely City: Adventures in the Art of Being Alone*. London: Canongate, 2016.
Latour, Bruno. *An Inquiry into Modes of Existence: An Anthropology of the Moderns*. Cambridge, MA: Harvard University Press, 2013.
Lawrie, Alexander. *The Beginnings of University English: Extramural Study 1885–1910*. London: Palgrave Macmillan, 2014.
Lazarus, R. and S. Folkman. *Stress, Appraisal and Coping*. New York, NY: Springer, 1984.
Leung, Ka-heung. "The Relationship of Stress & Depression: A Study Among Secondary Students in Hong Kong." MA Dissertation. 1992. http://hdl.handle.net/10722/65139.
Lee, Kim-ming, Hung Wong, and Kam-yee Law. "Social Polarisation and Poverty in the Global City: The Case of Hong Kong." *China Report* 43, no. 1 (2007): 1–30.
Li, Chenyang. "Shifting Perspectives: Filial Morality Revisited." *Philosophy East and West* 47, no. 2 (1997): 211–32.
Li, S. K. and R. N. K. Ng. *Life Stressors Help Seeking Behaviour of Secondary School Students in Kwun Tong Comparative Study of Students' and Their Teachers'*

Perception. Hong Kong: Kwun Tong District Committee on Promotion of Mental Health Education, 1992.

Li, Yiyun. *Dear Friend, from My Life I Write to You in Your Life*. London: Penguin, 2017.

Lieberman, Mathew D. *Social: Why Our Brains Are Wired to Connect*. New York, NY: Crown, 2013.

Lipsky, David. *Although of Course You End Up Becoming Yourself: A Road Trip with David Foster Wallace*. New York, NY: Broadway Books, 2010.

Lissitsa, Sabina and Svetlana Chachashvili-Bolotin. "Life Satisfaction in the Internet Age—Changes in the Past Decade." *Computers in Human Behavior* 54 (2016): 197–206. http://www.sciencedirect.com/science/article/pii/S0747563215300790.

Lubin, Gus. "This City Has by Far the Most Inequality in the Developed World." *Business Insider*. June 26, 2012. http://www.businessinsider.com/inequality-in-hong-kong-2012-6.

Lukács, Georg. *Realism in Our Time: Literature and the Class Struggle*. New York: Harper & Row, 1971.

Lynch, K. "Carelessness: A Hidden Doxa of Higher Education." *Arts and Humanities in Higher Education* 9, no. 1 (2010): 54–67.

Mansfield, Katherine. *The Garden Party and Other Stories*. London: Penguin, 1966.

Manthei, R. J. and A. Gilmore. "The Effect of Paid Employment on University Students' Lives." *Education and Training* 47, no. 3 (2005): 202–15.

Marginson, S. "The Worldwide Trend to High Participation in Higher Education: Dynamics of Social Stratification in Inclusive Systems." *Higher Education* 72, no. 413 (2016). DOI: 10.1007/s10734–016–0016-x.

Marsh, Stefanie. "Teenagers on Loneliness: We Want to Talk to Our Parents. We Need Their Guidancle," *The Guardian*. April 8, 2017. https://www.theguardian.com/society/2017/apr/08/teenagers-loneliness- social-media-isolation-parents-attention.

Mayer, F. W. *Narrative Politics: Stories and Collective Action*. New York, NY: Oxford University Press, 2015.

Max, D. T. *Every Love Story Is a Ghost Story: A Life of David Foster Wallace*. London: Granta, 2012.

McCullers, Carson. *The Heart Is a Lonely Hunter*. Boston, MA: Houghton Miflin, 1940.

Mead, Rebecca. "How 'The End of the Tour' Nails a Whole Profession." *The New Yorker*, August 20, 2015.

Menand, Louis. *The Metaphysical Club: A Story of Ideas in America*. New York, NY: Farrar, Strauss and Giroux, 2001.

Merton, Thomas. *No Man Is an Island*. New York, NY: Harvest, 1983.

Mettler, Suzanne. *Degrees of Inequality: How the Politics of Higher Education Sabotaged the American Dream*. New York, NY: Basic Books, 2014.

McGurl, Mark. "The Institution of Nothing: David Foster Wallace in the Program." *boundary 2* 41, no. 3 (2014): 27–54.

Michie, F., M. Glachan, and D. Bray. "An Evaluation of Factors Influencing the Academic Self-Concept, Self-Esteem and Academic Stress for Direct and Re-Entry Students in Higher Education." *Educational Psychology* 21, no. 4 (2001): 455–72.

Mijuskovic, Ben Lazare. *Loneliness in Philosophy, Psychology and Literature*, 3rd ed. New York, NY: Universe, 2012.

Mitchell, W. J. T. *Cloning Terror: The War of Images, 9/11 to the Present*. Chicago: University of Chicago Press, 2011.

Montaigne, Michel De. *On Solitude*. Great Ideas. London: Penguin, 2009.

Moretti, Franco. *Distant Reading*. London: Verso, 2013.

Moretti, M. M. and M. Peled. "Adolescent–Parent Attachment: Bonds that Support Healthy Development." *Paediatric Child Health* 9, no. 8 (2004): 551–5.

Mortenson, Tom. "Regressive Social Policy and Its Consequences for Opportunity for Higher Education in the United States, 1980 to Present." In *Aspirations, Access and Attainment: International Perspectives on Widening Participation and an Agenda for Change*. Ed. Neil Murray and Christopher M. Klinger. London: Routledge, 2014, pp. 20–40.

Moustakas, Clark E. *Loneliness*. New York, NY: Prentice-Hall, 1961.

Murakami, Haruki. *Men Without Women*. Trans. Philip Gabriel and Ted Goossen. London: Harvil Secker, 2017.

Murata, Sayaka. *Convenience Store Woman*. Trans. Ginny Tapley Takemori. New York, NY: Grove Press, 2018.

Murthy, Vivek. "Work and the Loneliness Epidemic: Reducing Isolation at Work Is Good for Business." *Harvard Business Review*, September 28, 2017. https://hbr.org/cover-story/2017/09/work-and-the-loneliness-epidemic.

Ngo, Jennifer. "Working Poor Households Increase Alarmingly Despite Hong Kong Government's Attempts to Reduce Poverty since 2013." *South China Morning Post*, September 30, 2015.

Ngo, Jennifer. "Hong Kong Lawmakers Launch 'Blood-Stained' TSA Paper Protest over Student Suicide Tragedies." *South China Morning Post*, March 16, 2016.

Nishida, Kitarō. *Last Writings: Nothingness and the Religious Worldview*. Trans. David A. Dilworth. Honolulu, HI: University of Hawaii Press, 1993.

O'Connor, Frank. *The Lonely Voice: A Study of the Short Story*. New York, NY: Melville House, 2004.

OECD. *Education at a Glance 2012: Highlights*. Paris: OECD Publishing, 2012. doi: 10.1787/eag_highlights-2012-en

O'Faolain, Sean. *The Irish: A Character Study*. New York, NY: Devin-Adair, 1947.

Oliver, Kelly. *Technologies of Life and Death: From Cloning to Capital Punishment*. New York: Fordham University Press, 2013.

O no Yasumaro. "Kojiki." Trans. Chamberlain Hall Basil. *Internet Sacred Text Archive*, 2005. www.sacred-texts.com/shi/kj/index.htm.

O no Yasumaro. "古事記. 上 (Kojiki First Volume)." *National Diet Library*. 2011. dl.ndl.go.jp/info:ndljp/pid/772088/1. DOI: 10.11501/772088.

O'Sullivan, Michael. *Michel Henry, Incarnation, Barbarism and Belief: An Introduction to Michel Henry*. Oxford: Peter Lang, 2006.

O'Sullivan, Michael. *Academic Barbarism, Universities and Inequality*. London: Palgrave, 2016.

O'Sullivan, Michael and Michael Yat-him Tsang. "Educational Inequalities in Higher Education in Hong Kong." *Inter-Asia Cultural Studies* (2005): 454–69. Published online: 30 Sep 2015.

Pang, Laikwan. *The Art of Cloning*. London: Verso, 2017.

Piketty, Thomas. *Capital in the Twenty-First Century*. Cambridge, MA: Belknap Press, 2014.

Poole, Adrian. *Henry James. Harvester New Readings*. Hempstead, NY: Harvester, 1991.

Poon, A. Y. K. and Y. C. Wong. "Governance in Education in Hong Kong: A Decentralizing or a Centralizing Path?" In *One Country, Two Systems in Crisis*. Ed. Y. C. Wong. Lanham, MD: Lexington Books, 2001, pp. 137–66.

Primack, Brian A., Ariel Shensa, Jaime E. Sidani, Erin O. Whaite, Liu yi Lin, Daniel Rosen, Jason B. Colditz, Ana Radovic, and Elizabeth Miller. "Social Media Use and Perceived Social Isolation Among Young Adults in the U.S." *American Journal of Preventive Medicine* 53, no. 1 (2017): 1–8. http://www.sciencedirect.com/science/article/pii/S0749379717300168.

Pryjmachuk, S. and D. A. Richards. "Predicting Stress in Pre-registration Nursing Students." *British Journal of Health Psychology* 12 (2007): 125–44.

Qian, Zhaoming. *The Modernist Response to Chinese Art: Pound, Moore, Stevens*. Charlottesville, VA: University of Virginia Press, 2012.

Quigley, Megan. *Modernist Fiction and Vagueness: Philosophy, Form, and Language.* Cambridge: Cambridge University Press, 2015.

Radcliffe, C. and H. Lester. "Perceived Stress during Undergraduate Medical Training: A Qualitative Study." *Medical Education* 37, no. 32 (2003): 32–8.

Raftery, A. E. and M. Hout. "Maximally Maintained Inequality: Expansion, Reform and Opportunity in Irish Education, 1921–1975." *Sociology of Education* 66 (1993): 41–62.

Ricoeur, Paul. *Living Up To Death.* Trans. David Pellauer. Chicago: University of Chicago Press, 2009.

Riesman, David, Nathan Glazer, and Reuel Denney. *The Lonely Crowd: A Study of the Changing American Character.* Abridged and revised edition. New Haven, CT: Yale University Press, 2001.

Roberts, R., J. Golding, T. Towell, and I. Weinreb. "The Effects of Students' Economic Circumstances on Mental and Physical Health." *The American Journal of College Health* 6 (1999): 23–35.

Robotham, David. "Stress among Higher Education Students: Towards a Research Agenda." *Higher Education*, 56 (2008): 735–46.

Rorty, Richard. *Philosophy and Social Hope.* London: Penguin, 1999.

Roth, Michael. *Beyond the University: Why Liberal Education Matters.* New Haven, CT: Yale University Press, 2015.

RTHK. "40% Interviewed HKDSE Students Found It Difficult to Make Post-Result-Release Choices." July 9, 2016. http://news.rthk.hk/rthk/ch/component/k2/1271641-20160709.htm.

Sagan, Olivia and Eric D. Miller, eds. *Narratives of Loneliness: Multidisciplinary Perspectives from the 21st Century.* London: Routledge, 2018.

Saroson, I. G., J. H. Johnson, and J. M. Siegel. "Assessing the Impact of Life Changes: Development of the Life Experiences Survey." *Journal of Consultant Clinical Psychology* 46 (1978): 932–46.

Sartre Jean-Paul. *Nausea.* New York, NY: New Directions, 1969.

Sato, Hiroaki. "The Transient Rasping that Captivates the Poets." *The Japan Times.* May 27, 2013.

Schiller, J. C. Friedrich. "Letters Upon the Aesthetic Education of Man." *Literary and Philosophical Essays.* The Harvard Classics, 1909–14. www.bartleby.com.

Severs, Jeffrey. *David Foster Wallace's Balancing Books: Fictions of Value.* New York, NY: Columbia University Press, 2017.

Shaughnessy, K., E. S. Byers, S. L. Clowater, and A. Kalinowski. "Self-Appraisals of Arousal-Oriented Online Sexual Activities in University and Community

Samples." *Archives of Sexual Behavior* 43, no. 6 (2014): 1187–97. DOI: 10.1007/s10508-013-0115-z.

Siedentop, Larry. *Inventing the Individual: The Origins of Western Liberalism*. London: Penguin, 2015.

Sijie, Dai. *Balzac and the Little Chinese Seamstress*. London: Vintage, 2002.

Sijie, Dai. *Once on a Moonless Night*. London: Anchor, 2009.

Soseki, Natsume. *My Individualism and The Philosophical Foundations of Literature*. Trans. Sammy I. Tsunematsu. Intro. Inger Brodey. Boston, MA: Tuttle, 2004.

Soseki, Natsume. *Sanshiro*. Penguin Classics. London: Penguin, 2009.

Soseki, Natsume. *Kokoro*. Trans. Meredith McKinney. Penguin Classics. London: Penguin, 2010.

Silver, Curtis. "Patents Reveal How Facebook Wants to Capture your Emotions, Facial Expressions and Mood." https://www.forbes.com/sites/curtissilver/2017/06/08/how-facebook-wants-to-capture-your-emotions-facial-expressions-and-mood/#6c39b2256014.

Siu, Phila. "Salaries of Hong Kong's University Graduates Dropped 20 Per Cent in Last 20 Years, Study Finds." *South China Morning Post*. July 29, 2015.

Sparrow, Tom. *The End of Phenomenology: Metaphysics and the New Realism*. Edinburgh: Edinburgh University Press, 2014.

Stanley, N. and J. Manthorpe. "Responding to Students' Mental Health Needs: Impermeable Systems and Diverse Users." *Journal of Mental Health* 10, no. 1 (2001): 41–52.

Storr, Will. *Selfie: How the West Became Self-Oobsessed*. London: Picador, 2018.

Sun, Jiandong. *Educational Stress among Chinese Adolescents: Measurement, Risk Factors and Associations with Mental Health*. Unpublished PhD Dissertation. Queensland University of Technology, 2012.

Sun, Jiandong, M. P. Dunne, X. -y. Hou, and A.-q. Xu. "Educational Stress Scale for Adolescents: Development, Validity, and Reliability With Chinese Students." *Journal of Psychoeducational Assessment* 29, no. 6 (2011): 534–46. DOI: 10.1177/0734282910394976.

Svendsen, Lars. *A Philosophy of Loneliness*. London: Reaktion Books, 2017.

Tanabe, Hajime. Trans. Yoshinori Takeuchi and James W. Heisig, *Philosophy as Metanoetics*. Nagoya: Chisokudō, 2016.

Taylor, Charles. *A Secular Age*. Harvard, MA: Harvard University Press, 2007.

Thaler, Richard. *Misbehaving: The Making of Behavioral Economics*. New York, NY: W.W. Norton, 2015.

Tung, C.-H. *New Elitism*. Speech. December 18, 2001. www.info.gov.hk/ce/speech/cest.htm.

Twenge, Jean M. *iGen: Why Today's Supe-Connected Kinds Are Growing Up Less. Rebellious, More Tolerant, Less Happy, and Completely Unprepared for Adulthood*. New York, NY: Simon & Schuster, 2017.

UNESCO. *Higher Education in Asia: Expanding Out, Expanding Up: The Rise of Graduate Education and University Research*, 2014. http://www.uis.unesco.org.

UNITE Student Living Report. UK Government Publication (2004).

University Grants Committee. "Student Enrolment of First-Year-First-Degree (FYFD) Places of UGC-Funded Programmes, 1965/66 to 2015/16."

Verhaeghe, P. *What About Me? The Struggle for Identity in a Market-Based Society*. London: Scribe Books, 2014.

Wallace, David Foster. *The Broom of the System*. London: Penguin, 1987.

Wallace, David Foster. "*E Unibus Pluram*: Television and U.S. Fiction." *Review of Contemporary Fiction* 13, no. 2 (1993): 151–94.

Wallace, David Foster. *Infinite Jest*. New York, NY: Back Bay Books, 1996.

Wallace, David Foster. *Oblivion*. Stories. London: Abacus, 2004.

Wallace, David Foster. *Consider the Lobster: And Other Essays*. New York, NY: Back Bay Books, 2007.

Wallace, David Foster. *Fate, Time, and Language: An Essay on Free Will*. New York, NY: Columbia University Press, 2010.

Wallace, David Foster. *The Pale King: An Unfinished Novel*. London: Hamish Hamilton, 2011.

Wallace, David Foster. *The David Foster Wallace Reader*. New York, NY: Little, Brown and Company, 2014.

Wallach, Wendell and Colin Allen. *Moral Machines: Teaching Robots Right from Wrong*. Oxford: Oxford University Press, 2009.

Wang, Ban. "The People in the Modern Chinese Novel: Popular Democracy and World Literature." *Novel* 47, no. 1 (2014): 43–56. DOI: https://doi.org/10.1215/00295132-2414057.

Watsuji, Tetsuro. *Watsuji Tetsuro's Rinrigaku: Ethics in Japan*. Trans. Robert Carter and Seisaku Yamamoto. New York, NY: SUNY Press, 1996.

Whaite, Erin O., Ariel Shensa, Jaime E. Sidani, Jason B. Colditz, Brian A. Primack. "Social Media Use, Personality Characteristics, and Social Isolation Among Young Adults in the United States." *Personality and Individual Differences* 124 (2018): 45–50. https://doi.org/10.1016/j.paid.2017.10.030.

World Happiness Report Update. Ed. John Helliwell, Richard Layard, and Jeffrey Sachs. 2016. http://worldhappiness.report/wp-content/uploads/sites/2/2016/03/HR-V1_web.pdf.

Wu, Alice. "Hothouse Hong Kong Is Spawning a New Breed of Monster Parents." *South China Morning Post*. June 26, 2016.

Yan, Mo. *Red Sorghum*. Trans. Howard Goldblatt. New York, NY: Penguin, 1994.

Yates, Richard. *Eleven Kinds of Loneliness*. London: Vintage, 2008.

Yates, Richard. *Revolutionary Road*. London: Vintage, 2009.

Yuen, Tik Chi. "Hong Kong Students Need More Options—and Less Stress." *South China Morning Post*. July 15, 2015.

Zagury, Daniel. *La Barbarie des Hommes Ordinaires: Ces criminels qui pourraient être nous*. Paris: Éditions de l'Observatoire/Humensis, 2018.

Zhang, Longxi. *From Comparison to World Literature*. New York, NY: State University of New York Press, 2016.

Zhang, Jane. "More Hong Kong Students Taking Their Own Lives, Study by Jockey Club Research Suicide Centre Finds." *South China Morning Post*, September 10, 2018.

Žižek, Slavoj. *Organs without Bodies on Deleuze and Consequences*. London: Routledge, 2012.

Index

A History of Loneliness (John Boyne) 74, 83, 193
academic barbarism 5, 15, 95, 112–14, 173–87
Agamben, Giorgio 198–9
Agassiz, Louis 38
algorithms 7, 8, 17, 22, 23, 25
amae 93, 116–19
Anthropocene 151, 198
artificial intelligence 17, 23, 27

bad faith 5, 90, 96, 143
Balzac and the Little Chinese Seamstress (Dai Sijie) 164–5
barbarism 18, 21, 97, 163
Barth, John 90, 100
Bauman, Zygmunt 2–3, 16, 19–20, 100
Beckett, Samuel 81, 90, 99
Benjamin, Walter 69–70
biopolitics 190–1
Bolaño, Roberto 104, 136
boredom 90, 91–2, 94, 96, 98, 108–11
Bourdieu, Pierre 16
Bowen, Elizabeth 59, 71, 98, 171
Boyne, John 74, 83, 193
Buddhism 155

Cacioppo, John 1, 3, 24, 60
Cacioppo, John and Sarah 189–90
Camus, Albert 67, 92, 93, 107, 129
Cao, Xueqin 172
    The Dream of the Red Chamber 157, 159–62
Chemero, Anthony 10–11, 28
cloning 4, 12–13, 15, 16, 21
Cohen, Daniel 18, 19, 22–6
Confucianism 138, 154–5, 158
Convenience Store Woman (Sayaka Murata) 82, 83, 115, 136–43
Cultural Revolution 159, 165–6

Daoism 155–6
Dear Friend from My Life I Write to You in Your Life (Yiyun Li) 170–2
death 59, 60–1, 68–72, 125–6, 220n. 143
Deleuze, Gilles 195–6
Deleuze & Guattari 196–9
De Man, Paul 60, 69–70
Derrida, Jacques 39, 60, 124, 125–6, 149
desire 189–99
Dewey, John 10, 38, 45
Doi, Takeo 93, 113, 116–19
Dollimore, Jonathan 193
Drucker, Peter S. 64

Eleanor Oliphant Is Completely Fine (Gail Honeyman) 74, 83, 140–1
Eleven Kinds of Loneliness (Richard Yates) 12, 41, 83–4, 88, 207n. 22
Emerson, Ralph Waldo 38, 48
Epictetus 168–9
erotic 189–99
existential loneliness 3, 5–8, 14, 28, 29, 61, 81–4

Facebook 1, 2, 23, 24, 25, 27, 28
filial piety 151–70
Floridi, Luciano 27, 191
    information ethics 27
Fludernik, Monica 151, 169–70
Foucault, Michel 168–9, 190–1

GAFA (Google, Amazon, Facebook, Apple) 1, 3, 21, 25, 26
Guinier, Lani 104

Ha Jin 166–8
Hardt, Michael & Antonio Negri 11–12, 58
Harman, Graham 18
Henry, Michel 50, 124
Hikikomori 116

Hitorigami 147
homo digitalis 18, 25–6
Honeyman, Gail 74, 83, 140–1
Hong Kong 122, 137, 152, 154, 156, 173–87
  inequality 176–7, 180
  Universities 173–87
Hopper, Edward 77, 78, 81

iGen 8, 24, 111, 194
inequality 104, 173, 174, 176–8, 180
Infinite Jest (David Foster Wallace) 91, 95, 105–8
information ethics 27–9
infosphere 27, 190–1
"interconnected loners" 2, 4, 7, 123, 157, 173–87
Internet use 7, 9, 17, 19–26, 189, 192–5

James, Henry 35–56
  essential loneliness 35, 37, 41, 42–3, 44, 47, 51, 56
  The Ambassadors 41, 44–5
  The Portrait of a Lady 36–8, 50–1, 53
  The Sacred Fount 36, 41, 48–9
  The Tragic Muse 50–6
James, William 13, 45
Joyce, James 58, 59, 62, 65, 68–72, 130
  "The Dead" (James Joyce) 58, 59, 68–72

Kaag, John 8, 191
Kafka, Franz 42
Keegan, Marina 79
Kipling, Rudyard 58–9, 65
  essential loneliness 58–9
knowledge worker 64
kodokushi 116
kojiki 144, 146, 149
Kokoro (Natsume Soseki) 117–20
Kurosawa, Akira 132–3

Laing, Olivia 32, 77, 78, 82
Latour, Bruno 113, 114, 115
Leavis, F. R. 63
Lieberman, Matthew D. 27
Li, Yiyun 157, 170–2
Lukács, Georg 156

Mansfield, Katherine 57–60, 63, 65–6, 68, 70
Mao, Zedong 15, 157, 166, 167–8
May Fourth Thinkers 154–5
McCullers, Carson 73–82
  The Heart Is a Lonely Hunter 73, 75–81
Men without Women (Haruki Murakami) 115–16, 128–31, 136
Menand, Louis 38, 48
Mencius 158
mental health 82, 83, 108–11
Merton, Thomas 8, 9, 191
MGMT 22
Mijuskovic, Lazare 29
Mitchell, W. J. T. 4
Mo Yan 119, 158, 162–4
Montaigne, Michel de 8, 9, 10, 111
Moretti, Franco 151–3, 159, 192
Moustakas, Clark E. 3, 11, 12, 14, 28, 81, 82, 83, 84, 89, 93
Murakami, Haruki 115, 116, 128–30, 131, 136
  Men without Women 115–16, 128–31, 136
Murata, Sayaka 3, 81, 82, 83, 115, 136–43
  Convenience Store Woman 82, 83, 115, 136–43

narrative 41, 44, 74, 83, 151–8, 169–70, 171–2, 182
  loneliness 86–90
natural narratology 169–70
Nausea (Jean-Paul Sartre) 6–8
Nietzsche, Friedrich 8, 10, 191
Nishida, Kitaro 93, 115, 116, 119, 124–8

Oblivion (David Foster Wallace) 91, 101, 102, 111
O'Connor, Frank 3, 12, 14, 41, 57–72, 82, 154, 171
  The Lonely Voice 3, 12, 41, 57–72
O'Faolain, Sean 66–7
Once on a Moonless Night (Dai Sijie) 165–6
OSAs (arousal-oriented online sexual activities) 189–90, 192, 194

Patočka, Jan 125
phenomenological loneliness 31, 39, 127
Piketty, Thomas 104
pornography 189, 190, 194
possessive individualism 12, 165
prosopopoeia 60, 69
Proust, Marcel 40, 49, 65, 134, 153

Qian, Zhaoming 155–6

radical embodied cognitive loneliness 1–33
radical loneliness 144–50
Red Sorghum (Mo Yan) 157, 158, 162–4
Revolutionary Road (Richard Yates) 76, 82, 84–90
Ricoeur, Paul 60, 103
robots 23, 106, 194
Roethke, Theodore 81
Rorty, Richard 108
Roth, Michael 38

Sanshiro (Natsume Soseki) 128, 130, 131–6
Sartre, Jean-Paul 5–8, 31, 80, 89–90, 143
Schep, Tijmen 3, 16
Schiller, J. C. Friedrich 49–50
school banding 176–80
school competition 182–7
sentimental loneliness 3, 61, 62, 82, 84–90
Shintoism 117, 144–8
Siedentop, Larry 56, 113, 114, 115
Sijie, Dai 151, 164–6
social cooling 3, 16
social fixation 179
social stratification 182, 183, 186
solitude 8–10, 28, 29–33, 41, 53, 60, 86, 93, 120–2, 134, 141, 157, 170, 191–4
Soseki, Natsume 115, 116, 117, 118, 119, 120–4, 130–6
speculative realism 16, 18, 50, 101
Stevens, Wallace 155–6
student stress 173–87
suicide 5, 42, 96, 119, 135, 144, 146, 170, 173, 193
Svendsen, Lars 29–33, 85

Tanabe, Hajime 116, 148, 149
Tanguy effect 24

Taylor, Charles 125
teledildonics 194
Tisseron, Serge 23
The Ambassadors (Henry James) 41, 44–5
"The Dead" (James Joyce) 58, 59, 68–72
The Dream of the Red Chamber (Cao Xueqin) 157, 159–62
The Heart Is a Lonely Hunter (Carson McCullers) 73, 75–81
The Lonely Crowd (Riesman, Glazer & Denney) 3, 12, 13, 14, 67–8, 74–6, 194
The Lonely Voice (Frank O'Connor) 3, 12, 41, 57–72
The Pale King (David Foster Wallace) 91, 92, 93, 97, 98, 108–11
The Portrait of a Lady (Henry James) 36–8, 50–1, 53
The Story of the Stone (Cao Xueqin)
  see *The Dream of the Red Chamber* 157, 159–62
"The Stranger" (Katherine Mansfield) 58, 59, 68–9
The Tragic Muse (Henry James) 35, 50–6
Twenge, Jean M. 24, 190, 193, 194

university admissions 106–7, 173–4, 175, 177, 180, 182–7
university rankings 15, 16, 103, 104, 176, 182

Veblen, Thorstein 90
Verhaeghe, Paul 174, 177, 182
VIRP (virtual intercourse with real people) 194

Waiting (Ha Jin) 166–8
Wallace, David Foster 61, 83, 91–111
  bliss 92–3
  boredom 83, 90, 92, 96, 109–11
  Infinite Jest 91, 95, 105–8
  Internet 93–4
  mental health 108–11
  Oblivion 91, 101, 102, 111
  philosophy 96, 101–2, 103
  self 91
  The Pale King 91, 92, 93, 97, 98, 108–11
  University 96–7, 101, 104–8
  writing 99–100

Warhol, Andy 23
Watsuji, Tetsuro 145, 147, 148, 149
Weil, Simone 20
Wordsworth, William 28

Xi Jinping 156

Yates, Richard 3, 12, 41, 62, 73, 74, 76, 82–90

Eleven Kinds of Loneliness 12, 41, 83–4, 88, 207n. 22
Revolutionary Road 76, 82, 84–90
young adults 21, 24, 189–95

Zagury, Daniel 18–22
Zhang, Longxi 151, 152
Zhuangzi 155
Žižek, Slavoj 195–6

www.ingramcontent.com/pod-product-compliance
Lightning Source LLC
Chambersburg PA
CBHW052032300426
44117CB00012B/1792